Cleo

Programming
in REXX

J. Ranade IBM Series

Programming in REXX

Charles Daney
Quercus Systems, Saratoga, California

McGraw-Hill, Inc

New York St. Louis San Francisco Auckland Bogotá
Caracas Lisbon London Madrid Mexico Milan
Montreal New Delhi Paris San Juan São Paulo
Singapore Sydney Tokyo Toronto

Library of Congress Cataloging-in-Publication Data

Daney, Charles.
    Programming in REXX / Charles Daney.
        p.   cm.
    Includes index.
    ISBN 0-07-015305-1
    1. REXX (Computer program language)   I. Title.
QA76.76.R48D36   1992
005.13'3—dc20   92-7025
                                                 CIP

2 3 4 5 6 7 8 9 0   DOC/DOC   9 8 7 6 5 4 3 2

ISBN 0-07-015305-1

The sponsoring editor for this book was Jerry Papke, and the production supervisor was Donald F. Schmidt. It was composed in Century Schoolbook by North Market Street Graphics.

Printed and bound by R. R. Donnelley & Sons Company.

To Jeanne and Meghan

Contents

Preface

REXX has been around since 1979. Mike Cowlishaw's authoritative and lucid book on the language appeared in 1985, though it was based largely on his language definition which had existed in written form for several years.

Various REXX books have come out since 1985, but, oddly, it seems to me, none appears to have been designed to teach the language in a discursive way and with a platform-independent viewpoint. Mike's book is very good, but it is a language definition, and often doesn't go far enough in the area of explanation and motivation. All the other REXX books of which I am aware miss the mark in one way or another. There are tutorials which are superficial and somewhat lightweight. Other books are full of tables and syntax diagrams, but offer little in-depth explanation of how REXX actually works and why. Still other books are limited to particular REXX implementations. (O'Hara and Gomberg's *Modern Programming Using REXX* is an exception from these observations. But it is a special case in that its aim is more to teach programming than to teach REXX.)

This situation is unfortunate, as I have heard many wistful requests over the years for the recommendation of a good book from which to learn REXX. The best answer available was, "Read Cowlishaw." Now, there should be no mistake about this: REXX is a very approachable language, and most people get into it easily with the help of available documentation and some good examples. It was designed to be easy to learn and to use.

But mastery of the language is another matter. It has shimmering blue depths that, I have found, very few users ever seem to plumb. In truth, REXX has some very unusual features and concepts, which are found in few other languages, especially the better-known ones. These aspects of the language are often inadequately understood even by quite proficient users of REXX, including implementors of the language. (And I have been no exception.) The very existence of some of these subtleties, of course, goes unnoticed by the more casual users of REXX.

I hope the present book will help illuminate the language in general, as well as some of its more arcane details. The time certainly seems right for this, because REXX now appears to be catching on, even though it is rather late in the game for a new language to stand much of a chance to break into the ranks of popular programming languages.

Charles Daney

Acknowledgments

I became involved in REXX as an implementor of the language rather than as a user. I had written most of a REXX interpreter before I wrote very many lines of code in REXX itself. After all, one must have such an implementation before one can write programs, and no implementation existed on personal computers, which is what I was primarily using at the time.

This was around 1984. I realized that a clean, high-level procedure language would be a great asset in conjunction with other applications I wished to develop. The synergy of this coupling of an application and a general-purpose programming language is a fact which is only now beginning to be widely understood. I had heard about REXX from a presentation Mike Cowlishaw made in 1981, when I was still working with large mainframe computers. I quickly became convinced that REXX was the right language for my purposes.

Around the same time, Kevin Kearney had similar ideas, related to the programmer's editor, called KEDIT, that he was developing. Though I already knew Kevin, Dave Gomberg acted as a catalyst at a critical time, bringing us together in collaboration on a new version of the language (called "Personal REXX") which we introduced in 1985. This was the first implementation of REXX developed outside IBM.

Over the years, Mike Cowlishaw has patiently and insightfully answered, via electronic mail and in personal conversation, innumerable questions about the fine points of REXX and his overall vision of the language. Mike is a gentleman and a credit to the programming profession.

However, I owe my greatest debt concerning REXX to the community of REXX users in general, and to the users of Personal REXX in particular. These people, who have had the good sense to recognize a decent language when they saw it, have contributed in many ways. They have helped promote a worthy tool against the understandable skepticism of those who wonder why the world needs yet another programming language. They have informed each other and their colleagues about the finer points of the language. And they have instructed me, countless times, by their questions and their suggestions, in both the strengths and weaknesses of the language, and also in how it can best be used.

By the way . . . I am a REXX user, too. Though the language isn't perfect, it is good enough to use for everything from small personal programming chores to large-scale application prototyping. It has proven to be the right choice as a scripting language for the communication program (REXXTERM) I developed to use with it. And now that this book is completed, I am eagerly looking forward to having a little more time to develop some of the other applications I originally wanted to before I had written my first line of REXX.

Charles Daney

Introduction

REXX is, preeminently, a language for personal programming. It is quick, easy to maneuver, and fun to drive—like a sports car. It excels at the kinds of things an individual computer user needs to do for his or her own purposes: menu systems, customized front-ends to other programs, personal utilities, prototyping of new ideas, and so forth.

All popular programming languages have their own distinctive place and personality. C, for instance, is a pickup truck with standard transmission and 4-wheel drive. C++ is a pickup truck with automatic transmission, leather upholstery, and a cellular phone. Ada is a World War II battleship, and so on.

But for writing code quickly, easily, and enjoyably, REXX is hard to beat.

WHAT REXX IS

REXX is a modern, structured, high-level programming language that was consciously designed for ease of both reading and writing. It was designed and first implemented between 1979 and 1982 by Mike Cowlishaw of IBM. Though it was primarily developed by one individual, it was widely disseminated within IBM during that time, and improved by the feedback of hundreds of users. REXX was first made commercially available as the system procedure language for IBM's VM/CMS operating system in 1983.

When IBM's Systems Application Architecture was announced in 1987, REXX was included as the standard system procedure language. By that fact, IBM indicated that REXX would eventually be implemented in a standard way on all of their strategic computing systems. An implementation for the MVS system appeared in 1988. In 1990, an implementation of REXX from IBM appeared on personal workstations in version 1.2 of OS/2.

Long before then, REXX had been implemented by others on various computers and operating systems. The first such implementation, known as Personal REXX, was developed for MS-DOS by the author and Mansfield Software Group in 1985. We followed this with a version of REXX for OS/2 in 1989. ARexx for the Commodore Amiga made its debut in 1987.

At the present time, IBM has widened the availability of REXX in its systems to include OS/400. Other vendors have developed versions of REXX for Unix and for Tandem computers. Thanks largely to the relative clarity and completeness of Mike Cowlishaw's original definition of REXX, there is a high degree of compatibility among existing versions of the language.

Ease of use in end-user personal programming was the predominant objective in the design of REXX. Several key characteristics contribute to this ease of use. They include:

character-string orientation

dynamic data typing (no declarations)

reliable, machine-independent arithmetic

automatic storage management

protection from "crashing"

content-addressable data structures

straightforward access to system commands and facilities

few artificial limitations

In this introductory section, we will touch on each of these points. It should be mentioned, also, that REXX's ease of use does not limit its appeal to end users only. The same characteristics make it useful to professional programmers as a utility programming language for "quick and dirty" jobs, because REXX programs can be developed and debugged much faster than programs in most conventional languages, even if the user is an experienced programmer.

In overall appearance, REXX is a fairly conventional language, not too much unlike Pascal, C, or other languages which trace their ancestry to Algol. This is in contrast to languages like Snobol, LISP, or Smalltalk, which explore very different approaches to programming.

Thus, REXX has much in common with other Algol-like procedural languages—variables, expressions, control structures, subroutines, and I/O facilities.

The following is a complete REXX program that prompts for a file name, then asks the user to make a selection from a menu, and executes a command corresponding to the selection. The fact that the program should require no further explanation to be understood illustrates the naturalness and readability of the language.

```
/* execute file utilities */
say 'Enter file name:'
pull file_name
say 'Choose a file operation by number:'
say '  1 - Edit'
say '  2 - Print'
say '  3 - Delete'
pull response
select
   when response = 1 then
      'edit' file_name
   when response = 2 then
      'print' file_name
   when response = 3 then
      'erase' file_name
   otherwise
   say response 'is an incorrect choice.'
   end
exit
```

One important point about this program arises from the fact that REXX originated as a system procedure language. Specifically, the capability of executing system or application commands is an integral part of the language, rather than a function which is available (if at all) only through library routines. In other words, like a Unix shell language or the MS-DOS and OS/2 batch language, REXX automatically passes commands to the surrounding "environment" for execution. We'll have more to say about this when we explain how REXX can be used as a universal macro language.

Perhaps the most noteworthy departure of REXX from other Algol-like languages is its "natural" data typing. All data is treated as character strings. Numbers, including both integers and reals, are just special cases of strings. Numbers need to be recognized as such for computational purposes only, but no explicit conversion, no "formatting," is required for communications with humans. This alone is a major aid to usability, as any novice who was ever baffled by a "format" statement can testify.

Another consequence of this approach is that data declarations are never required (or even possible). Data declarations in other languages are really provided for the convenience of the computer, not the user. They are an accommodation of the fact that computers use a variety of internal data representations for different purposes and must be told which representation to use for a given data item. REXX isolates the user from all concern with these internal representations.

A further side effect of treating all data as character strings is that there need to be no inconvenient limits on the magnitudes of numeric data items. Although seldom required, hundreds of digits can be handled in REXX as easily (for the user) as five or six. Errors both gross and subtle that result from the inability to represent a number in a particular word size simply aren't possible. This also makes REXX programs much more portable between widely different computer architectures.

In particular, REXX does not cause a program failure when a computation exceeds a user-definable maximum precision. It does not even generate wildly incorrect results, as other languages usually do, when an "overflow" occurs. Instead, it discards the least significant digits of a result in order to stay within the specified degree of precision.

In conventional languages, data declarations not only specify internal representations to use, but also define storage allocation. Since there are no declarations in REXX, it is not necessary to worry about allocation issues (at least as long as enough storage is available). This is another great simplification. All data items, even elements of arrays, are allocated storage automatically when, and only when, they are required. They are also deallocated automatically as soon as possible.

Another pleasant benefit of REXX's dynamic memory management is that REXX is almost crash-proof, even on a CPU without memory protection. One of the most unpleasant experiences in programming for end users (or professionals) is the tendency for undebugged programs to crash themselves, or even the operating system, because they have overwritten their own code, or code belonging to other applications or the system. This is essentially impossible in REXX. (The exception is such things as functions provided explicitly to give access to external memory.)

Another unusual feature of REXX is the way *arrays* are handled. In REXX, data variables have names which are either *simple* or *compound*. A *simple* name is just a sequence of alphanumeric characters that contains no periods. A *compound* name is composed of two or more simple names connected by periods, for example, age.fred. The portion of a compound name before the first period is called the *stem;* it is taken literally. The remaining portions of the name are themselves variables which can be substituted. In effect, these are subscripts.

In order to work with arrays of any number of dimensions, one uses a stem followed by the appropriate number of subscripts. For instance, `temperature.x.y.z` is an element of a three-dimensional array called `temperature`. If the variables `x`, `y`, `z` have values 1, 2, 3, respectively, this element is `temperature.1.2.3`.

There are several important points here. The first is that no storage is allocated except for array elements that have actually been assigned values. The subscripts may be as large as necessary, but as long as there are only three elements having values, only three are stored, so the array can be very sparse.

But more importantly than that, the array subscripts need not be numeric—they can have any data value at all. This permits *associative indexing,* in which the subscripts are general nonnumeric data. For instance, one can have an `age` array whose elements include, in particular, `age.fred`, `age.sally`, etc. A computation can deal with a data reference like `age.person`, where `person` is a variable that ranges over values `fred`, `sally`, etc.

It should be apparent by now that the uniform representation of data as character strings is very important in REXX. This is connected with another design objective of the language, which is to place a great emphasis on symbolic manipulation. Since most system commands and application programs interact with users—or with REXX—much more with arbitrary strings of symbols than just with numbers, this is very appropriate for a system command language.

The most basic operation possible with character strings is concatenation, so REXX makes it as easy as possible to express. There are several flavors of this. The following example illustrates two of them:

```
'The date is:' month'/'day'/'year'.'
```

Here, strings enclosed in quotes are literals, while `month`, `day`, and `year` are variable names. In this expression, all of these parts are simply concatenated together, just as written. The extra blank before `month` is even retained, because it is actually the operator for "concatenate with a blank in between." No explicit operator is required to express direct concatenation. (An explicit operator, " | | ", is provided for cases where juxtaposition alone would be ambiguous.)

A large number of other character-string manipulation primitives are provided in REXX by means of built-in functions. Indeed, this is one of the most agreeable features of REXX. Included are such operations as substring, replacement, translation, verification, insertion, searching, and the like. There are even operations to reverse the characters of a string or to center a string in a given field. Since it is frequently useful to treat a string as a sequence of "words" delimited by blanks, there are a number of functions to count and extract such words.

THE APPLICATION PROGRAMMING INTERFACE

There's a lot more to REXX than what we've been able to describe so far. There will be time enough for that later. For now, let's turn our attention to how REXX facilitates end-user computing by providing a universal macro language.

REXX cannot be fully understood or comprehended in terms of its language features alone. There is an aspect to REXX that is ordinarily not even considered to be a part of other programming languages. Namely, all reasonable implementations of REXX come equipped with an *application programming interface*. This is a set of defined interfaces that allow applications written in other languages to communicate with REXX programs in various ways. Although the details of the interface necessarily differ from one implementation to another (at least in different operating systems), certain core functionality is always present.

Of course, it's not unusual for professional programmers to be able to build a single application using several different languages. However, application users do not ordinarily have the privilege of adding their own code to the application with conventional languages like C. If users are permitted to add code at all, it is in the form of special-purpose "macro" or "script" languages provided by—and specific to—the application.

What REXX offers, rather uniquely with its well-defined application programming interface, is the ability to allow end users to write application extensions in a single language—for any application that supports the interfaces.

The special-purpose languages embedded in applications today are variously called *macro languages, script languages, batch languages, shell languages,* and so forth. Macro languages (for applications like spreadsheets and word processors) and script languages (for communications programs) are especially well known. They are designed with little but their own application in mind and usually are not very suitable for general-purpose programming. Yet, because such languages are used by far more people than just professional programmers, they actually represent the most widely used computer languages today.

Though there are some fortunate exceptions, many of these languages are just as hard to use as traditional programming languages. Even so, because they were conceived and implemented with one particular application in mind, they don't have the power and flexibility of traditional languages.

Furthermore, since these languages are "captives" of their respective applications, they cannot be used for other applications. They have no concept of a general-purpose, standardized interface that can be used effectively by any application or by the operating system itself. In contrast to such macro languages, and to traditional programming languages as well, REXX includes a definition of how to interface to other system components at a functional level.

Probably the most unfortunate thing about such macro languages is how many of them there are—each application has its own. Yet there is no useful purpose served by having a different language for each application.

While these problems are coming to be recognized and better understood, it is less well known that the problems were addressed and solved long ago with REXX. What had to be done was to define both a sufficiently rich and powerful language and a set of interfaces for communicating between that language and other applications. For this to work, the interfaces are probably more important than specific details of the language.

The important thing is that REXX can communicate with any application that implements the required interfaces, so it can act as the single "macro" language used by all such applications. Therefore, a user need only learn a single language in order to write procedures that control a number of applications.

This is precisely what happened in VM/CMS with REXX, and even more dramatically with ARexx on the Amiga. In order for this approach to achieve its purpose, many software vendors must support the same interfaces in their own applications. As a result, in VM/CMS and on the Amiga there are now many applications and development tools—editors, word processors, spreadsheets, database systems, and communications packages—that use REXX as their macro language.

Something even better than being able to use a single language to control multiple applications sequentially is to be able to do this simultaneously. A language such as REXX (and the associated interfaces) that supports this can then be a "glue" that permits combining powerful, general tools together in useful and interesting ways. It is an integrating agent that makes it easy to build larger systems out of simpler building blocks. It facilitates and encourages a modular, building-block approach to application development.

So, the application programming interface of REXX is a feature of importance equal to the details of the language itself. Unfortunately, this is the last we can speak of it here, because the purpose of this book is to provide a comprehensive exposition of programming in REXX.

The details of how to use the programming interface to communicate between REXX and an application form an interesting subject in themselves. But they inevitably vary from one operating system where REXX is implemented to the next, so they are best described separately for each specific environment.

Hopefully, though, an awareness of the existence of this interface and what it means for the ability to use REXX as a universal macro language will help motivate learning of the language itself, because, once you've learned REXX, you will be able to use the same language in many different applications.

WHAT'S IN THIS BOOK

Given that caution about what is not in the book, it is appropriate to say a little about what is. To begin with, the reader may well wonder how this book relates to Mike Cowlishaw's *The REXX Language* (which I will subsequently refer to simply as TRL). As the inventor of REXX, Mike's words are authoritative. His book is a very well-written, clear, and concise definition of the language. Unlike most language definitions, it is eminently readable. It has formed the basis of IBM's documentation on REXX from the beginning, up through IBM's latest "Systems Application Architecture" (SAA) language specification. My debt to Mike's book is obvious.

However, it is a language definition. As such, it organizes information in a way that is not optimal for actually learning the language. For instance, all keyword instructions are described in one long chapter, and all built-in functions in another. This sort of organization tends to obscure natural functional groupings. Certain instructions and functions are ordinarily used in close association, and it is sometimes difficult to perceive such affinities in TRL. In this book, on the other hand, I have tried to group language features together by function and purpose. Character string handling, for example, occupies two consecutive chapters (string handling per se and the PARSE instruction). All information on I/O is collected into another chapter. And so forth. I hope that this effort to put related information together as much as possible will be a substantial advantage in learning REXX.

In a few cases, experience with TRL has revealed areas of the definition that are simply unclear and incomplete. This is most especially so in the treatment of I/O. In writing my own chapter on this, I struggled time and again with questions that were just not answered by Mike's book. In this case, I have tried to point out what the open questions are. It is not up to me to provide the final answers, though often my opinion will not be well concealed. The answers will come from users of the language and will ultimately be rendered into language standards by the

ANSI X3J18 committee (about which I will have a few more words later).

Historically, the reason for the problems with I/O in REXX is clear. This is the only area of the language which was not part of Mike's original VM/CMS implementation of REXX. Consequently, it was not subjected to the same degree of iterative refinement that benefitted other parts of the language so markedly. It is true that Mike developed a function package for VM/CMS which implemented his specification, but it never became part of the released product.

There are just a few other areas where I believe I have been able to improve on the treatment in TRL. One of these is exception handling. I believe that the exposition of this was a bit too concise and did not really explain all of the issues. Another is the PARSE instruction. It is generally recognized that Mike's presentation was just a little too informal for a language definition and has allowed a great deal of misunderstanding over the years. My own exposition is also informal, but I hope it is a little more complete and that it presents the mechanics of PARSE a little more clearly.

I have in some cases decided to use new terminology or terminology that differs in minor respects from that used in TRL. The primary example of this is my choice in Chap. 3 to introduce the term *statement* for what was previously called an *instruction,* and to restrict the latter term to what was previously called a *keyword instruction.* I have also tried to make a greater issue of the distinction (in Chap. 2) between the name of a variable and the symbol used to refer to it.

All that being said, I must confess that in some respects I have deliberately attempted to be less thorough and precise about some things than TRL is. The purpose of this book, after all, is to offer instruction and advice on how to write REXX programs. It does not need to bear the burden of being a complete prescriptive document on exactly what the language is. I highly recommend that the reader turn to Mike's book for that. In fact, ideally, TRL should be read along with my book and, while it is quite possible to learn REXX without TRL, no education in REXX is complete without it.

One of the facets of REXX that I don't treat rigorously is arithmetic and the precise definitions of the arithmetic operators. I feel that, for the most part, users will find that REXX does "the right thing" as far as arithmetic is concerned, and that it is no more necessary to know the exact rules REXX employs in order to use it than it is to know the exact rules of a calculator. I feel that excessive preoccupation with these rules may be a stumbling block to actually learning the language.

I have not attempted to give all the details for each built-in function of the language. That is, I have not tried to define exactly what all legal arguments are for each of the functions, nor how they will behave in all cases. That kind of thing is just plain boring. It's in TRL. And the best way to learn it is by experimenting with each new function as you use it.

I won't have much to say about debugging beyond Chap. 13. REXX is rather unusual among programming languages in that it includes a precise, formal definition of its debugging commands. It is unquestionably a good thing for a language to have built-in debugging capabilities, since that is a very necessary language feature which is often slighted. Having debugging commands included in the very definition of the language tends to ensure that all implementations will contain a consistent minimum level of debugging functionality. However, it is also true that most programming environments today have debugging tools of far greater sophistication than the minimal features that REXX prescribes. At the time of this writing, such tools have not yet become common for REXX. But it is certain that they will.

THE REXX STANDARDIZATION PROCESS

A moment ago I alluded to the ANSI X3J18 subcommittee which at the time of this writing had just recently begun to draft a standard for REXX. Many present users of REXX will wonder why this is necessary, given the existence of TRL, or at least whether substantial work is needed to turn TRL into a standard. I think the answer, unfortunately, is that quite a bit of work is going to be needed. And this is true despite the high quality of the definition in TRL, and despite the fact that REXX has suffered much less from divergent implementations than have most other languages which have been in active use for a decade.

One reason for this is, as I have stated, that there are certain areas like I/O that just aren't adequately defined in TRL. I/O, of course, is something that is notoriously hard to standardize across diverse operating systems. However, the purpose of X3J18 is to produce a standard which will to the greatest extent possible enable true portability of REXX programs from one environment to the next. I/O is such an important part of any program that portability is a hollow and meaningless ideal if it does not extend to I/O. Exception handling is another area in need of greater precision in order to ensure a standard for a truly portable language.

Portability has, rather suddenly, become a matter of much more urgency, because just in the last two or three years implementations of REXX have appeared on so many new platforms. Since REXX has been designated as IBM's SAA "Procedures Language," IBM has introduced versions for MVS, OS/2, and OS/400. Other vendors have added versions for OS/2, Amiga DOS, Unix, and other systems. The genuine need now exists to make many REXX programs run in several of these environments.

Portability of REXX programs is of the greatest importance. Even though REXX is essentially a language for personal programming, you should not assume that means you won't have to port programs that you write in REXX to different environments. In fact, if anything, it may mean a higher likelihood of the need to port a program once or more in its lifetime. You may well find that computer technology is moving so rapidly, and computing environments are diversifying so much, that the tools you write in REXX today for VM/CMS are needed tomorrow on MVS, and the day after that on MS-DOS or OS/2 or Amiga DOS or Unix. It is the charter of X3J18 to make that work as easily as possible.

REXX already has a good head start in the portability area. As we will see, arithmetic in REXX is intentionally defined so as not to be machine dependent. This is very unlike most other languages, which rely on hardware-specific data formats and arithmetic operations. It would be unfortunate to use this inherent advantage in portability by failing to promote it in other areas, like I/O.

Another reason the REXX standardization is becoming a more urgent issue than in the past is that, with increasing usage, various shortcomings in the language have become apparent. These involve a variety of things, such as the absence of a true subscript notation, difficulties in dealing with the scope of variables, and inability to iterate over all variables sharing a common stem.

On top of that, the value of many of the constructs of *object-oriented* programming is beginning to reveal itself to programmers working in both traditional and the newer *graphical user interface* (GUI) computing environments. It is inevitable that some of these constructs will become available in REXX within the next two or three years.

So REXX may well experience much more rapid evolution in the next few years than it has in the last ten. These evolutionary changes need to be made in a principled way, and with the participation of the entire (rapidly expanding) community of people and organizations now interested in REXX. Though individual language implementors will usually spearhead the introduction of particular language innovations, it is important for these changes to be subject to impartial professional scrutiny and peer review very early on, before they become de facto standards.

By ANSI rules, formal participation in subcommittees like X3J18 is open to all interested parties. Even though you or your organization must bear your own expenses of participation, you should be aware that the option is available to you—even if you are representing only yourself. If you do become interested in bringing issues to the attention of the X3J18 committee, an option that will be more practical to most is to raise your concerns directly with members of the committee.

X3J18 members are accessible through a large number of electronic networks: the Internet, BITNET, the UUCP network, and commercial networks like CompuServe, BIX, and MCI mail. (My most accessible mail addresses are cgd@well.sf.ca.us and 72777.2554@compuserve.com.) I, or any other committee member, can provide you with mailing addresses of other X3J18 participants. Please get in touch with us if you have concerns about the language.

GETTING STARTED

It is assumed that you have access to one or more REXX implementations through your work or on your personal computer. The very best way to learn REXX is by starting immediately to use it and write programs. Since REXX is a language for personal programming, it is very likely that you already have one or more pet projects for which REXX would be a very suitable language. I recommend that you plan to begin implementing these ideas in parallel with the reading of this book. You may be surprised at how easy it is to write REXX without already knowing it!

Another good approach is to take some of the examples from this book or elsewhere, enter them on your computer, and start to run them and modify them to see how they work. (Copies of all the programs in this book are, of course, available in machine-readable form from the author.) Use the SAY and TRACE instructions liberally to step through the examples one instruction at a time, and observe how values change and results are produced. Modify the examples and improve them.

Chapter 2 provides an overview of REXX that, hopefully, is sufficient to let you fruitfully begin to work with the examples in the rest of the book. Unless you already know a little REXX, Chap. 2 is required reading. The material in Chaps. 3, 4, and 5 contains the remainder of the absolute "must know" details of the language. Beyond that point, you can read the rest of the book in just about any order. There are interdependencies among chapters, as well as forward and backward references (though hopefully more of the latter). But each of the later chapters has been written to offer, as much as possible, a free-standing treatment of its topic.

A good candidate for the very first example to work with is the REXXTRY program at the beginning of Chap. 12. It occurs late in the book because it takes some prerequisites to explain exactly how it works and the language features that it uses. But it can be run without full understanding. What it allows you to do when you run it is to enter REXX statements, one or more at a time, for immediate execution.

This lets you see right away what each statement does and observe the effects of simple variations. You can see at a glance how substitution of variable values works and how REXX expressions are evaluated. It is very good for working with built-in functions to get a hands-on feeling for how each works.

And so, all that remains here is to say: I hope you find REXX and this exposition of it to be useful.

Language Overview

Learning a new language can be intimidating, whether it is a natural language or a computer language. For computer languages, the actual difficulty of the learning process depends a great deal on the nature of the language itself. Because ease of use was a primary consideration in the design of REXX, learning it should prove to be as easy as learning almost any other computer language, and probably easier.

Many readers will already know one or more computer languages. Since REXX uses concepts which are widely used in other popular, contemporary languages, it should be especially easy to learn. That is, language constructs in REXX such as literals, variables, arithmetic expressions, conditional statements, subroutines, and so forth are very similar to their counterparts in other languages like C, Basic, or Pascal. There are, however, some constructs in REXX which are both powerful and not present in most common languages. These include such things as compound variables and the PARSE instruction. Experienced programmers can use much of their present programming knowledge and will want to focus on the distinctive features of REXX.

On the other hand, for beginning programmers there are many concepts that have to be learned regardless of which language one starts with. Since REXX is intended to be used as a system command language (among other things), it will in fact be the first serious programming language that many people learn. The book *Modern Programming Using REXX* by Robert O'Hara and David Gomberg is highly recommended. It uses REXX to provide an introduction to programming. While it is beyond the scope of the present text to teach programming, beginners will find that much of the REXX language is simple, intuitive, and a natural step from using operating system batch files and application macros.

GETTING STARTED

A complete REXX program may consist of as little as a single line, for instance:

```
say "hello world"
```

This program displays the words hello world on the screen. Here, SAY is a REXX reserved word that begins an output instruction. "hello world" is a literal string. A single blank separates the verb from the literal. SAY is not always a reserved word in REXX. It is reserved and has a special meaning only when it is the first word of a *clause*. SAY could be used elsewhere in the program, even in the same clause, without any conflict (though this may not be good REXX style).

There are two fundamental program units in REXX: the *statement* and the *clause*. There are three types of statements: REXX instructions which begin with keywords such as SAY, assignments of some value to a variable, and commands to external environments. A clause is a slightly smaller unit of executable code. Most statements, including assignments and commands, are single clauses all by themselves. Most keyword instructions are also single clauses, but a few (such as IF and DO) are more complex and consist of multiple clauses. Also, for technical reasons, a label is considered to be a clause which is neither a statement by itself nor part of a statement. We will go much further into these details in this chapter and the next, but for now you can think of a REXX program as a sequence of statements.

In REXX terminology, the example above consists of a single statement which is also a single clause. Although clauses and lines are not the same thing, in general, REXX programs tend to be written as if they were. That is, the usual practice is to put at most one clause on a line. Multiple clauses can be written on a single line by ending each clause with a semicolon, but this usually decreases the readability of the program. It is possible to write REXX programs consisting of thousands of clauses with each one on a separate line and without using a single semicolon.

So, the end of a line normally means the end of a clause as well. However, most REXX implementations place a limit on the length of a single line. Most editors or word processors used to write programs do, too. And for readability (always a very important concern with REXX), it is desirable to keep lines shorter than the width of the screen or editing window. The length of a clause in most REXX implementations is also limited, but it is usually longer than 80 characters, which is the width of most screens. Therefore, some mechanism is necessary for continuing a single clause onto additional lines. This is done by ending each line to be continued with a comma:

```
say "To be or not to be:",
    "That is the question."
```

This example will display the two quoted phrases on the same line of the screen, because it is really just one clause as far as REXX is concerned. It is equivalent to:

```
say "To be or not to be: that is the question."
```

Blanks play a very special role in REXX—several roles, actually. One or more blanks separate individual tokens in a REXX clause, just as in the preceding example where a blank separated the verb and the literal. Except within literals, it is irrelevant whether one or more than one blank is used to delimit tokens. Therefore, it is common to use blanks to help format a program for greater readability. Above, for instance, they were used to line up the quoted phrases.

One of the design goals of REXX was to make a language in which it is especially easy to work with character strings, and to do so in as natural a way as possible. One of the most frequent operations on character strings is concatenation, in which two strings are joined together. This is expressed in REXX simply by writing the two strings together with one or more blanks in between. So, a third way to write the example we have been using is

```
say "To be or not to be:" "that is the question."
```

Here, there are three *tokens* in the clause: the verb and two literal strings. When this statement is executed, the two literals are concatenated, and a single blank is inserted between them. Only one blank is inserted in the concatenation regardless of how many blanks separate the literals.

A REXX clause can contain other types of tokens. The verb SAY is a special case of a symbol token. Such a token begins with an alphabetic character and extends to the next delimiter. Delimiters are either blanks or special characters like ":", ";", "*", "+", and "\". Such delimiter characters may be tokens all by themselves (as are each of the ones just mentioned), or they may be the start of longer operator tokens such as "\=" (not equal). Operator tokens include the standard arithmetic operators ("+", "–", "*", "/", "**"), string operators such as "||" (concatenation) and ">" (comparison), and logical operators such as "&" (logical and) and "\" (negation).

Numbers are the other major sort of token. A number is delimited like a symbol, but it consists only of numerals, ".", "+", "–", and "e". Numbers can be integers, decimals, or in exponential notation, and may be signed. The following are all valid numbers in REXX:

```
666
2.718281828
-32768
6.63E-27
```

PUTTING THE ELEMENTS TOGETHER

We now have enough terminology to examine a more interesting REXX program. The task is to convert temperature expressed as Fahrenheit to Centigrade. The program should ask the user to enter a number representing the Fahrenheit temperature and display the corresponding Centigrade value. It should terminate when the user enters nothing but blanks. Here is the program:

```
/* Convert Fahrenheit to Centigrade */
do forever
    say 'Enter temperature in Fahrenheit:'
    parse pull fahrenheit
    if fahrenheit = '' then
        exit
    centigrade = 5 * (fahrenheit - 32) / 9
    say 'Temperature is' centigrade 'degrees C.'
end
```

Let's look at what's new here, line by line. The first line is a comment. As in C and PL/I, comments in REXX begin with /* and end with */. Comments may extend over as many lines as necessary without the need to do anything special to indicate continuation. Beginning every program with a comment is recommended as good programming style. It is also required in some implementations of REXX in order to distinguish the file from others that may use a different language.

The second line (do forever) contains the REXX reserved word DO as its first token. This begins a loop which extends to the matching END instruction on the last line. Any other REXX statements can occur between the DO and the END. This includes other DO statements, so that loops can be nested up to an implementation-defined limit, each beginning with DO and terminated with END. A DO statement may have a number of optional modifiers that specify a control variable to be incremented on each iteration, or define conditions on when the loop should be ended. In this case, the keyword FOREVER means that the DO statement itself has no specified terminating condition. Other instructions within the body of the loop can cause it to terminate. In this example, that is the function of the EXIT instruction on the sixth line.

The third line is a SAY instruction. In this case, the literal string has been delimited with single quotation marks (') instead of double ones ("). This is done as a convenience in case quotation marks need to be part of the literal, as in

```
'"Jump!" he said.'
```

That is, all literal strings are terminated with the sort of quotation mark with which they began. An exception to this is made if the quotation character is doubled. Within a literal that begins with the same sort of quotation mark, the doubled one is treated as if it were a single one that is part of the literal, so that

```
"""Jump!"" he said."
```

is exactly the same literal.

The next line, parse pull fahrenheit, reads user input. It is the most common input instruction in REXX, corresponding to the output SAY instruction. PARSE PULL causes a read to the keyboard, which is terminated when carriage return (Enter) is pressed. Everything typed up to (but not including) the carriage return is assigned to a REXX variable, fahrenheit in this case.

There is actually a shorter input instruction, PULL. This does input just like PARSE PULL, but has the additional side effect of converting the input to uppercase. (PULL is shorthand for PARSE UPPER PULL.) Sometimes this is useful; more often it is annoying. Here it doesn't matter, since the input should be a number.

A REXX variable like fahrenheit is any symbol beginning with an alphabetic character, except for a reserved word occurring at the start of a clause. (In certain kinds of statements, such as DO, there may be reserved words after the first token.) Variable names may be very long—up to 250 characters in most implementations of REXX.

REXX is generally not sensitive to alphabetic case. So symbols can be written in either upper- or lowercase, or any mixture, and no distinction is made. The convention in this book will be to use lowercase in most examples and uppercase for REXX reserved words mentioned outside of an example (for emphasis). The most obvious instance in which case matters is in character string literals. Internally, REXX converts the whole program (except for literals and comments) to uppercase.

The next two lines of the example,

```
if fahrenheit = '' then
   exit
```

begin with an IF instruction that performs a test and executes other instructions according to the results. Technically, REXX considers this statement to consist of several clauses. The first begins with IF and concludes with an expression that must evaluate to 1 or 0. 1 represents *true,* and 0 represents *false.* In the present case, the expression uses the "=" operator to compare the value of the variable FAHRENHEIT to the literal string " (null or empty string). One of the convenient characteristics of the "=" (equality) operator when comparing strings is that leading and trailing blanks are ignored.

This behavior of ignoring blanks in circumstances where they are not meaningful is common throughout REXX; it is one of the ways in which REXX tries to be helpful. In the present instance it is useful because the user is expected to type either a number or nothing. Several blanks are taken as equivalent to nothing; it is considered irrelevant whether any blanks are entered before or after the number. Blanks are in fact stored internally. The "=" operator just happens to ignore them. Blanks in the middle of a string are not ignored. If it is important to recognize leading or trailing blanks, another operator ("==", exact equality) can be used.

THEN is a reserved word in an IF clause. In fact, it is considered to be a separate clause all by itself. Its purpose is to mark the end of the conditional expression. The statement immediately following THEN is executed if (and only if) the expression after IF evaluates to 1. Here, that is the case, provided that the expressions on either side of "=" are the same except for leading and trailing blanks. (Alphabetic case is significant to the "=" operator.) The expression here is evaluated by taking the value of the FAHRENHEIT variable and comparing it to a null string. If this value contains any nonblank characters, the value of the whole expression is 0, and the statement after THEN would not be executed.

In the present example, the clause after THEN is another REXX reserved word, EXIT. This instruction terminates not only the DO loop but the entire REXX program, and allows control to return to the operating system. The statement after THEN could be any legal REXX statement, including another IF statement. In case several statements need to be executed when the condition is true (i.e., 1), they can be enclosed between a DO ... END pair.

The end of the IF statement is recognized because the line following EXIT begins with a token other than the reserved word ELSE, which would be used if there were a statement to be executed in case the conditional expression has the value 0. Since there is no such statement in this example, the next statement will always be executed. The next statement here

```
centigrade = 5 * (fahrenheit - 32) / 9
```

is an assignment, recognized by the presence of the assignment operator as the second token in the clause. Here, the variable named CENTI-GRADE is given the value of the expression on the right-hand side.

In this case the expression is purely an algebraic one. Although that value of the variable FAHRENHEIT was stored as a character string, and could be used as such if appropriate, here it is automatically treated as a number. This illustrates one of the key characteristics of REXX: as little distinction as possible is maintained between different data types until they are actually used. REXX neither requires nor even possesses data type declarations. All data is stored internally as a character string (at least in principle). Only when values are actually used are any conversions made—if necessary and if possible. Of course, only certain character strings represent numbers, and conversion may not be possible. In our example, the user may have entered a nonnumeric value such as OK, which would cause an error when the expression is evaluated. Although the example has no error checking, REXX has various ways to do checking, and a serious program certainly should have appropriate checks.

Since the algebraic expression involves division, the result will probably not be integral. REXX takes care of the decimal part automatically, even though no declarations were used to distinguish between integral, fixed point, or floating point numbers. The default precision that REXX supports is implementation dependent, but frequently it is nine digits (apart from the exponent, if any). If more or less precision is required for a particular purpose, it can be requested. The maximum precision that REXX supports depends on the implementation, but can be very large, even thousands of digits.

The last interesting line in the example is

```
say 'Temperature is' centigrade 'degrees C.'
```

The part of the clause after SAY is actually an expression consisting of the concatenation of two literal strings with a variable value. The value of centigrade is a computed number, but, because it occurs in a character string expression, it is automatically converted to the printable character representation of the number. Concatenation of strings is implicit in the expression; no explicit operator is required. The string concatenation automatically includes a blank between each operand as a convenience. The result displayed by this instruction might be, for instance,

```
Temperature is 37.7777778 degrees C.
```

This would be the result of converting 100 degrees F. The result has been expressed with exactly nine digits of accuracy and has even been rounded up appropriately. No complicated formatting directions are required to produce this output, so such common forms of output are simple and natural to write. However, there are ways to display the answer with less precision if desired.

Concatenation works the way it does in order that the form of the expression in the program resembles the final output as closely as possible (i.e., with blanks inserted). In case concatenation without intervening blank is required, an explicit operator ("| |") can be used. Thus,

```
say 'Temperature is '||centigrade||' degrees C.'
```

would produce the same results. Notice that the blanks have simply been moved inside the literal strings. In many cases (and this is one of them), the explicit operator can be dispensed with, so that

```
say 'Temperature is 'centigrade' degrees C.'
```

also produces the same results. REXX parsing rules still allow this expression to be resolved into three tokens (literal, symbol, literal) with an implied concatenation operation between tokens. But because there is no blank between the tokens, none is added by the concatenation operator. Although the detailed rules of how REXX handles such expressions are somewhat complicated to fully enumerate, the net result is intuitively just what it should be, with a minimum of required symbols.

PROGRAM STRUCTURE

Viewed from a top-down perspective, a REXX program consists of a series of *statements*. There are several different kinds of statements. The example we just examined consisted predominantly of *instruction* statements beginning with REXX keywords like DO, SAY, PULL, and IF. The only other statement type present was one *assignment,* distinguished by the presence of the = sign as the second token.

There are a couple of other program elements not illustrated yet. *Labels,* which consist of a symbol followed by a colon, may be mixed in among statements. Labels are used to define the start of an internal subroutine or function.

Finally, there is a third type of statement, the *command,* which is unique to REXX among popular languages. This is literally the "everything else" category. REXX assumes that anything which is not an instruction, assignment, or label is a command. A command is not interpreted by REXX itself. Instead, it is passed to an external environment like an operating system or application program that is equipped to process commands. In a typical operating system like MS-DOS or OS/2, COPY, ERASE, and SORT are examples of commands.

REXX's ability to handle commands is very important, since it makes it possible to write *batch* procedures and application *macros* or *scripts* in REXX. Although other languages may provide such capability through library functions, it is seldom an intrinsic part of the language as in REXX. Hence, other languages are unable to handle commands as naturally as REXX does. Since a command is just another type of statement, commands in effect provide a way to extend the language by introducing new directives. For instance, when REXX is used as a language for writing scripts for a communication program, the program itself may provide commands like SEND and WAIT. In use, these can be regarded almost as part of REXX itself. The benefit to an application program in employing REXX as a script or macro language is that the application needs to supply only its own specific commands, while all of the standard language facilities like variables, arithmetic, looping, and subroutines are provided by REXX.

Although REXX doesn't ultimately execute operating system or application commands, it can process command statements by substituting variable values and evaluating arithmetic or character string expressions. An example of this might be

```
'copy' source_file destination_file options
```

This statement is actually a REXX expression that begins with a literal string and is followed by three symbols. The symbols are variable names for which the current values are substituted. Finally, all strings are concatenated with single intervening blanks to produce a result. This statement is a command because it is not any of the other three types, so it is then passed to the default execution environment for execution.

Since commands are application-specific, they play no further part in the structure of a REXX program as such. The other three clause types (instructions, assignments, and labels) do, so we will concentrate our attention on them. There are currently about 25 (depending on how they are counted) different instruction types. Some of these instructions, specifically CALL, DO, EXIT, IF, ITERATE, LEAVE, RETURN, SELECT, and SIGNAL, define the flow of control within a REXX program. That is, they provide for testing, iteration, and subroutines. The remaining instruction types perform diverse functions like I/O (SAY, PULL), string parsing (PARSE), variable handling (DROP), and debugging (TRACE). Assignment statements can conveniently be regarded as another type of variable handling instruction, even though an assignment doesn't begin with a REXX keyword.

Testing is the simplest control flow construct. As illustrated in the earlier example, REXX uses an IF ... THEN ... ELSE ... format for this fundamental operation. The ELSE part of this construct is optional. There is no specific keyword (such as ENDIF in other languages) required to end an IF statement. Context and REXX syntax rules are sufficient to handle IFs unambiguously. A complete IF statement might be:

```
if time = 0 then
    say "Cannot compute speed."
else
    say "The speed is" distance/time "Km/Hr."
return
```

Here, RETURN (to return from a subroutine or main program) will always be executed, because only one statement can ordinarily follow THEN or ELSE. The exception to this, if multiple statements are required to follow THEN or ELSE, is a series of statements bracketed by DO ... END. For instance:

```
if time = 0 then
    say "Cannot compute speed."
else do
    say distance "travelled in" time "hours,"
    say "The speed is" distance/time "Km/Hr."
    end
return
```

As always, the indentation is used only for clarity. As far as REXX is concerned, all statements could begin at the left margin. It is, however, necessary to place the ELSE on a new line unless the clause following THEN is terminated with a semicolon.

IF statements can also be nested, as is commonly done when several alternatives must be handled:

```
if hour < 12 then
   say "Good morning!"
else if hour < 18 then
   say "Good afternoon!"
else
   say "Good evening!"
```

Here, the second IF statement occurs following the first ELSE. DO . . . END pairs can also be nested within each other and within IFs as appropriate.

When a program must provide for testing many alternatives, a better way to do it than with nested IF statements is with the SELECT instruction. As with IF, the SELECT instruction really begins a compound statement, which might be something like:

```
select
   when country = 'Austria' then
      composer = 'Mozart'
   when country = 'Russia' then
      composer = 'Tchaikovsky'
   when country = 'Finland' then
      composer = 'Sibelius'
   otherwise
      composer = 'Beethoven'
   end
```

Here, after SELECT there is a series of WHEN . . . THEN . . . pairs, concluding with an OTHERWISE and finally an END. As with IF, some true/false condition follows each WHEN, and a statement to be executed when the corresponding condition is true follows THEN. Only the statement following the first true condition is executed. If none of the WHEN conditions is true, the statement following OTHERWISE is executed. If multiple statements need to be executed for each condition, they are grouped within DO . . . END pairs after THEN. SELECT statements can be nested within themselves and IFs in any combination up to some implementation-defined level of complexity.

The next major type of control flow is iteration, i.e., looping. All REXX loops begin with a DO instruction. By itself, DO is used together with END to group statements. In that case, the enclosed statements are executed only once. However, there are more complex forms of DO that provide for a wide range of loop control. Loops may repeat the statements within their range a specific number of times (or forever). Loops may have a control variable that is incremented each time through. Loops may, finally, have logical conditions that cause them to terminate.

For instance, to sum N terms of a geometric series of powers of a variable X:

```
sum = 0
do i = 1 to n
   sum = sum + x ** i
   end
```

($X**I$ is the expression for exponentiation.) Here I is the control variable. It is initialized explicitly to 1 and incremented (implicitly) by 1 each time through the loop, terminating at the point where it would exceed the value of the variable N. Expressions could be used instead of constants or variables for the initial and limit values. Increments other than 1 can be specified explicitly.

If initial values, increments, and limits for a control variable are specified by a variable or expression instead of a constant, the quantities are evaluated only once, before the loop is first executed. Sometimes it is desirable to decide whether to continue a loop based on quantities that are evaluated each time through. In that case, a subclause consisting of either of the keywords WHILE or UNTIL (or both) followed by an expression may be used. Thus, if we wanted to sum a geometric series up to the point where each summand is less than some limit, we might revise the preceding example to read:

```
sum = 0
do i = 1 by 1 until x ** i < 1e-10
   sum = sum + x ** i
   end
```

(X must have a value less than 1 for this to work. And, of course, this example is needlessly inefficient because it evaluates $X**I$ twice.) Conceptually, the difference between WHILE and UNTIL is that the former is tested at the top of the loop and the latter at the bottom. Note that no limit value for the control variable was supplied with a TO expression, but an increment was explicitly specified with a BY expression.

A DO loop does not need to have a control variable. Instead, it may simply specify how many times the loop is to be executed, using a constant, variable, or full expression. As we saw in the temperature conversion example above, this repetition count can even be forever. In this case, some means is still required for getting out of the loop. Any DO loop will be terminated by a RETURN instruction (which returns from a subroutine) or an EXIT instruction (which ends the REXX program). Another, less drastic way to get out of a DO loop is provided by the LEAVE instruction. It is particularly useful in a loop that is processing user input, for instance:

```
do forever
   say 'Enter next command:'
   pull command
   if command = 'QUIT' then
      leave
   /* other command processing */
   end
```

Here, if the user types quit, the response is converted to uppercase by
PULL, the LEAVE instruction is executed, and control passes to the next
statement after the END instruction.

A similar requirement in a loop is to be able to go back to the start
of the loop from somewhere in the middle, i.e., before the END instruction. This need is also frequently encountered when processing user
input:

```
do forever
   say 'Enter a number between 1 and 10:'
   pull number
   if number < 1 | number > 10 then do
      say 'Number entered was out of range.'
      iterate
      end
   /* process the number entered */
   end
```

In this example, "|" is the symbol for logical or: the compound condi-
tion in the IF instruction is true if either NUMBER < 1 or NUMBER > 10 is
true. If the condition is true, the two instructions bracketed by a DO . . .
END pair are executed. The second of these is ITERATE, which goes back
to the start of the repetitive DO instruction. Note that the DO instruction
on the fourth line of the example has no control variable, repetition
count, or UNTIL/WHILE condition. So it is not a repetitive DO; it does not
introduce a loop; and it is ignored by LEAVE and ITERATE instructions.
These instructions always refer to the innermost repetitive DO loop in
which they occur.

The third and last type of control structure in REXX is the procedure. A distinction is sometimes made between two types of procedures: subroutines and functions. A function must return a value,
while a subroutine usually does not. However, in REXX the same procedure may sometimes return a value and sometimes not, so this distinction isn't always relevant.

In most languages, procedures are identified unambiguously by the
language syntax, by using special keywords or symbols. This is not the
case in REXX. A procedure must begin with a label (i.e., a symbol followed by a colon), but not all labels introduce procedures. Whether or

not a given label actually introduces a procedure depends on how it is used.

There are two ways a label can be used so as to be the beginning of a procedure, corresponding to the distinction between subroutines and functions. A subroutine procedure is invoked with the CALL instruction:

```
call get_user_input
/* other processing */
...
get_user_input:
say 'Enter data:'
parse pull data
return
```

The name of the procedure here is get_user_input, which is the label before the first instruction of the procedure. A function procedure is invoked by using the name of the procedure in a *function reference* within a REXX expression. A function reference consists of a symbol followed immediately (with no blank spaces) by a left parenthesis. The preceding example could be modified slightly to use a function reference instead of a subroutine call:

```
answer = get_user_input()
/* other processing */
...
get_user_input:
say 'Enter data:'
parse pull data
return data
```

There are several things to notice about this example. Although the procedure has no parameters, it was necessary to use parentheses around an empty argument list in order to identify it as a function reference. Also, the RETURN instruction that ends the procedure contains an expression (here just a variable name) that is returned as the value of the function. In the example, the returned value is then assigned to another variable.

There is one subtle point to note about REXX procedures. Unlike the END of a DO . . . END pair, the RETURN instruction in a procedure does not have a syntactic function. That is, the RETURN does not necessarily constitute the last line of the procedure. This is particularly true if the RETURN occurs inside some conditional (IF or SELECT) construct. In fact, in REXX it's not really possible to identify syntactically where the end of a procedure is to be found. The end of a procedure, as well as the beginning, is defined purely by the flow of control during execution rather than by syntax. This circumstance can be a source of confusion and errors in REXX programs, so programmers need to take extra care, using comments and blank lines, to make it very clear to a reader where a procedure begins and ends.

It is not necessary that all procedures used in a REXX program be defined (by a label) within the program. In the first place, REXX comes with a large number of predefined built-in functions. These functions deal mostly with input/output and with character string manipulation. The character string functions are noteworthy because they augment the already strong support REXX provides for working with character strings. Many character string operations, like substring, character replacement, and blank-delimited token parsing, are implemented as built-in functions. Many less common operations are, also. This support adds up to a great deal of power and flexibility for handling character strings with REXX.

In addition to built-in functions, REXX also allows for external procedures, i.e., procedures defined in other files. This gets into an area of the language that is implementation dependent. Most implementations of REXX allow invoking an external procedure as either a subroutine or function by using the file name in the CALL instruction or function reference. Procedures that are internal to another file, i.e., defined by a label within the file, usually cannot be invoked in this way. However, other implementation-specific mechanisms such as *function packages* are usually available for allowing REXX programs to access external procedures, which may be either system-wide or part of a specific application, and which may be written in other languages.

THE REXX DATA MODEL

Now that we know at the highest level what the structure of a REXX program is, it's time to look more closely at how REXX manages data. There are two primary facts to remember about the REXX data model. The first is that all data is stored (conceptually at least) as character strings. That is, REXX in general does not recognize data types. All data in REXX, without exception, can be handled as a character string. It can be concatenated with other strings. String operations like substring can be performed on it. All data can be input and output without the need to perform conversions.

Certain operations in REXX, like arithmetic, do require the data to be understandable as a number, and will give an error if it isn't. But conversions in such cases are implicit and automatic. Even when data has to be treated as numeric, the user is relieved of the requirement present in other languages to be concerned with the internal representation of the number. That is, there is no distinction made between integer, binary, decimal, or floating point representations. Indeed, there is little need to be concerned with the precision of a number, i.e., the size or number of significant digits in it. By default, REXX allows for nine significant digits. If necessary, this default limit can be raised, subject only to limits of the specific implementation and available space.

The second primary fact about data in REXX is that the language makes no provision at all for declaring data. In other languages, data must usually be declared for at least three reasons: to specify the type of the data, to specify the amount of storage required for the data, and to specify the name used to access the data. All of these reasons are in reality designed for the convenience of the language processor rather than for the convenience of the user. REXX handles each of these details automatically. As just explained, it handles any necessary conversions implicitly. It automatically manages storage allocation. And it can always recognize variable names from context. Since REXX eliminates these needs for declaration of data, the language does not have any data declarations.

All data items in REXX are referred to with a symbolic name. REXX has no other way, such as pointers, to access data. This makes REXX very safe to use, since it is impossible to reference memory that has not been allocated. REXX symbols are tokens that contain only the upper- and lowercase alphabetic characters, numerals, and certain special characters ("!", ".", "?", and "_"). Not all valid REXX symbols can be used as the name of a variable, but the precise rules are not important at this point. Variable names can usually be quite long, though this is implementation dependent. Commonly the limit is 250 characters or more. REXX always converts symbols to uppercase before interpreting them.

A REXX variable acquires a value when it is the target of an assignment or in a few other specific cases such as PARSE. Such a variable is said to be initialized. It is legal in REXX to use uninitialized variables. This is because any uninitialized variable is assumed to have a value that is the same as its name. Although there are a few times where this convention is convenient, it is usually not any more advisable in REXX than it is in any other language. While a REXX program will never crash simply because it refers to an uninitialized variable (as can happen in many languages), it certainly may malfunction and give incorrect results. Though not the default, it is possible to force REXX to raise an error condition when an uninitialized variable is used inadvertently.

There are two kinds of variables in REXX: simple and compound. So far, all examples we have presented use simple variables. These behave much like variables in any other language. The other kind of variables, compound variables, is one of the most significant and characteristic features of the language. Compound variables are similar to arrays in other languages, but with significant differences (as well as advantages and disadvantages).

A compound variable is referred to with a symbol that contains one or more periods in it, such as:

```
array.i
two_dimensional_array.i.j
database_record.type.field.name
```

Each part of such a symbol is a simple symbol. We may speak of simple and compound symbols as (respectively) those that do not or do contain a period. There is a fundamental distinction in REXX between the symbol that refers to a variable and the actual name of the variable, although it is relevant only for compound variables. While it is true for simple variables that the symbol which refers to the variable and the variable's name are the same, this is not true for compound variables.

Let us agree to call each portion of a compound symbol delimited by periods a *node*. The first node, up to the first period, is called the *stem*. The rule for mapping a symbol to a variable name is as follows: for each node in the symbol except the stem, substitute the value of the variable named by the corresponding simple symbol. As a special case, for each node corresponding to a simple symbol which names an uninitialized variable, substitute the name in uppercase. (This is, after all, the "value" of an uninitialized variable.) The stem does not undergo substitution (but it is uppercased). The result is the name of a variable. (The periods are retained, too, so the name contains at least as many periods as the original symbol.) This name, sometimes called the *derived name,* is then used just like an ordinary (simple) name in whatever way is appropriate for the context.

To take the simplest example, suppose

```
x = 1
```

and y is undefined. Then

```
foo.x = 'Renoir'
foo.y = 'Monet'
```

assigns values to two variables, having derived names FOO.1 and FOO.Y, respectively. The statement

```
say foo.x foo.y
```

displays Renoir Monet. Many different symbols can refer to the same variable if they produce the same derived name. For instance, if

```
z = 'Y'
```

then

```
say foo.1 foo.z
```

produces the result `Renoir Monet` as before. Keep in mind that there are symbols which cannot be the names of (simple) variables. Such symbols include numbers, or any symbol that begins with a number. When symbols like this occur in a node of a compound symbol, they are used literally (after being uppercased). The symbol `foo.1` is an example of this.

For additional examples of the general process, suppose the following assignments have been made:

```
i = 100
j = -30
type = '01abc'
field = 'salary'
name = 'H. P. Lovecraft'
```

Then the symbols

```
array.i
two_dimensional_array.i.j
database_record.type.field.name
```

correspond to the following derived names:

```
ARRAY.100
TWO_DIMENSIONAL_ARRAY.100.-30
DATABASE_RECORD.01abc.salary.H. P. Lovecraft
```

Note that the values of the simple variables that are substituted may contain lowercase letters which are not uppercased. In fact, those values may contain any characters at all, even blanks, special characters, and extra periods. So variable names may contain arbitrary characters.

Because variable names may contain arbitrary characters, there are many names which cannot appear explicitly in a program. This is the case, for instance, with names that contain blanks or operator symbols. Such names can be referred to only when derived from an appropriate compound symbol.

The periods occurring in the original compound symbol remain in the compound name, and additional periods may occur if they form part of the value of one of the simple variables being substituted. Unlike a compound symbol, however, a compound name should be thought of as having only two parts: the initial part up to and including the first period (the stem), and everything else (which may contain additional periods).

When REXX goes to look up the value of a compound variable, it first searches for the stem. Then under the stem it searches for the suffix consisting of the remainder of the name, just as if this suffix named a simple variable in a private *name space* defined by the stem. This suffix is called the *tail*. If the resulting name is not found, the original compound symbol still refers to a value which is the derived compound name, according to the normal rules by which REXX handles undefined variables.

Though the details of this process for working with compound variables are somewhat involved, REXX compound variables turn out to be a very powerful and useful facility of the language. Compound variables can be used very much as arrays are in other languages. Even so, the REXX approach has several advantages. It is not necessary (or possible) to determine the size of an array in advance; storage is allocated as needed, and there can even be large gaps in the array without wasting space. Also, though compound variables can be used as if they were arrays of a specific number of dimensions, they can also be used without any specific fixed dimensionality if that is convenient.

REXX compound variables have the significant advantage over arrays in most other languages in that the "subscripts" need not be numeric; they can be any valid character string (up to some implementation-defined maximum length). This permits very useful associative retrieval of data. For instance, database records pertaining to individuals can be retrieved directly by the name of the individual:

```
individual_birthday.name
individual_email_address.name
individual_job_title.name
```

These symbols might be used to work with a personnel file. To access any piece of data, it is necessary to have only the actual name as the value of the variable NAME. (All current REXX implementations keep data in memory only; they do not refer directly to external files. Therefore, this example assumes the data has been loaded in from some sort of file. But in principle REXX could transparently use disk files for its data.)

SCOPE OF VARIABLES

A second important aspect of the REXX data model involves the scope of variable names. To begin with, each separate REXX program maintains its variables independently of every other REXX program. In other words, REXX variables named in one program file are completely unrelated to those named in another file. In fact, one REXX program's variables are completely inaccessible from any other REXX program's variables. This is usually an advantage in working with a system of multiple REXX programs, since naming conflicts cannot occur. On the other hand, it can also be an inconvenience when sharing data is necessary.

Within a single REXX program, the scoping rules have to do with exactly when the same variable name refers to the same data. The only time the scope of a name is an issue is when internal procedures are invoked. In the examples of procedures already given, there has been just a single scope for all names. That is, names used in one procedure will refer to the same data when used in other procedures that the first procedure either calls or is called from. Such names are "global," and this is the default in REXX.

It is often convenient, however, to use the same name for different data in different procedures. For instance, it is common to use variables like I and J as loop control variables. In fact, it is both a nuisance and a frequent source of errors to have to provide unique names for loop variables in all procedures. Further, to avoid unintended side effects, it is usually good practice to isolate separate procedures from each other by giving each a unique "name space" and eliminating the possibility of variable naming conflicts. Therefore, REXX provides a way for any procedure to hide its own variables from any procedure which invokes it. This is done with the PROCEDURE statement. If used, it must immediately follow the label which names the procedure:

```
/* compute the area of a circle */
area:
procedure
arg radius
pi = 3.14159
return pi * radius ** 2
```

In this example, there is one new instruction, ARG, whose purpose is to assign the procedure's argument to the variable RADIUS. Because of the PROCEDURE instruction, all variables in this procedure (RADIUS and PI) are local to the procedure and distinct from any variables with the same name in the calling procedure. In particular, they are undefined

until they receive a value from an assignment or an instruction like
ARG. The variables used in the calling procedure are hidden from the
called procedure and from any procedure which the called procedure
might call in turn. Likewise, the variables of the called procedure are
hidden from the caller. However, the variables of the called procedure
are not necessarily hidden from any procedure it calls, unless the latter also begins with a PROCEDURE statement.

Although purely local variables are probably preferable as the rule,
global variables are often very useful as an exception. It is possible to
use an option on the PROCEDURE statement to explicitly name variables
that are to be shared. For instance, it's inconvenient and inefficient to
assign a value to PI in every procedure that uses it, since PI is really a
constant. Therefore, one would normally assign its value just once in
the main procedure and use the EXPOSE option to make it available in
procedures that need it with the instruction

```
procedure expose pi
```

If there is a chain of several calling procedures, each must EXPOSE
any variables that are to be shared. REXX scoping rules are dynamic
in nature, rather than static. This means that it is not possible to
determine by a syntactic analysis of the program when a given name
actually refers to the same data. Instead, this always depends on the
exact sequence of procedures which are called. In this case, assuming
PI is first assigned in the main procedures, the same data will be available to the AREA procedure only if all other procedures in the calling
hierarchy either do not use a PROCEDURE instruction or else explicitly
expose PI.

A related issue is the way in which arguments are passed to procedures. Every procedure (or function) call may supply zero or more
arguments. For a function call, the arguments are in the form of a list
of values, separated by commas, and all enclosed in parentheses. For
instance, to use the area function defined above, one might have:

```
pull radius
say 'The area of the circle is' area(radius)
```

In REXX, arguments are always passed *by value*. This means that
arguments are evaluated when the procedure is called and only the
resulting value is available to the procedure. The procedure can
change the value of a variable which happens to be used as an argument only if no PROCEDURE statement occurs in the procedure or if the
variable is explicitly exposed. Even if the value of a variable is changed
in this way, the value passed as an argument is not changed, since it
was computed when the procedure was called. Notice that in the cur-

rent example, the symbol radius refers to different variables in the called and calling procedures because of the PROCEDURE statement, and the fact that the same symbol is used is merely a (possibly confusing) coincidence.

REXX procedures which are not functions, i.e., do no return values, are invoked with the CALL instruction, and their arguments are also specified as a list of values, but the list is not enclosed in parentheses. (This is a source of frequent confusion in REXX.) If we changed the area example slightly so that it was simply a procedure invoked only for its side effect, it might look like this:

```
pull radius
call area radius
/* other code... */
...
area: procedure expose pi
arg radius
say 'The area of the circle is' pi * radius ** 2
return
```

There are several ways of accessing the arguments passed to a procedure. So far, we have illustrated only the ARG instruction. Although it has the appearance of a declaration, it is not. Instead, ARG is an executable instruction which causes the assignment of the first argument to the named variable, just as if an "=" assignment operator were used. If the variable in question happened to be exposed, its value would be changed even in the calling procedure.

If the procedure has more than one argument, then more than one variable name can be used in the ARG instruction, each name separated from the others by commas. For instance, we might modify our example to display the area of a rectangle instead of a circle:

```
pull height width
call area height, width
...
area: procedure
arg ht, wd
say 'The area of the rectangle is' ht * wd
return
```

ARG assigns arguments to variables in the same order as they occur in the argument list. ARG, like PULL, is a special case of the general REXX PARSE instruction, because it is just shorthand for PARSE UPPER ARG. Hence, it can do interesting character string parsing as well. But in the most common case, as illustrated here, there is a one-to-one correspondence between arguments passed and variables. In this case, you might just remember that there should be as many commas in the list following ARG as there are in the argument list that is passed.

The other main way of accessing arguments is with the ARG( ) built-in function. The argument passed to ARG( ) is the number of the argument passed to the current procedure, and its value is the value of that argument. Here is a completely equivalent form of the last example:

```
pull height width
call area height, width
...
area: procedure
say 'The area of the rectangle is' arg(1) * arg(2)
return
```

STRING MANIPULATION AND PARSING

One of the most important strengths of the REXX language is its character string handling ability. As noted earlier, REXX has no explicit data types and all data can be manipulated as character strings. This is not a limitation for most applications where REXX is naturally used (application macros, command procedures, prototyping, etc.), and is actually quite convenient. Further, because REXX specializes in handling character strings, it does it very well and offers many built-in facilities for this purpose.

The most frequent string operation, concatenation, can be expressed with a simple operator ("| |") or in many cases none at all (direct abuttal of tokens). Equality and comparison operators for strings are the same as for numeric values, and the distinction is usually immaterial. REXX even tries to work with strings in a way that is most natural in ordinary applications, so leading and trailing blanks are ignored in the standard equality and comparison operators. Alternative "exact" equality and comparison operators are also available when leading and trailing blanks should not be ignored.

String handling is greatly facilitated by the fact that storage allocation and management in REXX is completely automatic. It is never necessary to specify the (maximum) length of a string or to allocate space for it. Providing temporary storage for intermediate results is also handled transparently, and there is no need for "garbage collection."

REXX has two other significant features designed for manipulating character strings. The first is a collection of string-oriented, built-in functions and the second is the PARSE instruction.

A number of REXX's string handling functions provide services commonly available in other programming languages. Some examples are:

```
SUBSTR()     substring of argument string
LENGTH()     length of argument string
POS()        position of one argument string in another
COPIES()     arbitrary number of copies of argument string
```

REXX string functions extend far beyond such standard capabilities, however. One interesting group of functions is based on the frequently occurring situation of regarding a string as a sequence of words delimited by blanks. Strings of this sort include natural language text (after punctuation is removed) as well as short lists ("bread eggs butter onions tomatoes"). In this category are functions like WORD(string,n), which returns the *n*th word in the string, and WORDS(string), which returns the total number of words in the string.

There are quite a few other string functions for miscellaneous purposes, some of which have surprisingly powerful capabilities. Among these are COMPARE(), which determines whether or not two strings are identical and otherwise returns the first position in which they differ; INSERT(), which inserts one string at an arbitrary position in another; STRIP(), which removes any specific character from the beginning or end of a string; VERIFY(), which tests a string for the occurrence or nonoccurrence of a specific set of characters; and TRANSLATE(), which replaces any desired characters with specific others.

To show a bit of the flavor of string handling in REXX, here is a little program that takes a time in the form HH:MM (hours and minutes) and displays the value in English:

```
pull hours ":" minutes
numbers = "one two three four five six seven eight",
    "nine ten eleven twelve"
teens = "eleven twelve thirteen fourteen fifteen",
    "sixteen seventeen eighteen nineteen"
tens = "ten twenty thirty forty fifty"
hr = word(numbers,hours)
select
    when minutes = 0 then
        min = "o'clock"
    when right(minutes,1) = '0' then
        min = word(tens,minutes%10)
    when left(minutes,1) = '0' then
        min = "oh-"||word(numbers,minutes)
    when left(minutes,1) = '1' then
        min = word(teens,minutes-10)
    otherwise
        min = word(tens,minutes%10)"-"||,
            word(numbers,minutes//10)
```

```
      end
say 'Time is' hr min'.'
```

For instance, when the input is 10:33 this program displays

```
Time is ten thirty-three
```

There are a few features of REXX used here which haven't been explained yet, such as the use of a literal in the PULL instruction and the "%" (integer division) and "//" (remainder) arithmetic operators. However, apart from illustrating string handling in REXX, the main point to be made here is how transparently REXX deals appropriately with data as either numbers or strings. Arithmetic can be performed directly on character strings when appropriate. In particular, notice how the variable minutes can be used as easily with string functions (RIGHT( ), LEFT( )) as with numeric operators. Of course, a real program would have error-checking to ensure that only valid numbers are involved.

This example also illustrates how one often uses lists of words separated by blanks instead of arrays. The WORD( ) built-in function is used to access specific elements of the list.

The use of the PULL instruction here also bears further discussion. PULL is really just a shorthand form of the PARSE instruction. The example could have been written equivalently with the line

```
parse upper pull hours ":" minutes
```

instead. The full interpretation of this instruction is: "read a line of input from the user, assign everything before ":" to the variable hours and everything after ":" to minutes."

The PARSE instruction (or its equivalents implied by PULL and ARG) is used frequently in REXX programs. It is able to take strings from a number of possible sources and break them apart into constituent parts using a fairly natural notation. The part of the instruction that tells how to parse the string is called the *parse template*. The simplest form of a template is just a list of variable names. The input string is divided into blank-delimited words which are assigned, in order, to the variables. If there are more words than variables, the entire remaining part of the string is assigned to the last variable. If there are more variables than words, the excess variables are assigned the null string. This construct is useful in reading several numbers from a user, or tabular data from a file. For instance:

```
do i=1 by 1 while lines(file) \= 0
   parse value linein(file) with avg.i.1 avg.i.2,
```

```
        avg.i.3 avg.i.4
    end
```

uses the `linein()` function to read a line at a time from a file into compound variables with the stem `avg`. Each line of the file contains four numbers separated by blanks, but otherwise in a free format. The file is easy to maintain with a text editor because there is no need for a restriction to specific column numbers. (The `lines()` function is nonzero until the end of the file is reached, which makes it convenient for terminating input loops.)

It is often helpful to be able to automate the processing of computer files produced by various applications. When such files are in a report format suitable for reading by people, they are more of a problem to process by another program. For instance, a report may have on a single line:

```
Name: Sam Spade Birth-date: 10/4/57 SSN: 000-00-0000
```

In many languages, this would require a lot of work to interpret, because (for instance) the name might be a variable number of words. A single PARSE instruction,

```
parse var line 'Name:' name 'Birth-date:' birthday,
   'SSN:' ssn
```

handles the whole thing and assigns each data item to an appropriate variable.

OTHER FEATURES OF REXX

REXX has many additional surprises. You already know enough of the language to begin writing interesting and useful REXX programs. But there are a number of useful features of the language we haven't had time to describe yet. We have the rest of the book for that. We'll just give a few indications here of some of the highlights.

One of the most important is the extensive library of built-in functions. The fact that there are a large number for character-string manipulation has already been mentioned. But there are many others in the standard list. And most REXX implementations add many more of their own which are specialized for specific environments. Some of the standard functions are:

DATE()	returns the current date in a variety of formats
TIME()	returns the current time in a variety of formats and permits elapsed timing

VALUE( )	allows access to variables whose names are determined at run-time
SYMBOL( )	indicates whether a given variable has been initialized or not
DATATYPE( )	returns the character or numeric type of a variable

There are also a number of built-in functions for file I/O. Though REXX's I/O model is relatively simple, it does encompass files which are organized as either a sequence of characters or a sequence of records. Subject to the capabilities of the underlying file system, the I/O functions permit random access to any location in a file. More specialized I/O functions are usually provided with each particular REXX implementation.

REXX has a simple but convenient model of exceptional event handling. This allows programmers to make their code more robust by providing *handlers* for a variety of exceptional circumstances, such as uninitialized variables, I/O errors, and user-generated interrupts. The handlers can either attempt to recover from the condition, or at least permit graceful termination of the program, with appropriate error message and cleanup of any resources that may have been in use.

Lastly, REXX has simple debugging capabilities as part of the language definition. Through the TRACE instruction, it is possible to trace program execution at varying levels of detail. You can request a trace of each statement executed, the evaluated results of an expression, or even the intermediate results during expression evaluation. The trace can be nonstop, or interactive. During interactive tracing, you can execute any REXX statement, so you can display and change variables, call subroutines, issue system commands, and so forth. It is also possible to reexecute most program statements during interactive tracing, so that debugging can often continue after errors without a need to rerun the program.

Program Structure and Syntax

In this chapter we begin a more formal introduction to the REXX language. The purpose is to lay out the basic rules by which all REXX programs can be written and understood. There will be a number of definitions of terms that have already been introduced informally. There will also be lists of such things as possible *token* types that can occur in a REXX statement and valid operators. This will be the most formal chapter in the book. Later chapters will return to a more expository style that focuses on specific kinds of language features like control structures, built-in functions, and string handling facilities.

Even so, this treatment will not amount to a precise formal definition of the language, which can be found in Cowlishaw's *The REXX Language* or IBM's SAA documentation. Instead, our objective is to present the features of the language organized according to how they are employed to do useful work.

Bear in mind, too, that although REXX is a fairly well-standardized language, there are many details which have been left to the discretion of each implementation. You should consult your implementation's *User's Guide* for information on such specifics.

PROGRAM FORMAT

In general, a REXX program is contained entirely in a single file. There are no language provisions (as there are in C, for example) for dividing a program into multiple files while still allowing a procedure in one file to access procedures and variables in another file. This is not to say that a large program cannot be broken down into a number of separate files. It is just that such files can invoke each other only as external procedures which have no straightforward means of using the data and internal procedures of each other.

Some implementations of REXX may provide a way to allow more interaction between external programs. In addition, an implementation may allow for multiple independent programs in a single file, as a sort of "library." For our purposes, however, we will always assume that a REXX program is coextensive with one file.

The most fundamental unit of a REXX program is the token. There are basically four types of tokens:

Symbols

Symbols consist of a group of legal symbol characters (alphanumeric characters and a few special ones like "_" and "."), delimited by blanks, operator characters, or other special characters. Numbers are a special case of symbols. Other than numbers, symbols are usually variable names, but may simply be used as literals if they are not valid as either a name or a number.

Literal strings

Literal strings begin with a quote character: either ' or ". They continue until a matching quote. There are three subtypes: character, hexadecimal, and binary strings.

Operators

Operators are groups of consecutive operator characters (such as "+", "*", "–"). Two operator characters, even if separated by blanks (or even a comment), are part of the same operator token.

Special characters

Special characters are punctuation like ",", ":", ";", "(", and ")" and are tokens by themselves. They act as delimiters and also have additional syntactic functions.

In order to separate a program into its constituent statements, any REXX language processor (compiler or interpreter) performs a process called tokenization. This process involves examining a source program character by character in order to identify symbol, literal, and operator tokens. Users of REXX should know a bit about how tokenizing works in order to understand various features of the language (such as how statements are recognized!), so we will describe the tokenizing process in more detail a little further on.

CLAUSES AND STATEMENTS

The next syntactic level of a REXX program is the *clause*. This is the most important unit from the standpoint of understanding program execution. Every REXX program consists of a sequence of clauses which are processed as units, one at a time. In general, a clause is indivisible and will always be executed fully if it is executed at all (unless errors occur). There are four types of clauses. One is a label (a symbol followed by ":"). Labels are not executable; they merely identify a location within a program. The other types of clauses are executable and are better understood in terms of a related program unit that we call a *statement*. Statements are the basic units of work in a REXX program. A REXX program consists of a sequence of statements, some of which are preceded by labels. Statements themselves consist of one or more clauses. Some statements (such as DO . . . END) may even contain other statements nested within.

There are three types of statements:

Assignments

Any statement whose first token is a symbol and whose second token is the assignment operator "=" is an assignment statement. If the first token is a symbol that is not a valid variable name (i.e., if it begins with a number or a period), the statement is still formally an assignment, though it is in error. (If the first token is a literal or an operator, the statement is technically not even an assignment.) The first token may be a valid REXX keyword, such as SAY. In this case, a variable named SAY is assigned a value. This is legal REXX; it does not affect the keyword SAY, and should cause no problems (but it may be confusing to read).

Here are some examples of assignment statements:

```
name = "Peter Jairus Frigate"
address = "10 Downing Street"
1 = 2    /* will cause an error! */
```

And these are not assignments:

```
'stuff' = 'nonsense'/* evaluates to 0 */
* = 'asterisk'      /* syntax error */
```

Instructions

Any statement that is not an assignment but whose first token is a REXX keyword (there are about 25 of these) is an instruction. Instructions are directives which are part of the REXX language, and which are used mostly to determine flow of control (IF, DO, CALL), perform I/O (SAY, PULL), manipulate character strings (PARSE), or set options (NUMERIC).

Commands

Any statement that isn't an assignment or instruction is, automatically, a command. Such a statement is first evaluated as a REXX expression, and the evaluated result is passed to some other program (an application or the operating system) as a command to be handled by that program. In REXX terminology, a program that handles commands is called a *command environment* or simply an *environment*. (This is unfortunate, as various operating systems often use the term to mean something quite different.)

Given this typology of statements we can list two other types of clauses: assignments and commands. Every assignment or command is considered to consist of a single clause. Most instructions are also just single clauses. The sole exceptions are instructions that begin with the keywords IF, DO, and SELECT. These instructions always consist of several clauses and may even contain other statements. For instance, in the statement

```
if today = 'Tuesday' then
    say 'This must be Belgium.'
else
    say 'This must be France.'
```

`if today = 'Tuesday'` is a clause, `then` and `else` are each clauses, and both `say` instructions are clauses. The `say` instructions are also statements that are embedded within the `if` statement. The fourth type of clause, `then`, consists of individual instructions except for IF, DO, and SELECT, as well as certain specific constituents of the latter three. (For instance, the THEN in an IF statement is always a clause by itself.)

The reader should note that we have adopted a terminology which is somewhat different from Cowlishaw's in *The REXX Language* and other references based on it. The latter use the term *keyword instruction* to mean the same thing as what we have called simply an *instruction*. They use the term *instruction* to mean what we have called a *statement*, i.e., a more general concept encompassing assignments, (keyword) instructions, and commands. We have found that users easily confuse Cowlishaw's terms *instruction* and *keyword instruction*, so we have decided to use *statement* for the more general concept.

To illustrate further: a statement like `say "Hello"` is also, simultaneously, a clause and instruction, and we may refer to it interchangeably as statement, clause, or instruction. An assignment or an operating system command is a single clause and also a statement, but not an instruction. A keyword like THEN, ELSE, or OTHERWISE is a clause but is neither an instruction nor a statement.

A label, also, is a clause that is neither an instruction nor a statement. Any statement may be preceded by one or more labels. A label is simply a symbol followed by a colon (":"). Labels are used as the names of internal procedures, i.e., the target of a function reference or a CALL instruction. Labels are also used to name the target of a SIGNAL instruction. Labels are not required to be unique within a file, but only the first occurrence of a label is used as the target of a function reference, CALL, or SIGNAL.

Since, in our terminology, a label is not a statement, we can exclude the possibility that a label may occur within a DO, IF, or SELECT statement, if we provide that only statements may be embedded within DO, IF, or SELECT. Although one can construct contrived examples of programs that have labels inside a DO loop, for instance, and where the example might even be expected to execute properly, it doesn't seem like there is any useful purpose in allowing this possibility. (Most current implementations do not rigorously enforce this limitation, however, thereby treating labels as if they were also a type of statement.)

MORE ABOUT CLAUSES

The concept of clauses is very important in REXX, since the clause is the basic execution unit. In writing REXX programs you need to be aware of clauses, because of the rules that specify when semicolons or continuation characters are required. For instance, since

```
say "Enter today's date"; say "Use mm/dd/yy form."
```

contains two clauses on one line, the semicolon has to be used to separate them. But

```
say,
    "Enter today's date. Use mm/dd/yy form."
```

is a single clause. The comma must be used after say to continue to the next line. The code is syntactically valid without the continuation, but will not work as intended. REXX tends to require more use of line continuation characters than do other languages, such as C, where a positive indication (the semicolon) of the end of a statement is required. So the occasional need for continuation characters is the price we must pay for being able to leave out semicolons most of the time.

Another reason for paying attention to clauses is that implementations typically have limits on the length of a single clause. Simply continuing a clause to extra lines will not overcome such limits.

Yet another reason is that statement type recognition depends on certain details which are revealed at the clause level of analysis. For instance, keywords like SAY are recognized only at the beginning of a clause, so it is important to know where clauses begin. This isn't always obvious. In an IF statement like

```
if n > 100 then
    say "Value of 'n' is out of range."
```

there is an explicit REXX rule which says THEN is a clause by itself, which makes it possible to recognize the SAY instruction. (This rule also means that an IF statement can be continued to another line before or after THEN without a continuation character being required.)

Finally, several features of REXX are tied to the definition of a clause. For instance, during interactive tracing one clause at a time is executed before a pause. Certain events, such as external conditions like HALT, are recognized only at clause boundaries. And the built-in functions DATE() and TIME() are synchronized so that they give consistent results within one clause.

But, as we have seen, the concept of a clause includes a hodgepodge of different things. We can, perhaps, clarify the concept somewhat by examining how clauses are delimited. Basically, a clause is just a sequence of tokens that is terminated by one of five things, whichever comes first:

a semicolon.

the end of a line (provided the last token on the line isn't a comma).

the keyword THEN, if the first token of the clause is IF or WHEN. (In this case, THEN is a separate clause and not part of the clause it terminates.)

the keywords THEN, ELSE, and OTHERWISE are clauses by themselves when they occur in the appropriate context (after IF or SELECT).

a colon (if it is the second token of a clause).

This definition seems somewhat legalistic and complex, since it involves several alternatives and special associated exceptions or special conditions. However, as is true generally in REXX, while the formal rules of the language are sometimes a little convoluted, this is because of an attempt to codify rules that are in practice intuitively simple and clear. The intention of the rules is just to make things work out "the way they ought to." In this case, the intent is to allow clauses to be, for the most part, identified with separate lines of a program, and yet to allow for several short clauses to appear on one line and for long clauses to be continued across several lines.

Normally, the end of a line defines the end of a clause, with no special punctuation required. The next line of the program is automatically interpreted as the start of a new clause. The maximum length of a line in REXX is implementation dependent, but is usually at least 250 characters. However, it is usually inconvenient to edit or print programs whose lines are longer than the width of a screen or editing window, so it is more normal to use lines no longer than 80 characters. Many REXX expressions involve character-string literals or other lengthy elements, so it is common to need to continue a single clause to two or more lines. This is done by ending the line with a comma. This must be in addition to any comma that is required for syntactic purposes (as in function references or CALL instructions).

String literals (enclosed in quotation marks) must be complete on one line and cannot be continued to additional lines. Concatenation of strings solves the problem of dealing with very long literals.

Unlike literals, comments can span multiple lines. In fact, in the middle of a comment, a continuation character is not even required at the end of a line. Therefore, ending a line with an open comment is another way to force continuation.

Line continuation by means of commas is handled during the tokenizing process, before any syntactic analysis is done. When a comma is detected at the end of a line, the REXX language processor replaces the comma with a blank and continues reading the next line of the file. Because blanks are sometimes significant characters in REXX, it is important to observe the effect that continuation has, since it can change the meaning of an expression.

In this example:

```
say "ruby",
    "emerald",
    "amethyst"
```

the line that is displayed is `ruby emerald amethyst`, because the strings are concatenated with a blank in between each, since blanks are significant when they occur between two literals. If it were necessary to break a line between two strings and not concatenate them with a blank, then the first line should have a concatenation operator ("| |") before the comma, since blanks are not significant on either side of an operator. Thus

```
say "ruby"||,
    "emerald"||,
    "amethyst"
```

displays `rubyemeraldamethyst`.

Also, because the comma that indicates continuation is removed, you should be careful with CALL instructions or expressions involving function references, where the comma has a syntactic function. So, if `area` is a function of two arguments, the statement

```
say "The area is" area(height,,
    width)
```

requires two commas in order that the `area` function isn't passed a single value consisting of the concatenation of `height` and `width`.

Sometimes it is convenient to place several clauses on the same line. In this case it is necessary to separate each clause from the preceding one with a semicolon. This might be done with several short assignments:

```
a = 0; b = 0; c = 0
```

In general, however, placing several clauses on the same line makes a program harder to read and modify, so it's best not to get into this habit.

There is one case where you may need to be careful to use a semicolon. The `IF` instruction has the form:

```
IF condition THEN statement; [ ELSE statement]
```

REXX views this as several clauses. The first clause is `IF condition`. In an `IF` instruction, `THEN` is a reserved word. It automatically marks the end of the first clause without requiring a semicolon, but it cannot be used as the name of a variable. In contrast, `ELSE` is not a reserved word. Therefore, `ELSE` can be used as the name of a variable (though it's not a good idea), but a semicolon is required just before it. For readability, it is generally advisable to write an `IF` statement on several lines, in a consistent manner. For instance,

```
IF condition THEN
    statement
ELSE
    statement
```

is a format that uses indentation to reveal clearly the separate parts of the instruction. In this format the semicolon is unnecessary, since the clause before `ELSE` is terminated by the end of the line.

TOKENIZATION OF STATEMENTS

Tokenization is the process of building meaningful program elements out of the smallest identifiable elements of a file, i.e., characters. Tokenization is the first step that a language processor performs in interpreting a REXX program. It is important to understand a little about tokenization in order to correctly read and write REXX statements.

For the purposes of tokenization, characters are classified into one of several types:

Symbol characters
These are the characters which can occur in REXX symbols. The class includes upper- and lowercase alphabetic characters (A–Z, a–z), numerals (0–9), and a few other "special" characters ("!", "?", ".", "_"). This constitutes the minimal set of allowable symbol characters. Different implementations of REXX may include others, such as currency symbols ("$") and characters of non-English alphabets. For portability, it would be best to avoid using characters outside of the minimal set in symbols.

Operator characters
This class includes all the characters which may occur in REXX operators, specifically "+", "–", "*", "/", "%", "|", "&", "=", "<", ">", and "\". Some implementations also recognize alternatives for the negation symbol ("\"), such as "~", "^", or "¬". (The negation symbol has proven especially troublesome in ASCII-EBCDIC conversion. You should probably stick with "\" unless it presents a conversion problem.)

Special characters
There are a few other characters which are used as punctuation by REXX: ",", ":", ";", "(", ")", " " (space), and both single (') and double (") quotes.

Invalid characters
All other characters are not valid in REXX programs except in comments or quoted strings. If used outside comments or quoted strings, such characters will be flagged as errors. Even in comments and quoted strings, certain control characters (such as *newline*) may not be used transparently.

During tokenization the following operations are performed:

1. The occurrence of any symbol character marks the beginning of a REXX symbol or number. All subsequent characters up to the first nonsymbol character are part of a single symbol or number. (A number is considered to be a symbol.) All alphabetic characters in a symbol are converted to uppercase.

2. The occurrence of any operator character marks the beginning of a REXX operator. Spaces adjacent to any operator character are ignored and removed from the program. All subsequent characters up to the first nonoperator character (other than a space) are part of a single operator. (Whether a particular multicharacter operator is actually valid isn't determined until later.)

3. Special characters are always treated as tokens by themselves. Adjacent blanks are always removed, except for a blank preceding a left parenthesis or following a right parenthesis. Such blanks are meaningful, since they distinguish a function reference from a symbol or literal followed by a parenthesized expression.

4. Comments are recognized as beginning with the sequence /* (as in PL/I and C). Inside a comment, any characters are valid. No character sequence except for /* or */ has any special meaning inside a comment. Comments may be nested, so the sequence /* can occur in a comment only if it introduces a nested comment. Comments can be continued on as many lines as desired without requiring a continuation character. A comment is terminated by the sequence */. Once a complete comment has been recognized, it is removed from any further processing, except for source code displays. A comment marks the end of any symbol it happens to follow, but it can occur in the middle of a multicharacter operator such as "**" (not necessarily a good idea!).

5. The occurrence of either quote character marks the beginning of a REXX string literal. Either kind of quote character may be used, so that if one is required inside a literal, the other kind can be used to delimit the literal. Alternatively, a quote character can be used inside a literal that it delimits by doubling the character. Except for this rule, any sequence of characters is valid inside a literal, including /* and */. The literal is terminated by the first undoubled quote character of the same kind as used to begin the literal. If a B or an X (either case) follows the final quote character and is followed by a nonsymbol character, it is also part of the literal (binary or hex string).

6. Some special cases are handled on an ad hoc basis. For instance, if E or e immediately follows a number and is immediately followed by "+", "−", or another number, then the whole is taken as a single symbol which is a number in exponential notation, such as 6.023E+23.

A few examples should illuminate the significance of these tokenization rules. In the statement

```
say "The price is $"price
```

there are three tokens: say, "The price is $", and price. The fact that the last two tokens are adjacent to each other means that concatenation is implied (the "abuttal" operator).

```
say "The price is $"/* display the price */price
```

also has three tokens and is completely equivalent to the previous example.

In the statement

```
if amount > = 100 then
    say "Value is out of range."
```

there is only one operator (`>=`) rather than two, because blanks adjacent to operator characters are removed.

The statement

```
say +3
```

contains three tokens: `say`, `+`, and `3`. `+3` is not a single numeric token, but rather an operator (unary +) followed by a number.

Parenthesized expressions behave like symbols or literals, in that adjacent blanks are treated as a *blank concatenation operator* rather than being ignored. Thus the statement

```
say "The speed is" (d/t) "km/sec."
```

might display `The speed is 3.4 km/sec.` If it is necessary to concatenate a symbol or literal to a parenthesized expression with no intervening blank, the concatenation operator ("`||`") must be used to avoid producing a function reference:

```
say "The price is $"||(units * unit_price)"."
```

(Note that a concatenation operator isn't required after the right parenthesis.)

Based on these rules there are seven types of tokens recognized by REXX:

Symbols

A symbol is a string of consecutive symbol characters. A symbol may play various roles in REXX. It may be a keyword like `SAY` or `CALL` if it occurs at the beginning of a statement. It may be another reserved word like `THEN` or `WHILE` if it occurs in an appropriate context. Some, but not all symbols can be the names of REXX variables. (A variable name cannot begin with a numeral or a period.) A symbol which is neither a valid name nor a valid number is converted to uppercase and treated as a literal. Implementations usually have only a very loose limit on the length of a symbol, typically the same as the limit on the length of a clause (perhaps 250 characters or more).

Numbers

A number is a special case of a symbol or a literal string which obeys certain specific restrictions. A number can be composed entirely of numerals, or of numerals with one period (decimal point). It can also have an exponential suffix, which is E (or e) followed by a whole number or by "+" or "–" and a whole number. The following are valid numbers:

```
9999999999999999999999999
99999999999999999999e9999
6.023E+23
1.4142135
' 666 '
'+ 2'
'313233'x
```

Note that although the last three examples are written as string literals, they are also legal numbers. (Leading and trailing blanks and a leading plus or minus sign are allowed in a number, and '313233'x is the same as '123' in ASCII.)

The following are symbols that are not valid numbers:

```
1.05.03
100K
333e.5
```

As symbols, there is a maximum length of a number that can be expressed literally in a program. However, depending on the implementation, REXX may be able to compute numbers with a much larger number of digits. There are other computed character string results and character string literals which can also be used as numbers (i.e., are valid in arithmetic expressions). For instance, the string literal ' + 3' is a valid number, but not a numeric token.

Character string literals

A character string literal is a sequence of arbitrary characters enclosed between either single (') or double (") quotation marks. Either quotation mark may occur in the string provided it is doubled. String literals, like all other tokens, must be entirely contained on one line. The limit on the length of a string literal is usually the same as the limit on the length of symbol tokens. As with numbers, computed character string results may, in general, be much longer.

Hexadecimal literals

A hexadecimal literal is like a character string literal in that it is delimited by either single or double quotation marks. However, only the numbers 0 through 9 and letters A through F (upper- or lowercase), plus blanks, are allowed in the string. In addition, the ending quotation mark must be immediately followed by x or X, which in turn must be followed by a nonsymbol character. Blanks may be used in the string to improve readability. When blanks are used, characters must be grouped in pairs (except possibly for the first group).

The following are valid hexadecimal literals:

```
'68656c6c6f'x  /* equivalent to 'hello' (ascii) */
'88 85 93 93 96'x /* 'hello' (ebcdic) */
'1ff ff ff'x    /* the number 2**25 - 1 in binary */
```

Hexadecimal literals are ordinarily used to easily specify the exact machine representation of a given piece of data. This is a very non-portable feature! If the data in question involves character strings, the representation will depend on whether the encoding is ASCII or EBCDIC.

If the data is a binary number, the portability problems are even more severe, because the proper representation depends on the byte ordering used on a particular machine, and on how the data will be used as well. For instance, if the string is binary data that will be written to a file and read by another (non-REXX) program, the correct representation depends on the ordering assumed by the other program. Suppose you need to write the number 256, in binary, to a file. Nominally, the hexadecimal representation of 256 is '0100'x. But on some machines (e.g., the Intel 80x86 series) this is actually stored in memory as '0001'x, and that is how another program might expect to read it.

Hexadecimal literals are immediately converted internally to the equivalent character-string representation. They are supported merely as an alternative form of notation. In other words, as far as REXX itself is concerned, data is always a string of bytes, and a hexadecimal literal is just another way of writing a given byte string. Hexadecimal literals can be used in arithmetic provided they correspond to the character-string representation of a number. That is, '313233'x is exactly the same string as '123' (ASCII representation), whereas the binary representation of 123, i.e., '7b'x, cannot be used in an arithmetic expression, since it is the same as the string '{' to REXX. In fact,

```
say '7b'x
would display {.
```

Bit string literals

A bit string literal is also like a character string literal in that it is delimited by either single or double quotation marks. In this case, only 0s and 1s can occur within the quotation marks, and the closing quotation mark must be followed by b or B (to be followed in turn by a nonsymbol character). Like hexadecimal literals, bit string literals are supported as a notational convenience, and are internally stored as the equivalent character string.

For readability, the digits 0 and 1 may be written in groups of four and separated by blanks. The first group need not have a full four digits. If the total number of digits is not a multiple of eight, the string is assumed to start with 0s.

These are valid bit string literals:

```
'1'b
'110001 00110010 00110011'b  /* '123' in ascii */
'1111 0000 1111 0000'b        /* 'f0f0'x */
```

Bit string literals are used, like hexadecimal literals, when an exact binary representation of data is required, and they suffer from the same portability hazards. They are primarily of use in specifying bit masks for the REXX built-in functions BITOR(), BITAND(), and BITXOR().

Operators

An operator token is a sequence of consecutive operator characters. Blanks adjacent to any operator character are removed. Of course, not all operator tokens are valid REXX operators. The valid operators will be described in the next section on REXX expressions.

Syntactic symbols

A few characters which have syntactic functions are considered to be tokens all by themselves (when used outside of a string literal or comment). These are:

: identifies a label, when it follows a symbol.

; explicitly ends a clause.

(begins a parenthesized expression or function argument list.

) terminates a parenthesized expression or function argument list.

, separates arguments in the argument list of a function reference or CALL instruction.

REXX EXPRESSIONS

REXX expressions can occur in each of the three types of statements. In an assignment, everything to the right of the equal sign is one expression. In a command, the whole clause is an expression. In an instruction there may be zero or more expressions, depending on the type of instruction. For instance, a SAY instruction may have one expression (or none at all). A DO instruction may contain as many as five different expressions, separated by reserved words like TO, BY, FOR, WHILE, or UNTIL. (These words are reserved only in a DO instruction.)

A REXX expression consists of a sequence of operators and *terms* that follows syntactic rules like those in most other modern procedural languages. A term is the simplest unit of an expression. It can be either a symbol, a string literal (character, hexadecimal, or binary), a function reference, or an expression enclosed in parentheses.

Informally speaking, an expression begins with an optional unary operator ("+", "–", or "\") followed by one or more terms separated from each other by operators, and with optional parentheses to indicate grouping. More formally, a term is one of the following:

a literal string

a symbol

a parenthesized expression (consisting of other terms and operators, enclosed in parentheses)

a function call (a literal string or a symbol, followed immediately by a left parenthesis, zero or more expressions separated by commas, and a final right parenthesis)

REXX is slightly unusual in that sometimes two terms may be written adjacent to each other with no explicit operator in between. However, in this situation it is considered that there is an implicit operator which is either simple concatenation or *blank concatenation,* depending on whether there is not, or is, a blank between the terms. (Blanks in excess of one in a row are removed during tokenizing.) As illustrated in various preceding examples, the explicit concatenation operator can be omitted when there is no ambiguity. (For instance, two adjacent symbols with no intervening blank would be tokenized as a single symbol, so the blank is required in this case.)

An expression, formally, is one of the following:

term

unary_operator expression

term binary_operator expression

In evaluating a complete expression, REXX first evaluates all constituent terms in the expression as they are encountered and then combines them with the operators in an order that is determined by precedence rules (possibly) modified by parenthesization. Note that terms themselves, as well as expressions, have to be evaluated. A symbol is evaluated by substituting its value (which may involve substitution in the symbol itself if it is a compound symbol). Function references are evaluated by calling the function.

An important rule of REXX evaluation is that terms are evaluated from left to right insofar as is possible. We have to add that last qualification, because terms can be nested (e.g., one function reference may occur in the argument list of another). It's important to be clear about the order of evaluation whenever function references are involved, because functions can have side effects which alter the values of variables.

For instance, consider the program fragment:

```
/* test order of evaluation */
say p1 (echosub(p2, sub1(), p3) p4)
say 'should say "P1 P2 - THIRD FOURTH"'
exit

echosub:
return arg(1) arg(2) arg(3)

sub1:
p1 = first
p2 = second
p3 = third
p4 = fourth
return '-'
```

The purpose of this example is to illustrate the order of evaluation of the expression

```
p1 (echosub(p2, sub1(), p3) p4)
```

When REXX processes this it recognizes subexpressions in the following order:

```
p1
(echosub(p2, sub1(), p3) p4)
echosub(p2, sub1(), p3)
p2
sub1()
p3
p4
```

Note that the routine sub1 has the side effect of changing all four variables. The values used for P1 and P2 are determined before sub1 is called, so they enter the expression with their original value (which is uninitialized). But P3 and P4 are determined after the call to sub1, so their altered values are used.

CLAUSE TYPE RECOGNITION RULES

Given all of the foregoing definitions, it is possible to explain precisely how REXX classifies clauses into each of the possible types. Once clause boundaries have been determined in the tokenizing process, then each of the following rules is applied in order. Whichever rule is first found to be true determines the type of the clause.

Label rule
   If the first token of the clause is a symbol and the second token of the clause is a colon, the clause is a label.

Assignment rule
If the first token of the clause is a symbol and the second token of the clause begins with an = sign, the clause is an assignment.

Keyword instruction rule
If the first token of the clause is a symbol which is one of the reserved REXX keywords (ADDRESS, ARG, CALL, etc.), the clause is a keyword instruction.

Command rule
If none of the preceding rules applies, the clause is a command.

To bring these rules into focus, and to demonstrate the importance of understanding them, let's consider a few REXX statements that appear very similar, yet which are actually very different. These examples bear some close study, since they illustrate points which are frequently missed by new users of REXX.
Consider first these statements:

```
EXIT(1)

GOTO(1)

GOTO (1)
```

In the first of these, there are four tokens: EXIT, (, 1, and). Although EXIT and (are adjacent, they are separate tokens. The second step in processing a REXX program after tokenization is statement classification. At this stage, EXIT is recognized as a keyword. That leaves the rest of the statement, (1), as an expression which is evaluated at the time the statement is actually executed.

In the second example, tokenization produces four tokens, just as before. However, the statement is classified as a command, because the statement isn't an assignment, and GOTO is not a language keyword. Later, when the statement is executed, it is significant that the tokens GOTO and (are adjacent, because that means the expression is to be treated as a function call. After the function is called and the value is known, that result is used as a command to be passed to the default command environment.

In the third example, there are still four tokens. Internally, however, the blank between GOTO and (is remembered, and when it is time to evaluate the expression, it is treated as the concatenation of GOTO and 1 instead of a function call.
Here are four more examples which illustrate statement classification:

```
SAY A = B

SAY = B
```

```
'SAY' = B

SAY: A = B
```

The first statement is a SAY instruction, not an assignment, because the equal sign is the third token rather than the second one. The second statement is in fact an assignment rather than a SAY instruction, even though the first token is a keyword, because the rule for recognizing assignments is applied first. In this statement, SAY is just an ordinary symbol that names a variable being assigned a value. This will have no effect on any other SAY statements in the program because keywords are recognized, when they occur as the first token, before symbols are evaluated. SAY used elsewhere in a statement would be handled properly as a symbol, however. The third statement is merely an expression which is processed as a command after evaluation. It is not an assignment, because the first token is a string literal rather than a symbol. (The expression evaluates to 0 or 1 depending on whether the variable B has the value SAY.) The last example is an assignment preceded by a label. It is not a SAY instruction, because the label rule is applied first.

Getting down to really fine points,

```
1 = 'xyz'
```

is still an assignment statement, although it will cause an error when executed, and even though it makes sense as an expression which could be evaluated and executed as a command. This is because 1 is a symbol, so the assignment rule still applies. And both

```
x == 1
```

and

```
2 == 1
```

are also considered to be assignment statements, because all that is required of the second token is that it begin with =. They are again invalid assignment statements, to be sure, and will cause errors if executed. Although they would make perfect syntactic sense as expressions that could be evaluated and executed as commands, the rules of REXX prevent this. The rationale for this is interesting. If they were evaluated as expressions the value would be 0 or 1, which is very unlikely (though possible in some contexts) to be a valid system or application command. But it is considered much more likely for programmer errors such as

```
x =, /* compute the next approximation */
= x - f(x) / f_prime(x)
```

to occur, and it is better to generate a syntax error than to (perhaps silently) try to execute a nonsensical command.

If you really want an expression to be handled as a command, you could use (for instance)

```
(1 = x + 1)
```

CHARACTER STRING OPERATORS

The first kind of operation performable on character strings is concatenation. All other string operations, except comparison (substring, reversal, etc.), are done with built-in functions. Concatenation comes in two forms. *Blank concatenation* means to concatenate two strings with a blank in between. This mimics the way words are concatenated into sentences in a natural language. It is expressed by writing two terms together separated by one or more blanks.

Simple concatenation is the same except that no blank is inserted. It can always be expressed with the || operator. In many cases, when there is no possible ambiguity, it can also be expressed by writing the terms together with no intervening blank. The only time this isn't possible is when a symbol is being concatenated to another symbol or a parenthesized expression.

Here are some examples:

```
"Hello" "world."/* same as "Hello world." */
"Never"||"more!"/* same as "Nevermore!" */
"Price: $"amount
```

Concatenation can be performed on strings that are valid numbers. The result may itself be a number, but usually isn't. For instance:

```
'1234'||'5678' /* is a number */
123'.'456      /* is a number */
'1234' '5678'  /* is not a number */
```

The other kind of character-string operation that corresponds to an explicit operator is comparison. That is, REXX supports the notion of one string being less than, equal to, or greater than another string. There are two forms of comparison: ordinary and strict, supporting two possible senses of the meanings of *greater than* or *less than*. Both forms of comparison are binary operators that combine two strings to yield a value which is also a string. The resulting string, however, is either 0 or 1.

String comparison is another example in REXX of how the language attempts to "do the right thing," even though the precise rules for what this is can be very complex.

The ordinary comparison operators are:

= operands are equal

> first operand greater

< first operand less

>= first operand greater or equal

<= first operand less or equal

The negated forms of these are \=, \>, \<, \>=, and \<=. Some of these are redundant, of course. For example, \> is the same as <=.

In the case of ordinary comparison, REXX recognizes a special case when both operands are numeric—that is, when both are valid REXX numbers. In that case the comparison is done in the numeric sense. So the following expressions all have the value 1:

```
1 < 2

2 < 10

2 < 1e2
```

Note that in the latter two cases, if comparison were done as if the operands were character strings, the value of each expression would be 0, since 2 is higher in the character collating sequence than 1.

On the other hand, if either operand is not a valid number, then an ordinary comparison is done by first ignoring leading and trailing blanks and then comparing the strings, character by character, using the standard collating sequence of the hardware (usually ASCII or EBCDIC). Removal of leading and trailing blanks is an important part of this operation, since in practice one often works with strings in such a way that the blanks are there but irrelevant for the purpose at hand.

Notice that both ordinary and strict comparison are case sensitive. This is a source of nonportability, since lowercase letters are higher than uppercase letters in the ASCII collating sequence, but (more logically) lower in the EBCDIC sequence. If portability is important, operands could first be converted to lowercase, yielding a case insensitive comparison.

Ordinary comparison can be a source of errors, if you are really interested in the exact character strings. You may want to sort a number of strings that might incidentally include values that could (inadvertently) be interpreted as numbers. In such a case, the strict comparison operators should be used.

There is a strict comparison operator corresponding to each ordinary one. It is expressed by doubling part of the ordinary operator. Thus ==,

$<<$, $>>$, $<<=$, $>>=$ (and negated forms) are the strict counterparts of =, $<$, $>$, $<=$, and $>=$.

In strict comparison, leading and trailing blanks are not ignored and operands are considered only as strings, never as numbers. The comparison is still done character by character using the standard collating sequence. Strict comparison is not only safer if you are not interested in treating strings as numbers, but it is also faster since no preprocessing of the operands is required.

ARITHMETIC OPERATORS

REXX supports the standard binary arithmetic operators of addition ("+"), subtraction ("−"), multiplication ("*"), division ("/"), and exponentiation ("**"). It also supports unary + and −. These are defined to be the same as 0 + or − another quantity.

Since numbers are not inherently either *fixed-point* or *floating-point* in REXX, division of one number by another usually produces a fractional result. The number of digits of accuracy that are retained after a division is governed by the NUMERIC DIGITS instruction. The default number of digits is nine, which is usually enough for most practical computations. The REXX language doesn't place any limit on the number of digits that can be requested via NUMERIC DIGITS. If more digits are required to express the result than allowed by NUMERIC DIGITS, the result is rounded rather than truncated.

Sometimes an integer result of division is desired, with the fractional part truncated. There is a separate operator for this: %. (If you are a C programmer, this will annoy you, because % is used in C for the integer division operator.) It is meaningful even if both divisor and dividend are nonintegral. When negative numbers are involved in multiplication, division, or integer division, the sign of the result is determined by the *sign law,* which is that the result is positive (or 0) if both operands are the same sign, and negative if the operands are nonzero and of opposite sign.

One last operator ("//") produces the remainder after integer division. The remainder, R, of the division of A by B is defined by:

```
R = A - (A % B) * B
```

For instance, if A = −4 and B = 3, then A % B is −1 and R = −1.

Unlike the other arithmetic operators, which require only that their operands be numeric (except for division by zero), exponentiation requires that its second operand be an integer (since REXX doesn't support complex numbers). Like the other operators, exponentiation is said to *associate left to right.* That is, the expression A ** B ** C is interpreted as (A ** B) ** C rather than A ** (B ** C). This is somewhat unfortunate, since (A ** B) ** C can be expressed equivalently but more efficiently as A ** (B * C), and the normal way of writing exponents as superscripts implies right to left associativity.

LOGICAL OPERATORS

REXX supports one unary logical operator (negation), and three binary logical operators (and, or, exclusive or). The logical operators are used primarily in IF instructions, but could be used in any expression.

The operands of a logical operator can be only the strings '0' and '1'; any other operand will cause an error. Furthermore, this must be interpreted in the sense of strict comparison. That is, for instance, the strings ' 0 ', '00', and '0E10' are not valid operands of a logical operator. (But '31'x would be okay, in ASCII, since it's just another way to write '1'.)

Assuming that the variables A and B satisfy this restriction, then, the definitions of the logical operators are:

negation

   \A is 1 if A is 0, or 0 if A is 1

and

   A & B is 1 if both A and B are 1, otherwise it is 0

or

   A | B is 1 if either A or B (or both) equal 1, otherwise 0

exclusive or

   A && B is 1 if exactly 1 of A or B is 1 (but not both), otherwise 0

Unlike some languages (such as C), REXX does not have any short circuit rules for the evaluation of logical expressions. Such a rule generally says that only as much of an expression needs to be computed as is necessary to determine the result. Thus, if you have

```
(expression1) | (expression2)
```

you could avoid evaluating expression2 if you found that expression1 was 1. But REXX does not work that way, because it is felt that such rules are less intuitively natural. The REXX approach has the advantage that all terms in a logical expression will be evaluated, which may be important if any of these terms are function calls with side effects. On the other hand, it may be less efficient, since it can mean performing unnecessary computation, particularly when used in IF statements. Such statements can always be rewritten to avoid the inefficiency, but it requires effort on the user's part.

Another point about logical operators is that they have nothing to do with bitwise operations on the operands. Built-in functions BITOR(), BITAND(), and BITXOR() are provided for this purpose.

OPERATOR PRECEDENCE

As in most other programming languages, operators in REXX have associated with them the notion of precedence, which determines the order in which expressions involving several operators are evaluated in the absence of parentheses.

The precedence of operators, in decreasing order is:

unary operators

    +, -, \

arithmetic operators

    exponentiation

        **

    multiplication and division

        *, /, %, //

    addition and subtraction

        +, -

concatenation

    ||, <blank>, <abuttal>

comparison

    =, ==, <, >, \=, <=, >=, \==, <<=, >>=, etc.

logical operators

    and

        &

    or, exclusive or

        |, &&

The way to apply this table to an expression like

```
operand1 op1 operand2 op2 operand3
```

is to perform op1 first on its operands if op1 occurs higher in the table than op2, or else to perform op2 first. If both operators occur on the same line of the table, the leftmost in the expression is performed first. Parentheses, of course, can be used to modify the order of evaluation. That is, regardless of precedence,

```
operand1 op1 (operand2 op2 operand3)
```

means that op2 is to be performed before op1.

NUMBERS AND ARITHMETIC IN REXX

We have seen that REXX tries as much as possible to treat all data as character strings, yet makes provision for dealing with a special class of character strings which are valid numbers. When the strings involved are valid numbers, arithmetic operators may be used, and the comparison operators behave differently from the way they would for nonnumeric strings.

The REXX language places no inherent limit on the size of numbers which may be represented and used in computation, though specific implementations may do so. Ideally, any REXX implementation would allow numbers that are as long (measured in characters required for their representation) as the longest allowed character string. But even this is sometimes not the case, since some implementations use special internal representations (e.g., floating-point numbers), which place a definite limit on the number of significant digits that can be maintained. Notice that the crucial limit here is on the number of significant digits rather than the magnitude of the number, since exponential notation permits representation of very large or very small numbers, though perhaps with relatively few significant digits.

As a practical matter, however, efficiency requires working with no more digits than are actually required for the problem at hand. Therefore, REXX provides a means, with the NUMERIC DIGITS instruction, to specify how many significant digits of precision will be used. The default is nine digits, which is adequate for most purposes. Numbers that have more significant digits are rounded off before use, and results of operations (like multiplication) that increase the number of digits are also rounded. Rounding is unavoidable in some situations such as division, when the result cannot be expressed in a finite form. Thus the value of 2/3 is 0.666666667 with the default number of NUMERIC DIGITS.

The NUMERIC DIGITS setting is used for a variety of purposes in REXX. It controls not only the number of digits that will be retained in a result, but also the way numbers are formatted as strings and how large an integer can be to still be considered a *whole* number. See Chap. 13 for a full explanation of this and of REXX arithmetic in general.

The most commonly observed effect of NUMERIC DIGITS other than the rounding of numbers is the way large numbers are formatted. REXX will automatically convert results to exponential notation if the number of decimal places required to the left of the decimal point exceeds NUMERIC DIGITS, or if the number of places to the right of the decimal point exceeds twice NUMERIC DIGITS. Thus, for instance, the value of the expression 1000 * 1000 * 1000 is 1.00000000E+9 with the default value of NUMERIC DIGITS, since otherwise 10 digits of precision would be required. This rule affects the way results are represented; it places no limits on the size of numeric constants that can be used in a program. It is legal to use numbers with more precision than the current NUMERIC DIGITS value.

Rounding and possible conversion to exponential notation will occur only if and when an arithmetic operation or comparison is performed. Otherwise, numeric strings are not changed in any way. For instance,

```
numeric digits 5
say 123456789
say 0 + 123456789
```

displays 123456789 as the output of the first say instruction, but 1.2346E+8 as the output of the second. In other words, adding 0 to a numeric string constant may sometimes be a useful way to force it into the proper form for the current value of NUMERIC DIGITS.

When dealing with fractional numbers, it is often distracting to see results displayed with the full NUMERIC DIGITS of precision (for instance, 0.666666667 for 2/3). REXX has a built-in function called FORMAT() that can be used when more control over the appearance of output is desired. It takes three parameters: the number to format, the number of digits before the decimal point, and the number of digits after the decimal point. Thus

```
say format(2/3, 1, 4)
```

would display 0.6667.

REXX VARIABLES

The section in the last chapter on the REXX data model presented most of the important details about the nature and use of variables in REXX. To recapitulate, there are two types of REXX variables: simple and compound. Simple variables are *scalar* quantities, just like variables in most other languages. Simple variables in REXX are referenced by *simple symbols*, that is, symbols which do not begin with a digit (0–9) and do not contain any periods. In practice, the name of the variable and the symbol used to refer to it are one and the same. Alphabetic case of the symbol is ignored, as the symbol is converted entirely to uppercase during tokenization.

Compound variables, in contrast, have names that consist of a *stem* and a *tail*. Conceptually, the stem is the name of a group of related quantities, and the tail identifies individual members of the collection. So a compound variable is really much like a one-dimensional array in other languages. Compound variable names are referred to by compound symbols.

More precisely, a compound symbol is one of the form

$$s.t_1.t_2.t_3. - - - .t_n$$

where the first part, s. (including the period), is the stem, and each subsequent t_i is like a simple symbol in that it does not contain periods, but it may begin with a digit. t_i may also be null. This compound symbol refers to a variable whose name (the *derived name*) is

$$S.T_1.T_2.T_3. - - - .T_n$$

where each T_i is the value of the variable corresponding to the simple symbol t_i, if that symbol doesn't begin with a digit, or the symbol itself in uppercase, if it does begin with a digit. The stem part S is just s converted to uppercase; no variable value lookup is performed.

There is one important special case in this notation. It is that a symbol may consist of just a stem alone, that is, a simple symbol which ends in a period. LIST. would be an example. How REXX interprets this depends on the context. When a stem is used in a context that assigns it a value, the meaning is that all possible variables that have the same stem lose their existing value (if any) and take on the new value. This could happen in an assignment statement, a PARSE instruction, or in a call to the VALUE() built-in function. Similarly, in the DROP instruction, the meaning is that the values of all variables with the specified stem are dropped. And in the PROCEDURE EXPOSE instruction, all variables having the specified stem are exposed. On the other hand, in contexts where only the value of a variable is needed, a stem can be used just like a variable, and it is considered to have whatever value has been assigned to it, if any. You could even use a stem as the control variable in a DO loop, in which case the stem would be both assigned and evaluated. We will say a little more about this use of stems later in connection with an example.

There is no limit on the length of individual components of the compound symbol; the only limit is on the length of the whole symbol. An important special case is when t_i is a whole number; then it is much like a numeric array subscript in other languages.

The following are all legal compound symbols:

```
array.i
restaurant..address
a.b.c.d.e.f.g.h.i.j.k.l.m.n.o.p.q.r.s.t.u.v.w.x.y.z
```

It is possible to think of a symbol like A.i.j.k as equivalent to an array element, which would be expressed as A[i][j][k] in the C language, for instance.

There are, however, significant differences between such "arrays" in REXX and arrays in other languages. Some of these differences represent advantages of REXX, but others are disadvantages. The differences are both semantic and syntactic. The main semantic difference is that, despite appearances, a REXX array does not have a specific "dimension" like an array in other languages. The main syntactic difference is that a programmer cannot use expressions or even compound variable names in the "subscripts."

On the positive side, because of REXX's dynamic memory management, it is never necessary to declare in advance how large an array will be. It simply grows as needed, and (usually) does not consume storage for unused elements of the array. And because a REXX array does not have a true dimensionality, it is not necessary to decide even this in advance. We say that a REXX array does not have a specific dimension because the periods in a compound symbol have syntactic meaning only in the symbol. Once the derived name has been formed by substituting all values of simple symbols, there are really only two parts to it: the stem and the tail. For instance, if we have

```
i = 3
j = 4
```

then the symbol A.i.j actually consists of just the stem, which is A. and the tail, which is 3.4. At this point, the fact that the tail still contains a period is irrelevant. So, if we also have

```
x = 34
y = 10
z = x/y
t = "3.4"
```

then the symbols A.i.j, A.t, and A.z all refer to exactly the same piece of data, namely the value of the variable whose derived name is A.3.4. Useful programs can actually be written that take advantage of this ambiguity of the "dimension" of a REXX array.

The tail of a REXX variable can consist of completely arbitrary data, including blanks and unprintable ASCII characters. In contrast to the usual situation in REXX, blanks are significant in a variable tail. Thus, if

```
x = " "
y = "  "
z = "   "
```

then A.x, A.y, and A.z refer to three completely different data items, even though x, y, and z are "equal" when compared with the normal comparison operators. This is another respect in which REXX "arrays" differ from those in other languages.

Also, in connection with this example, note that the variable with the derived name A. is distinct from A. as a stem. Thus, in

```
x = ""
A. = "Newton"
A.x = "Leibniz"
```

the assignment to A.x affects only the variable A.; it does not affect other variables with A. as the stem. Any reference in a program to A. (alone) is assumed to be a reference to the stem.

In considering the syntactic difference of REXX arrays from those in other languages, we see that the REXX array notation is not as powerful, or at least as convenient. In particular, it is not possible to have expressions in a REXX "subscript." For instance, A.i+j is the sum of A.i and j, instead of an array with two subscripts. Even parentheses cannot be used to circumvent this problem, since A.(i+j) is actually a function call to a function named A. (In fact, Cowlishaw has stated that a distaste for complicated parenthesized expressions was one factor in not using the customary notation for subscripts.)

This notation is usually the most inconvenient when you simply want to use another compound symbol as a subscript. So if i.j is a value you wish to use as a "subscript," you cannot just refer to A.i.j. You must assign i.j to a simple variable first:

```
x = i.j
say A.x
```

Despite these syntactical inconveniences, the great power of REXX's notation lies in the fact that "subscripts" can be nonnumeric. This allows you to build data structures which easily associate data values with data names. Suppose, for instance, that you want to work with a database of books. In REXX you can do this by having a number of arrays, each of which is subscripted by the name of the book. The names of these arrays might be author, date_of_publication, publisher, call_number, and so forth. Then if the name of a particular book is stored in the variable book_name, you can retrieve all of the other information directly by referring to author.book_name, publisher.book_name, etc. Because of this direct association from a name to a value, such data structures are sometimes called *associative arrays*.

As far as the language user is concerned, there is no search process at all involved in looking up the author of a given book. In reality, of course, REXX does need to do a search to find each piece of data. The advantage is that this search process is all built in and transparent to the user.

An example may help clarify the usefulness of associative arrays. Suppose that we want to examine text files for the occurrence of specific key words. We would like to make a copy of only those lines in the file that contain one of the key words. The list of key words will be read from a separate text file in which they will be stored one or more to a line.

The following program does the job. It is written as a *filter*, i.e., a program which reads from *standard input* and writes to *standard output*. (*Standard input* and *standard output* are concepts originated in Unix that permit the output of one program to be used as the input of another.)

```
/********************************************************/
/* WORDFIND: a filter that copies only those lines  */
/* that contain a word from a list in another file. */
/********************************************************/

arg wordlist infile outfile
call dosdel outfile
dict. = 0

/* read wordlist */
do while lines(wordlist) > 0
    line = translate(linein(wordlist))
    do while line \= ''
        parse var line word line
        dict.word = 1
        end
    end
call lineout wordlist

/* search through infile */
do while lines(infile) > 0
    line = linein(infile)
    do i = 1 to words(line)
        word = translate(word(line, i))
        if dict.word then do
            call lineout outfile, line
            leave
            end
        end
    end

call lineout infile
call lineout outfile
exit
```

The program begins with an ARG instruction that picks up three file names from the program's single argument—the names of a word list file, an input file, and an output file. The second line calls a system function (which is not a standard part of REXX) to delete an existing file (if any) which has the same name as the output file. We will explain the assignment to dict. a little later.

The first loop in the program reads entirely through the word list file in order to create a table of keywords. How this table works is really the point of the example, so we will again defer the full explanation until we've finished an overview of the program. In this loop, the LINES() built-in function is used to allow the loop to terminate when there are no more lines to be read, and each individual line of the file is read with LINEIN().

We are assuming that each line of the file may contain more than word, so we have to extract each individual word. One REXX idiom to do this sort of thing, which may be of some interest, is the use of the instruction

```
parse var line word line
```

to isolate each word of the variable line in succession. In each iteration of the loop, line is updated with the portion following the first word. The TRANSLATE() built-in function is used to convert all words to upper-case, so that the program will not be case sensitive.

The second loop in the program has the same general structure. It reads one line at a time from the input file. Again, individual words are extracted from each line. Just for variety, we have used a different, more obvious (but usually less efficient) technique utilizing the WORD() built-in function to break a string of characters into words. The table created in the first loop is used in the second to identify words which were found in the word list.

In order to understand how the table works, the first important statement is

```
dict. = 0
```

This is a special kind of assignment, an assignment to a stem. Dict. is a very special case; it is not, strictly speaking, either a simple or compound variable, because it ends with a period. Assignment to a stem is defined to mean that all possible variables having that stem take on the new value, losing any previous value (if any). Of course, in practice REXX merely records the fact that a stem assignment has been done, rather than attempting the impossible feat of making an infinite number of assignments. But the effect is the same. Specifically, after an assignment to a stem, all possible values of variables having the same stem are now considered to be defined. And if they are used without any other assignment, the value of such variables is the value assigned to the stem.

The issue of whether a variable has been defined or, in other words, whether it has a value, is important in REXX. The language allows use of undefined variables, and gives them a value which is the same as the variable's name. In the case of a simple variable, this value is just the name (in uppercase). For compound variables, the value reflects the formation of the derived name from the corresponding compound symbol as described above.

For instance, in the following:

```
say dict.word
word = 'bah'
say dict.word
dict. = 0
say dict.word
dict.word = 'humbug'
say dict.word
```

The first SAY displays DICT.WORD, since nothing has been assigned yet. The second SAY displays DICT.bah (note lowercase), since the compound variable still does not have a value, though word has been assigned. The third SAY displays 0, reflecting the stem assignment. The last SAY displays humbug, because the specific compound variable DICT.bah has finally received a value apart from its assignment with all others having the same stem.

What we have done by making the stem assignment, then, is to make it possible to test very easily whether a given keyword has been encountered. The first nested loops in the example under discussion simply go through and set dict.word to 1 for each value of word which is found in the list of keywords read from a file. For all possible values of word that were not listed as keywords, dict.word is 0.

The second nested loops in the example use this information to determine quickly whether any particular word in the text file was contained in the list of keywords. Note that we were careful to convert words to uppercase, since a word might occur in the text with any combination of upper- and lowercase letters, and the variable DICT.something is not the same as the variable DICT.Something. (As symbols they would be equivalent, because of the rule that symbols are always treated as uppercase.)

Another thing that should be noted about stem variables is that they can be used in REXX expressions anywhere an ordinary (simple or compound) variable can be used. It is only when a value is assigned to a stem variable that something special happens. The value of a stem variable is, of course, whatever has been assigned to it, just as for any other variable, or else the (uppercase) symbol itself if nothing has been assigned. In this latter circumstance, compound variables based on the stem do not have the same value as the stem itself.

From this discussion, it is apparent that it is a matter of great importance in REXX whether or not a variable has been assigned, even though default values are supplied if the variable is undefined because no assignment has been made. You should, however, as a matter of good practice, never use a variable that hasn't been defined. REXX even allows you to enforce this convention by providing an instruction:

```
signal on novalue
```

which will cause a program trap in case an undefined variable is used. (Specifically, it causes the program to start executing statements beginning after the label novalue:.) Trapping of undefined variable usage is not the default, unfortunately, so you should include the above statement in all REXX programs of any significant size. Much more discussion of signals and how they work will be presented later.

One partial exception to the rule about use of undefined variables is that when they are referenced in the process of forming a derived name from a compound symbol they do not raise the NOVALUE condition. For instance, in the example discussed above, a reference to dict.word would be allowed even if word hadn't been assigned, provided the stem itself had been assigned. (The variable in question would then be named DICT.WORD.) Such a practice is still to be avoided, because of the hazard that word might inadvertently have a value though it was not expected to.

Given the importance of knowing when a variable is considered to be defined, we will mention the ways other than an assignment statement in which a variable can be assigned a value. One such way, of which we have seen a few examples, is the PARSE instruction (and its special cases ARG and PULL), which can assign a number of variables at once. Another way, the importance of which will become apparent later, is with the VALUE() built-in function. A DO instruction may initialize a control variable. Lastly, it is even possible for external programs to access REXX variables, depending on the application program interface supplied by each specific implementation. In fact, some implementations allow such external programs to create variables with names that are impossible in pure REXX programs—e.g., simple variables with names containing lowercase characters.

An assignment, or one of the other means of associating a value with a variable, also allocates storage for the variable. The reverse of this is also possible: the REXX DROP instruction releases a variable's storage and returns it to an uninitialized state. Both simple and compound variables can be dropped. A stem can also be dropped, which causes all variables having that stem to have their storage released and become uninitialized. This is obviously useful in an environment where storage is scarce and there are large data items or numerous compound variables which are no longer needed. It usually isn't necessary to use DROP when you are done with a particular variable or collection of compound variables, but it's handy to have the capability if little memory is available. Also, when a PROCEDURE statement is used in a subroutine or function, all variables which haven't been exposed are automatically dropped when the procedure returns.

More than one variable or stem can be dropped with the same DROP instruction. A typical example might be:

```
j = 10
drop list. bitmap model.j
```

The variables or stems to be dropped are listed in the DROP instruction, separated by spaces. In determining variables to be dropped, derived names are formed in the usual way, so in the above example the model.10 variable is dropped.

There is one thing to note about dropping specific compound variables. In the following:

```
stem. = 'something'
drop stem.1
say stem.1
```

the SAY instruction displays STEM.1 rather than something, because the value assigned to a stem should not be thought of as setting a default value for variables having that stem. Instead, conceptually, the stem assignment sets all possible variables having the same stem. The DROP statement above undefines just one of those variables, STEM.1, so like any other undefined variable, its uninitialized value is its name. Also, use of STEM.1 in an expression will raise the NOVALUE condition if it has been enabled.

4

Control Structures

A control structure is a programming language construct that determines the sequence in which instructions will be executed. There are several primary sorts of control structures. One is a selection structure which permits choices to be made in the flow of control based on the state of the program and its data. This is represented in REXX by the IF and SELECT instructions. A second type of structure is for looping. REXX has one instruction for this: DO, which has many variations. We will consider these control structures in this chapter, and also the SIG-NAL instruction, which is something like an unconditional "goto". In the next chapter we will look at a third type of control structure: subroutines.

SELECTION STRUCTURES

The IF instruction is REXX's basic conditional construct. Its general form is

```
IF expression THEN statement1 [ELSE statement2]
```

Here, expression must be a valid REXX expression that evaluates to 0 or 1 (a *boolean* expression). 1 represents *true* and 0 represents *false*. Therefore, statement1 is executed if expression has the value 1, and statement2 is executed if expression has the value 0.

This simple concept conceals a few subtleties. We will see these as we analyze this statement into the various clauses it contains. Recall that a *clause* is the basic unit of execution in REXX. Most REXX statements consist of just one clause, but IF is one of the exceptions. Let's consider a simple example:

```
if x >= 0 then z = x; else z = -x
```

If we wrote this with exactly one clause per line, it would be

```
if x >= 0
then
z = x
else
z = -x
```

so there are really five clauses here. Distinguishing the clauses becomes a matter of some importance when you are using REXX trace facilities to display the flow of execution. If you traced the above statement, you would see that there are indeed five separate clauses (though not all of them could be executed in any specific case). If you used the "interactive" trace option, REXX would actually stop after executing certain clauses, to allow you to display or change variables, and possibly even reexecute a clause. Clause boundaries are also important in that they represent opportunities for certain exceptional conditions to be raised.

But mostly, it's important to recognize the individual clauses in order to understand REXX's rules for the syntax of IF. The first important fact is that THEN is a reserved word in an IF statement. That is, THEN cannot be used as a symbol in the expression following IF, because THEN is specifically reserved to mark the end of the first clause. You could explicitly end the clause with ";":

```
if x >=0; then ...
```

or with the end of a line:

```
if x >= 0
then ...
```

but this is unnecessary, since THEN in this context explicitly ends the clause. THEN is also considered to be a clause by itself, so it may be followed by ";" or the end of the line.

A statement is required after THEN and may not simply be omitted. If you want to do nothing in the case the expression is true, then you must use the NOP (no-operation) instruction:

```
if x >= 0 then nop; else z = -x
```

However, the statement following THEN may be quite complex. It could be another IF instruction, a SELECT instruction, or a DO instruction. If you want to execute several statements in case the condition is true, this is done by enclosing them between DO and END:

```
if x >= 0 then do
    say 'Nonnegative value of x.'
    z = x
    end
else ...
```

The DO . . . END pair is considered to be a single statement, though it is composed of any number of other statements. This construct is also known as a *simple* DO group, as opposed to a *repetitive* DO group, which represents a loop that may possibly be executed many times. A repetitive DO group is also considered to be a single statement, and may be used following a THEN or ELSE.

In contrast to THEN, ELSE is not a reserved word within an IF instruction. Therefore it is required that the statement following THEN be terminated by ";" or the end of a line before using ELSE. If you like to write your IF statements to be complete on one line, this is one of the few times in REXX where you will be required to use ";". It is probably better style, however, to always put ELSE on a line by itself. Still, ELSE is like THEN in being considered to be a clause by itself.

The ELSE part of the IF instruction is optional. If you need to do something only when the condition part is true, then the ELSE and the statement following it may be omitted. But if ELSE is used it must be followed by a statement, which could be another IF statement, a DO group, etc.

You might also have to use the NOP instruction after ELSE. This is because if you use nested IFs, then any ELSE part is associated with the nearest incomplete IF. So in

```
if x >= 0 then
    if x > 100 then
        z = x
    else
        nop
else
    z = -x
```

we had to insert an extra ELSE NOP so that z = -x is executed only in case x < 0, rather than in case x <= 100.

There is an aspect of the way REXX handles conditional statements that has significant implications for performance. It involves the evaluation of logical expressions involving the *and* ("&") and *or* ("|") operators. Any expression which contains one of these operators is always evaluated fully. This is unlike the situation in some languages like C that have *short circuit* rules which guarantee that a logical expression is evaluated only far enough that its value can be unambiguously determined. For instance, the value of

```
x & y
```

could be determined just by looking at x, provided the value of x is 0. But REXX will always determine the value of y as well.

Logical expressions are used primarily in IF statements. You might naturally want to say

```
if something(x) & something_else(y) then call do_this
```

But if the function evaluations might take some time (and merely calling a function introduces some overhead), it would be better to rewrite this equivalently as

```
if something(x) then if something_else(y) then
   call do_this
```

Again, you may save time by ordering the clauses so that the function with the least overhead is called first, unless the other one is much more likely to determine the outcome.

Handling a logical expression that involves an *or* instead of an *and* is in principle the same, though slightly more awkward, since you must replace

```
if something(x) | something_else(y) then call do_this
```

with

```
if something(x) then call do_this
else if something_else(y) then call do_this
```

Many programming situations require you to test for any of a number of possibilities and take appropriate action. One way to do this is with a sequence of nested IF instructions, e.g.,

```
if choice = 1 then
   call show_help
else if choice = 2 then
```

```
      call edit_file
    else if choice = 3 then
      call finish_transaction
    else
      say "Invalid choice"
```

There is nothing especially wrong with this approach, but the situation is so common that REXX provides a separate SELECT instruction to deal with it. The preceding example could be written

```
select
    when choice = 1 then
      call show_help
    when choice = 2 then
      call edit_file
    when choice = 3 then
      call finish_transaction
    otherwise
      say "Invalid choice"
    end
```

A SELECT instruction works exactly like the corresponding nested IF, in that each condition is tested in turn. The instruction following THEN of the first case that is true (has the value 1) will be executed, and then control will transfer to the first instruction following END.

There is usually no particular limit to how many WHEN cases can occur in a SELECT instruction, but some REXX implementations do limit the depth of nesting of control structures. For this reason, the equivalent form using nested IF instructions is best avoided when there are more than a handful of separate cases.

The general form of SELECT is

```
SELECT when-list [OTHERWISE [statement-list]] END
```

where when-list is a sequence of one or more compound clauses of the form

```
WHEN expression THEN statement
```

This is just like an IF instruction (except there's no ELSE part). That is, the expression must have a value of 0 or 1.

THEN is a reserved word and cannot be used as part of expression. Instead, it marks the end of the expression. For instance, in

```
when pi * r ** 2 < 100 then
    call adjust_circle
```

REXX recognized the end of the expression

```
pi * r ** 2 < 100
```

by the presence of THEN. A semicolon could have been used to end the clause explicitly, too:

```
when pi * r ** 2 < 100; then
   call adjust_circle
```

Following THEN, statement can be any simple or compound statement, including a simple or repetitive DO group or another SELECT instruction. A nonnull clause is required after THEN. The NOP instruction should be used as the statement following THEN if nothing is to be done for one particular case.

OTHERWISE is not a reserved word, so if it is used, the preceding clause must be explicitly terminated with a semicolon or the end of a line, just as for ELSE in an IF instruction.

The OTHERWISE part of a SELECT instruction is optional. However, if none of the WHEN cases are found to be true, an error will be generated if there is no OTHERWISE. The list of statements following OTHERWISE can be empty, though—a NOP instruction isn't required. Therefore, if it is possible that none of the WHEN conditions in a SELECT is executed and you don't want to regard that as an error, you must include the OTHER-WISE, for instance,

```
select
   when author = "Twain, Mark" then
      author = "Clemens, Samuel"
   when author = "Carroll, Lewis" then
      author = "Dodgson, Charles"
   ...
   otherwise
   end
```

In addition, a list of two or more statements between OTHERWISE and END does not need to be enclosed in a DO . . . END pair.

LOOPING STRUCTURES

REXX has only one looping structure, but it has various forms. The general syntax of DO is:

```
DO [repetitor] [conditional]
   [statement-list]
   END [symbol]
```

The statement-list, which is sometimes called the *body* of the loop, is simply an arbitrary sequence of statements, separated from each other by semicolons (or line-ends). It can start on the same line as DO itself, provided that the DO [repetitor] [conditional] part is followed by a ";" to mark the end of the clause.

Both the *repetitor* and the *conditional* may be omitted, in which case the structure is called a *simple* DO group. The DO . . . END pair is merely used to group a sequence of statements to form a single statement for use with an IF or SELECT instruction.

The different forms that a repetitive DO group may take correspond to the use of different types of *repetitors* and *conditionals*. A repetitor can be one of three things. First, it can simply be FOREVER. DO FOREVER instructions are endless loops, except, of course, there should be some way in the body of the loop to terminate it, for instance:

```
do forever
   ...  /* processing */
   if string = '' then
     return
   ...  /* more processing */
end
```

In this example, some processing is done, and the internal logic calls for a return to a calling procedure if there's nothing left in string. The RETURN instruction terminates the loop in addition to returning to the caller. Notice (in this case) that the test occurred in the middle of the loop. Had it been possible to do the test at either the beginning or end of the loop, we could have used a conditional like WHILE string \= '' or UNTIL string = '' as part of the DO clause.

One other simple form of repetitor is an arbitrary expression that evaluates to a nonnegative whole number. This number tells explicitly how many times the loop should be executed:

```
do 3
   say 'Never!'
end
```

The third kind of repetitor is the most complex. It has the form

```
assignment [TO expt] [BY expb] [FOR expf]
```

Here assignment is just an ordinary REXX assignment of the form

```
symbol = expi
```

Expt, expb, expf, and expi are expressions. For instance, consider

```
do year = 1800 to 1990 by 10 for count
   call census_report year
   end
```

The target variable of the assignment (symbol) is the *loop control variable,* year. The initial value of the control variable (expi) is 1800. The terminating value of the control variable (expt) is 1990. The increment of the control variable (expb) is 10. And the number of times the loop can be executed (expf) is count.

The control variable assignment here is handled just like any other assignment to the variable named by symbol. When several loops having control variables are nested, it is possible to identify a particular one on a LEAVE or ITERATE instruction by naming the appropriate control variable. The control variable is just like any other REXX variable, and it can be either simple or compound—it could even be a stem.

The loop is executed with the control variable having the initial value given by expi. The loop will be terminated as soon as the control variable is greater than or equal to the quantity determined by expt if TO is present. This is true provided that there is no increment defined by expb, or the increment is nonnegative if present. However, if the increment is specified and it is negative, the terminating condition is that the control variable becomes less than the expt quantity.

The default for the increment, if none is specified, is 1. Thus

```
do i=1
   ...
   end
```

is just like a do forever loop, except that i is initially set to 1 and incremented by 1 every time through the loop.

It is possible, based on the original value, the limit, and the increment, that the loop may not be executed at all. In addition, FOR may be specified with a count (that must be a nonnegative value); if so, this acts as another way to terminate the loop before the limit is reached. If no limit is specified by TO, the loop will not terminate unless there is a FOR, WHILE, or UNTIL expression, or some explicit exit tests within the body of the loop.

The limit (expt), increment (expb), and maximum loop count (expf) may be specified in any order. Expressions in the repetitor are evaluated from left to right. (This is important to note in case any of the expressions involve functions that have side effects. For instance, a side effect might be a change to a variable used in another expression, or an I/O operation.) Further, they are evaluated only once, before the loop is executed, so the increment and limit cannot be changed by any action within the loop. All expressions must evaluate to valid numbers, and any necessary comparisons of the control variable to the limit are done in accord with the prevailing value of NUMERIC DIGITS.

TO, BY, and FOR are reserved words in the expressions expt, expb, expf, and expi, as are WHILE and UNTIL. That is, they cannot be used as the names of variables.

In addition to any of the three kinds of repetitors, one conditional of the form WHILE expw or UNTIL expu may be used. This provides yet another means of terminating a loop. The expressions associated with WHILE and UNTIL must evaluate to 0 or 1. But unlike the expressions associated with the limit, increment, and loop count, they are computed every time through the loop. This means that loops which use WHILE and UNTIL may be somewhat slower. For instance, in the two loops

```
do i=1 to 1000
   ...
   end
```

and

```
do i=1 while i<=1000
   ...
   end
```

the first will probably be faster than the second. The reason is that the termination condition can be tested more efficiently in the first case. In effect, use of WHILE or UNTIL requires that an expression (i<=1000) be evaluated every time through the loop, while a simpler numeric comparison can be performed in the first case.

The difference would be even more dramatic if the termination test involved a computation of some sort. Suppose the loop limit is computed by a function call like length(x). Assuming that x does not change within the loop then

```
do i=1 to length(x)
   ...
   end
```

would be much more efficient than

```
do i=1 while i<=length(x)
   ...
   end
```

since length(x) needs to be computed just once in the first case (the first time the loop is executed). However, if x may change within the loop, you would have to use the second form with WHILE in order to guarantee that i never exceeds the length of x inside the loop.

The difference between WHILE and UNTIL is that the WHILE condition is tested before the body of the loop is executed, but the UNTIL condition is tested afterwards. Consequently, use of WHILE may completely prevent the body of the loop from being executed, but UNTIL allows the body to be executed at least once.

When conditionals are combined with repetitors (including possibly both a limit and a loop-count condition), it may be important to know in precisely which order each of the tests will be applied. REXX guarantees that the control variable will be incremented and tests will be performed in the following order:

1. The control variable is assigned its initial value or incremented.

2. The control variable is compared against the limit, and the loop ends if the limit is exceeded.

3. The loop count is checked, and the loop ends if the value is exceeded.

4. The WHILE expression is evaluated and the loop ends if the value is 0. (An error occurs if it is not 0 or 1.)

5. Assuming none of these tests causes the loop to terminate, the body of the loop is executed.

6. The UNTIL expression is evaluated. If it is 1, the loop ends, but otherwise things begin again with step 1.

Hopefully you will avoid writing too many loops where details like this are critical, since it's easy to forget all these rules. The main time you might have to be aware of these rules is if you want to access the value of the control variable after the loop has terminated (quite a legal thing to do in REXX) or if you use functions that have side effects in the WHILE or UNTIL expressions.

Except that the value of the control variable has to be numeric, there is no other restriction. It could be fractional, as could the increment and limit. All arithmetic on the control variable is done in the standard REXX way, which means that the values of NUMERIC DIGITS and FUZZ may be significant. When nonintegral numbers are involved, note that the limit condition is defined comparatively, rather than in terms of equality. Therefore, a loop like

```
do x = 1.1 by 1.1 to 5
   ...
   end
```

will terminate, even though x never equals the limit value, since the loop ends as soon as x equals or exceeds the limit value.

One feature which is often helpful in a looping structure, but which is often missing in a language, is the ability either to terminate the loop or to begin another iteration of the loop from an arbitrary location within the body. Let's first consider leaving the loop. You might, for instance, be reading lines from a file and want to quit if some particular data item is read:

```
do while lines(file) \= 0
   x = linein(file)
   if x = '*** EOF ***' then
      leave
   ...
end
```

Here, as we will explain in the chapter on file I/O, the LINES() function returns 0 once the true end of the file has been reached, allowing the loop to terminate. But, perhaps for testing purposes, we also want to quit if a special marker ('*** EOF ***') is found. The LINEIN() function reads a line from the file. The next statement uses a LEAVE instruction to exit from the loop if the marker is found.

The rule is that LEAVE will terminate the innermost active repetitive loop in which it occurs. It is an error to use a LEAVE instruction that is not contained in the body of a repetitive DO loop in the current procedure. LEAVE would not terminate a simple DO group, and could not even legally be used there, unless the simple DO group were contained within an active repetitive loop. If the simple loop is nested within a repetitive one, however, then both are terminated by LEAVE. For instance, if we wanted to add a message to the previous example before ceasing to read the file, we might have

```
do while lines(file) \= 0
   x = linein(file)
   if x = '*** EOF ***' then do
      say 'Prematurely ending file scan.'
      leave
   end
   ...
end
```

Note that if you have one or more nested procedures (next chapter), only repetitive loops in the current procedure are considered to be *active,* so LEAVE has no effect on a loop which was active when the current procedure was called. In other words, LEAVE can't terminate a loop in the calling procedure.

The execution of a LEAVE instruction is like a jump to the first statement after the END which belongs to the active loop. This jump skips any incrementing of the control variable, which therefore will have the value current when LEAVE was executed. Any WHILE or UNTIL expressions are likewise skipped.

In case there are several active repetitive loops, only the one immediately containing LEAVE is normally terminated. However, it is possible to terminate an outer loop from within an inner one if the outer loop has a control variable (and if the control variable is different from that of the inner loop, as would normally be the case). This is done by using the symbol for the control variable on the LEAVE instruction:

```
do outer = 1 to 10
   ...
   do forever
      ...
      if something then
         leave outer
      ...
   end
end
```

This example terminates all DO loops illustrated, even though the inner one doesn't have a control variable. Any simple DO groups that happened to contain the LEAVE and be contained within the outer loop would also be terminated. If more than one repetitive loop has the same control variable, only the innermost one that contains the LEAVE is terminated.

The name that may be specified is treated as a symbol, in that no substitution is performed in case it happens to be a compound symbol. That is, the symbol must match the symbol used for the control variable exactly, except for case. In other words, something like

```
do a.3 = 1 to 10
   ...
   i = 3
   leave a.i
end
```

would not work. But it is rather uncommon, though legal, to use compound variables as loop control variables, so one isn't too likely to make this mistake.

ITERATE is the other instruction that can be used within a repetitive loop to alter the normal flow of control. Unlike LEAVE, which terminates the loop, ITERATE in effect branches to the END which closes the loop and therefore causes immediate incrementing of the control variable (if any) and application of the normal tests for loop termination. Unless one of these tests causes termination, the body of the loop is then entered again from the beginning.

If an UNTIL conditional is present on the DO instruction, it will be tested first, before the control variable is incremented. After that, the sequence of execution is as described earlier for incrementing the control variable and testing the loop conditions.

ITERATE is often used to skip the rest of the body of a loop if some condition indicates that to do so would be unfruitful. The only alternative would be to place the rest of the loop within a DO . . . END pair. For instance, if a program is prompting for input, a null input line would be a cause to ITERATE:

```
do forever
   say 'Enter a command:'
   parse pull input
   if input = '' then
      iterate
   . . .
   end
```

Or perhaps a program is scanning a file for lines of a particular type:

```
do while lines(file) \= 0
   parse value linein(file) with keyword .
   if keyword \= 'Name:' then
      iterate
   . . .
   end
```

The rules for use of ITERATE are just like those for LEAVE. For instance, it can only be used inside of an active repetitive DO loop. ITERATE will skip any enclosing simple DO groups to branch to the end of the nearest repetitive group. It has no effect on DO loops which are not active because they are not executing within the current procedure.

If ITERATE is contained within nested repetitive loops, it affects only the innermost one, unless the name of a control variable is included on the ITERATE instruction. In that case, it effectively branches to the END statement corresponding to the innermost containing loop which has the specified control variable. Any intervening repetitive (or simple) DO groups are thereby terminated, and their control variables are left with the values they had when the ITERATE was executed.

THE SIGNAL INSTRUCTION

The various control structures discussed so far cover most programming needs. There are times, however, when nothing less than a good, old-fashioned GOTO will do. REXX avoids the problem of implementing an instruction which some people view with suspicion by calling it SIGNAL instead of GOTO.

There are actually several forms of SIGNAL. One form is used to enable and disable the handling of exceptional conditions (sometimes called *signals*). This is discussed at length in Chap. 11. The other form of the instruction is provided to allow for explicit, direct transfer of control to another location in a program. You may think of this, if you like, as simply providing a way for the programmer to implement his or her own private exceptional condition types.

The syntax of this form of SIGNAL is

```
SIGNAL label
```

or

```
SIGNAL [VALUE] expression
```

In the first case, label is a symbol or a literal string. It is taken as a constant, and refers to a label within the program. This usage is exactly like the way labels are used in procedure calls. In particular, if the label occurs twice in the program, only the first occurrence is used as the target of a SIGNAL.

In the second case, the target of the SIGNAL is computed at run-time as the value of expression. VALUE needs to be used in the instruction if expression begins with a symbol or literal string (instead of a special character, such as a parenthesis). If you use a literal or an expression with SIGNAL, the literal or the value of the expression should be uppercase, since labels are always considered to be uppercase.

When SIGNAL is executed, control transfers immediately to the instruction following the specified label. There are, in addition, certain side effects of SIGNAL. Namely, any IF, SELECT, or DO instruction that may be active is terminated. This is true no matter how deeply such instructions are nested in the current procedure. If any INTERPRET instructions are active, they too will be terminated.

On the other hand, the current procedure is not terminated. There is no way by the use of SIGNAL alone to get out of a subprocedure. This can be a problem sometimes, since it means that there is no easy way to get back to the top of a program from inside a deep nest of subprocedure calls. This behavior is consistent with the way that signals are handled in connection with exceptional conditions (Chap. 11).

The fact that SIGNAL does not cause termination of the active procedure is one way in which it is slightly less powerful than an unconstrained GOTO. The fact that it does terminate active IF, SELECT, and DO instructions is another way, because it means that you cannot transfer control from one place to another within a DO or SELECT instruction. Actually, most implementations of REXX allow labels inside of IF, SELECT, and DO instructions, but there is little of use that can be done with them. You may even be able to use a SIGNAL instruction to such a label without immediate error. However, the DO instruction will actually have been terminated, and an error will occur when the first END statement is encountered.

You should be careful in placement of labels which will be the target of a SIGNAL. Although they may be anywhere in the program, even inside a remote DO loop, the context of execution will still be the *active* subroutine when SIGNAL is used.

The primary use of SIGNAL is to allow programmers to define their own *exceptional conditions* analogous to REXX's built-in conditions. For instance, in a data entry program, such a condition might be "invalid input". The condition could be *raised* any time the entry of invalid data is detected with

```
signal invalid_input
```

The code following the invalid_input: label would probably display an appropriate message, explain what the problem is, and request reentry of the data.

SIGNAL is often reserved for fairly serious problems. For instance, in a program that usually runs unattended, the code to which control is transferred by SIGNAL may simply record diagnostic information, perform clean-up, and then do an EXIT. (You could also call a subroutine to do this.)

Handlers for any of the REXX built-in conditions usually end with a SIGNAL to resume normal execution of the program. It is really the only alternative to EXIT or RETURN in this case.

There are other valid uses of SIGNAL completely unrelated to condition handling. For instance, it can be used to perform the equivalent of a very large SELECT statement with lower overhead. Remember that SELECT must test a number of logical expressions in turn until it finds one that is true. If there are scores, or even hundreds of them, this can be very time-consuming. SIGNAL can be used, instead, to construct an n-way branch:

```
signal value 'CASE'n
case1:
    . . .
```

```
    signal end_case
case2:
    ...
    signal end_case
case3:
    ...
    signal end_case
...
end_case:
```

is largely equivalent to

```
select
    when n = 1 then
        ...
    when n = 2 then
        ...
    when n = 3 then
        ...
    end
```

but much faster. Just remember that, unfortunately, SIGNAL cannot be used inside of a DO loop because it terminates the loop.

Subroutines and Functions

Most modern programming languages have, in addition to the control structures described in the last chapter, the concept of a subroutine. This is a special kind of control structure which allows a group of instructions to be *called* from many places within a program without having to actually be duplicated each time it is used (as is done with *macros* or *inline functions* in some languages). The use of subroutines makes it possible to decompose the design of a program into small functional units which are easily reusable. Because each subroutine (ideally) does one thing well and has explicit, well-defined interfaces to the rest of the program, it is easy to debug. A program can be designed as a hierarchy of subroutine calls in a way that matches the natural hierarchical structure of the problem being solved.

REXX, of course, supports subroutines. A distinction is made between subroutines that return a value and those that do not. However, in REXX this distinction is not very hard and fast. Generally, a subroutine is invoked with the CALL instruction, which has the format

```
CALL name [expression] [, expression] ...
```

Here, name is the name of the subroutine. Name may be a symbol or a character string literal. In either case, the value is taken literally— even if it is a possible variable name, it is not evaluated. The subroutine itself may be *internal, external,* or *built-in,* depending on where the code for the subroutine is located. A subroutine may return a value, but this is not required. If it does return a value, that value is left in the special variable `RESULT` after the `CALL`.

A function, on the other hand, is invoked by its occurrence in an expression. A function call is recognized as being a symbol or character string literal followed immediately (with no intervening blank) by a left parenthesis. This is followed in turn by zero or more expressions, separated by commas, and finally ends with a right parenthesis. Thus, a function reference has the form

```
name( [expression] [, expression] ... )
```

It is required that a function called in this way return a value, and an error will occur if it does not. The `RESULT` special variable is not assigned in this case. Functions, like subroutines, can be either internal, external, or built-in.

Note that there are no parentheses around the argument list in a `CALL` instruction (though there may be around each individual argument expression). This is a source of frequent confusion for beginning REXX users. You can fall into this trap unwittingly, because the following is legal:

```
call something (argument)
```

(since the parentheses merely enclose the first argument), while the similar statement

```
call something (argument_1, argument_2)
```

is definitely illegal.

Subroutines and functions are often simply called *procedures* when the distinction is not important. The reason that the distinction between subroutines and functions is less important in REXX than in other languages is that there are no declarations anywhere that limit a procedure to being one or the other. A procedure can very well return a value at all times and thus be usable as either subroutine or a procedure. Or it can return a value sometimes and not others. Or it can even determine (with the `PARSE SOURCE` instruction) how it was invoked and return a value only if necessary.

BUILT-IN, INTERNAL, AND EXTERNAL PROCEDURES

A much more important distinction turns on the location of the code for the procedure. Many procedures are an integral part of the language.

That is, they are always supplied with the language (if it is a complete implementation), they all accept the same arguments, and they (ideally) always operate in the same way. These are the *built-in functions,* and there are about 66 of them in standard REXX. (Different levels of the language specification have added or removed certain functions.) Specific implementations of REXX always provide additional built-in functions to take advantage of particular features of the environment. Although referred to as *functions,* these built-in procedures can always be called as subroutines.

Internal procedures are those which are supplied by the programmer in the same file as the rest of the program. In this case, the name of the procedure corresponds to a label within the file. A label is simply a clause which consists of a symbol followed by a colon, which marks the end of the clause. The label can be any valid symbol; it doesn't need to begin with an alphabetic character or be acceptable as a variable name. If there are duplicate labels within a file, only the first is ever used as the start of a procedure. The second occurrence of a label is not an error, but it can never be reached by a CALL statement or function reference. The procedure begins at the first clause following the label.

On the other hand, the end of a procedure is not syntactically delimited at all. That is, there is no syntactic indication of the end. Of course, the RETURN instruction causes control to return from a procedure, but it does not necessarily mark the end of the code of the procedure. By use of the SIGNAL instruction, control could jump all over the source of a program and still remain within a procedure (though this would be considered very bad form). Procedures can also overlap; that is, one procedure could "flow into" another without the label of the second procedure being invoked by a CALL or function reference. Technically, control would still be within the first procedure. While this would ordinarily be a suspicious usage, it could be employed to allow for alternate entry points to the same body of code (perhaps with different arguments).

External procedures, finally, are located somewhere outside the program source file. Exactly where is implementation-dependent. They may be written in REXX and contained in other source files, to be loaded by the operating system when required. Or they may be written in other languages and linked to by a variety of system-specific mechanisms (*function packages* in CMS and MS-DOS, DLLs in OS/2, etc.). The way that the name of the procedure as used in a program is related to the external function is also system-dependent. It might, for instance, be the same as the name on a particular file, or the name of an entry point in a dynamic link library.

As you can see, the same name might possibly be used to refer to a procedure that is any of these three types. So the language specifies a search order that defines the order in which each possibility will be tested for. The rule is that if the name of the procedure, as specified in the CALL or function reference, is a symbol, then internal procedures are searched for first, followed by built-in procedures, followed by external procedures.

This rule gives a programmer the freedom to override the definition of any built-in or external procedure at will, simply by coding an internal procedure of the same name. So if you don't like the way the SUBSTR() function works, for instance, you can write your own.

However, in writing your enhanced replacement for SUBSTR(), you may find that in many or most cases you just want to use the existing built-in function. This possibility is provided for by the rule that if the name of the procedure in the CALL or function reference is a quoted string, then internal procedures are excluded from consideration, and only built-in procedures (first) or external procedures will be invoked. There are no additional rules that would allow you to override built-in procedures with external ones. This generally works in your best interest, because stray files or libraries floating around in your computing environment can't accidentally subvert a working REXX program. (It also makes deliberate subversion by "Trojan horse" programs a little less likely.) But on the other hand, if you develop a whiz-bang extension to SUBSTR(), there's no way to incorporate it in all your REXX programs except by physically copying it into them.

PASSING ARGUMENTS
AND RETURNING VALUES

One thing that is common to the notion of a subroutine in most programming languages is the ability to pass values called *arguments* to the subroutine. This notion is derived from the mathematical concept of a function which computes some value based on the values of zero or more arguments. REXX, of course, supports argument passing.

It turns out that there are subtle differences in the ways that different languages implement the passing of arguments. Sometimes the arguments are said to be passed *by reference*. This means that the subroutine gets access to the actual variable in the calling routine and is able to modify it directly (assuming an actual variable was passed rather than a constant or some computed quantity). There are both advantages and disadvantages to this approach. One disadvantage is that the subroutine can have *side effects,* in that it can modify some of the caller's variables in addition to simply returning a value. But this can also be an advantage, especially when arrays are involved, since in many languages passing and returning entire arrays is inefficient or impossible.

An alternative is that arguments are passed *by value*. This means that only the values of variables are passed, and the subroutine is not able to modify the caller's variables by modifying the arguments. In REXX, arguments are always passed by value. There are other means, as we shall see, that enable a subroutine to modify variables belonging to the caller, if necessary.

Another consequence of passing arguments by value is that the argument values are completely determined at the time of the call. Even if a variable passed as an argument is changed within the subroutine, any reference to the argument will retrieve the original value. For example, in

```
x = 1
call example_sub x
...
example_sub:
arg y
say x y
x = 2
arg z
say x y z
```

the first SAY instruction displays 1 1, because y has been set to the value of the argument, which is 1. The second SAY displays 2 1 1. Although x has been reassigned the value 2, when the value of the argument is assigned to z, we find it is still 1. In other words, no matter what is done to the variable whose value was passed as an argument, the argument value itself does not change.

Further, variables which receive the argument value, like y and z, do not become "aliases" for x. In fact, it is incorrect to think of x as the argument. Strictly speaking, it is the value of x which is the argument. This is what call *by value* means.

There are basically two ways in REXX that a subroutine can gain access to the arguments that are passed. The first is with the PARSE instruction:

```
call example_sub this, that, the_other
...
example_sub:
parse arg first, second, third
```

PARSE is used in REXX for many things besides parsing character strings, and this is an example. PARSE is able to take one or more character strings and assign them, or portions of them, to variables. Where the strings come from is determined by the word following PARSE, in this case ARG. In the present case, ARG directs PARSE to operate on the argument strings passed to the subroutine. Here, the strings that are the values of this, that, and the_other are assigned to first, second, and third, respectively.

Notice the commas in the PARSE statement of this example. They are quite important. The example could have had

```
parse arg first second third
```

and still been perfectly legal. But what this does is to parse only the first argument string (i.e., the value of this). It assigns the first blank-delimited word to first, the second word to second, and the rest to third. The other two argument strings are simply ignored. This is a frequent problem for beginning REXX programmers. In general, you will stay out of trouble by remembering the rule that the PARSE ARG instruction should have as many commas as the corresponding CALL instruction or function reference. While there may be occasions when more or fewer commas would be called for, try to follow the rule unless you know exactly what you're doing.

There is an ARG instruction which is a shorthand form of PARSE UPPER ARG. It is intended to give the appearance, when used at the beginning of a subroutine, of being a declaration of the routine's arguments:

```
example_sub:
arg first, second, third
```

It is, however, just another executable statement, not a declaration, and it has the usually undesirable side effect of converting all strings to uppercase before parsing them and assigning to first, second, and third. (It is a holdover from an earlier era of computing when it was customary to deal mostly with uppercased characters and strings.) The ARG or PARSE ARG statement need not occur at the beginning of the sub-routine. It could be anywhere in the subroutine, and it could even be used several times to parse the arguments in different ways.

There is another, completely different, way for a subroutine to access its arguments: with the ARG() built-in function. This has the form

```
ARG([argument_number], [option])
```

Argument_number is the number of the argument to be returned. It must be a positive whole number. Thus

```
call example_sub this, that, the_other
...
example_sub:
```

```
first = arg(1)
second = arg(2)
third = arg(3)
```

is completely equivalent to the original example. In general, PARSE ARG will be slightly more efficient, but the use of ARG( ) is slightly less subject to introducing mysterious bugs due to forgetting a comma or two. Sometimes it is convenient to use ARG( ) directly in expressions. Also, ARG( ) makes it possible to distinguish between arguments that are null strings and arguments that are completely omitted.

First, we have to explain about omitted arguments. Syntactically it is always permissible to supply any number of arguments (up to some implementation-defined limit) to any procedure. Whether the procedure will use all supplied arguments, or may require more than have been supplied, is completely up to the procedure to decide. If arguments before the final one are to be omitted, this is indicated by supplying just the comma that separates one argument from the next. So in

```
call example_sub this, , the_other
```

the second argument has been omitted. If all arguments after some point are to be omitted, the commas can be left in or omitted, however you prefer. (Except you must remember that a comma which is the last thing on a line means continuation rather than an argument separator.) So

```
call example_sub this
```

passes just the first argument.

If the nth argument has been omitted, then the value of arg(n) will be a null string. This is the same as its value would be if a null string were passed explicitly. For example, in both

```
call example_sub
```

and

```
call example_sub ""
```

the value of arg(1) is "" (a null string). So how do you distinguish between these two cases? That is the purpose of the second optional argument of ARG( ): the value of option can be e ("exists"), or o ("omitted"). Arg(n, 'e') has the value 1 if the nth argument exists or 0 if it has been omitted. Arg(n, 'o') has the value 1 if the nth argument has been omitted or 1 if not. There is no way to detect omitted arguments with PARSE ARG. Variables corresponding to omitted arguments are simply assigned null strings.

If ARG( ) is called with no arguments at all, it returns the number of arguments passed to the procedure. More precisely, it returns the number of the last argument which was explicitly passed. So if you had

```
call example_sub this, , the_other
```

arg( ) would have the value 3 even though only two arguments were actually passed. You can use the value of arg( ) as a quick test for possibly omitted arguments, but you should use the above more elaborate test in most cases. In other words, if arg( ) has the value 3, you may be sure that the third argument was passed explicitly, and that nothing after the third one was; but you would not know about the first and second arguments.

Built-in functions have a special status as far as the omission of arguments is concerned. Part of the definition of a built-in function is a specification of which arguments are optional and may be omitted. In practice, all optional arguments occur after the required ones, though this is not a requirement of the language. If any required argument is omitted, an error will automatically be generated. For user-written procedures, either internal or external, it is up to the procedure itself to define what is meant by a "required" argument, and what to do if it has been omitted.

The process of returning values from a procedure is a much less complex matter than the passing of arguments. You simply use the RETURN instruction, which has the form

```
RETURN [expression]
```

The expression on a RETURN instruction is optional for a procedure invoked with CALL, but it is required if the procedure was invoked in a function reference. The expression is computed from values of the current generation of variables plus exposed variables (see the next section on scope of variables). All variables in the current generation are then dropped, and control returns to the point at which the procedure was invoked. If the procedure was invoked by a CALL statement, the special variable RESULT is assigned the value. Otherwise, the value becomes the value of the function reference, and RESULT is not changed. If the procedure was invoked by CALL and no expression is provided on RETURN, then RESULT is dropped and becomes undefined.

The EXIT instruction is like RETURN, except that it terminates the whole REXX program (contained in a single source file), and returns to the next higher level. The format of EXIT is just like RETURN:

EXIT [expression]

In case the current REXX program is an external routine called by another REXX program, the point of invocation of the external procedure is where control returns as a result of EXIT. Just as with RETURN, if the procedure was invoked by a function reference, the expression is required and its value becomes the value of the function reference, and RESULT is not affected. If invocation was by CALL, expression isn't required. RESULT is assigned the value of the expression if it is present; otherwise it is dropped.

If RETURN is issued from the topmost procedure in a REXX program (file), it behaves just like EXIT and terminates the program. If the end of the file is encountered when executing any procedure in a REXX program, that is considered to be an implicit EXIT, and the program will terminate. Since no return value was provided, an error will occur if the program was invoked as an external function by another REXX program.

REXX programs can also be invoked by other REXX programs in system-dependent ways. Sometimes the REXX programs are handled just like other system commands and are simply invoked in the usual REXX way via the ADDRESS instruction or because the statement is not an assignment and does not begin with a REXX keyword. In this case, the expression used on the EXIT or RETURN instruction may be assigned to the RC special variable, just like the return code from a system command. Depending on the system, it may be required to be a numeric value in this case.

SCOPE OF VARIABLES

Another important issue which arises with procedures in all languages which recognize the concept is that of the *scope* of variables. This is the question of whether instructions in a subroutine can "see" variables belonging to the caller. In some languages such as PL/I, a subroutine can see its caller's variables (at least if the subroutine is nested within the calling procedure), while this is not the case in other languages such as C. In those languages which have this feature, it is referred to as *lexical scoping,* because the region of the program within which variable names are recognized as referring to the same data is determined syntactically by the physical location of the code.

REXX in general pays little attention to the location of code. As we have seen, a subroutine can have code scattered all over a program, and subroutines can even overlap. The question of which subroutine has control at any particular time is therefore determined dynamically by the flow of control. The very same instruction may at one time be part of one subroutine, and later part of a different subroutine. (REXX is rather like assembler language in this regard.) Correspondingly, the scope of a variable name must be determined dynamically rather than statically.

REXX is, however, more like PL / I than C, in that a subroutine can in general "see" variables belonging to its caller. But it is recognized that this can be undesirable in practice, because it enables subroutines to have (unintended) side effects. For instance, it is common to use very simple variable names like I for loop control variables. If a subroutine is called in such a loop and also uses I, obscure bugs can easily be introduced.

To limit this kind of exposure, REXX provides the PROCEDURE instruction, whose purpose is to prevent access of a subroutine to its caller's variables. PROCEDURE is entirely optional, but, if used, it must immediately follow the label at the beginning of the subroutine:

```
x = 5
call some_sub
...
some_sub: procedure
x = -5
...
```

In this example, references to the variable X are to entirely different data items. The some_sub procedure cannot access any of its caller's variables. Although the appearance of PROCEDURE here is similar to a declaration in other languages, it is, like all REXX instructions, an executable statement. Only the rule that it must occur immediately after a label prevents PROCEDURE from being used in an IF statement (for instance). PROCEDURE actually does something when it is executed: it creates a new *generation* of variables, completely distinct from variables of the calling routine. All variables of this new generation that are created in the process of executing the subroutine are automatically dropped when RETURN is executed (as if the DROP instruction had been used).

But sometimes a subroutine has a real need to access a few variables of its caller, while desiring to avoid disturbing the majority of them. Normally, it would be best to pass such data to the subroutine through the argument list, as long as only a few variables are involved and they are merely to be read, not updated. However, if the caller's data has to be changed, or a number of variables are involved, some alternative is needed. So what PROCEDURE takes away with one hand it can give back with the other by means of the EXPOSE keyword. If the preceding example had been

```
x = 5
call some_sub
```

```
. . .
some_sub: procedure expose x
x = -5
. . .
```

then the symbol X refers to the same variable in both the calling and the called procedure.

The syntax of the PROCEDURE instruction is

```
PROCEDURE [EXPOSE name1 name2 ...]
```

where any number of variable names may be listed. The names may refer to simple variables, compound variables, or stems. It is immaterial whether the variables named have already been assigned a value or not. When a stem is used, every possible variable having that stem is exposed.

One or more variables in the list following EXPOSE may be enclosed in parentheses (only one variable per pair of parentheses). This has an additional effect beyond exposing the named variable. It is assumed that the variable has been assigned a value which is another list of variable names, similar in form to the list following EXPOSE, except that it may not contain further parenthesized names. All the variables named in that list are also then exposed.

There are several reasons for this provision of specifying parenthesized names in an EXPOSE list. First, it facilitates handling lengthy lists of variables to be exposed, at least if the same list is used repeatedly. The most important case where you might have a long list of variables is when you want a number of variables to be global to an entire program. Such variables might include initialized tables of data, constants (e.g., the number pi), quantities which are assigned only once but needed in many places, and any other kind of data that might have to be communicated between widely separated places in a program.

When a variable is named in an EXPOSE list, it effectively becomes a part of the current procedure's generation of data, so it can be accessed or reassigned at will, and all changes to it persist after return from the subroutine. It can also be exposed in calls to lower level routines. In fact, it must be exposed in every level of subroutine called if it is to be available at the lowest level. This is why it's especially convenient to be able to list the names of truly global variables as the value of a single variable, and expose them using the parenthesized name rule. Here's a skeletal example of handling global data this way:

```
/* my program */
parse arg main_arg1 main_arg2 main_arg3
call initialize
. . .
```

```
call sub1
...
sub1: procedure expose (globals)
...
call sub2
...
sub2: procedure expose (globals)
...
initialize: procedure expose (globals)
globals = 'main_arg1 main_arg2 main_arg3 '||,
    'screen_height screen_width message.'
parse value scrsize() with screen_height screen_width
message.1 = ...
message.2 = ...
...
```

(In this example, SCRSIZE() is a system-specific function which returns the height and width of the screen. It is not a standard part of the REXX language.)

Here the arguments to the main routine (main_arg1, main_arg2, main_arg3) may be referred to anywhere in the program. The use of a procedure called initialize allows data to be initialized at the beginning of a program, without cluttering up the main code with a lot of boring assignments. One or more data tables can be defined with essentially static data. (This is the closest you can get in REXX to what is called COMMON data in FORTRAN.)

There's another quite different use for parenthesized names in an EXPOSE list. It concerns the ability to write general-purpose subroutines that operate on arrays. The problem arises because REXX has no mechanism for passing arguments *by reference,* as we mentioned at the beginning of this chapter. It is not enough simply to pass the name of a stem to a subroutine. Consider the following attempt at writing a generalized sort routine:

```
array. = 0
array.1 = ...
array.2 = ...
...
call sort array.
...
sort: procedure
parse arg x
...
if x.i < x.j then ...
```

This simply does not work. In the first place, the argument passed to the subroutine is 0, which is assigned to x. We might not have done the assignment array. = 0, but then the string ARRAY. would have been passed and assigned to x. But that's irrelevant anyway, since a reference like x.i doesn't care about the value of x. If instead we had done parse arg x. in the sort routine, then the stem x. would have been initialized to the passed value, but it still would not help.

One solution to this problem involves the INTERPRET instruction, which creates a little REXX program on the fly and executes it. That is, we could say

```
interpret 'if' x'i <' x'j then ...'
```

In the expression following interpret, x is not part of a quoted string, so that it can be evaluated. If the value of x is array., then the whole expression evaluates to

```
if array.i < array.j then...
```

which is just what we need. This will work, but it's very clumsy, and very slow besides—not what one wants in a general purpose sort routine.

There is another solution which involves the VALUE() built-in function. VALUE() exists in large part to overcome some of the problems with INTERPRET in simple cases. With an optional second argument, VALUE() is able to set the value of the variable named in the first argument. So we could say

```
if value(x'i') < value(x'j') then...
```

and achieve the desired effect.

But one problem remains. Since there is a PROCEDURE instruction following the label sort, array.i in the subroutine isn't the same as array.i in the calling routine. We could dispense with the PROCEDURE, of course, or we could EXPOSE the name of every possible array we might want to sort. The alternative is:

```
array. = 0
array.1 = ...
array.2 = ...
...
argname = 'array.'
call sort
...
sort: procedure expose (argname)
...
if value(argname'i') < value(argname'j') then ...
```

At last we have something that is semireasonable. It's still clumsy, since the array name isn't passed in the call to sort itself, and we still have to use VALUE( ); but it works, and it's the best that can be done along these lines in REXX currently.

There are a couple of other subtleties to note in exposing variables. First, the names listed in an EXPOSE list are exposed in order from left to right. This is important, because the names exposed are actually the derived variable names, that is, the names obtained after any required substitution in the tail part of the name. In the statement

```
procedure expose name birthday.name
```

the simple variable NAME is first exposed. Suppose it has the value Suzy. Then the variable which is exposed next is BIRTHDAY.Suzy, which is the derived name. If instead we had

```
procedure expose birthday.name name
```

then BIRTHDAY.NAME would have been exposed instead.

The other tricky area with exposed variables is the issue of dropping them. Recall that the DROP instruction can be used to undefine particular variables, or all variables with a given stem. Any variables named or implied in a DROP instruction, and which happen to be exposed, are dropped not only in the subroutine, but in the calling routine as well. So if we had

```
a = 1
b. = 2
c. = 3
call mysub
say a b. b.2 c. c.1 c.2
...
mysub: procedure expose a b. c.1
...
drop a b. c.
return
```

then on return from mysub the SAY instruction will produce A B. B.2 3 C.1 3. Notice that the stem B. and all possible variables with that stem have been returned to an undefined state, since the whole stem was exposed. However, since only the single variable C.1 was exposed, it is the only one with the stem C. that becomes undefined in the calling procedure.

A similar effect occurs when values are assigned to a stem which has been exposed. The definition of assignment to a stem says that all variables having the stem are first dropped before the new value is assigned. So, if our example were slightly different:

```
a = 1
b. = 2
c. = 3
call mysub
say a b. b.2 c. c.1 c.2
...
mysub: procedure expose a b. c.1
...
a = 4
b. = 5
c. = 6
return
```

then the SAY statement would produce 4 5 5 3 6 3.

It is an important fact that all variables of a subroutine which starts with a PROCEDURE statement are dropped when the procedure returns, except those variables or stems which have been exposed. Conceptually, the exposed variables really belong to the earlier generation of variables, unlike the unexposed variables. So it is only the variables of the newest generation that are dropped when a procedure returns.

EXECUTION STATE PRESERVED AROUND PROCEDURE CALLS

The current generation of variables belonging to an active procedure may be considered to be a part of the state of execution associated with the procedure (assuming the procedure started with a PROCEDURE instruction). There are certain other things that are also part of the state of a procedure. These things are associated with a particular invocation of the procedure, and will in general be different if the procedure has multiple activations as a result of recursion.

When a procedure is called, the state of the calling procedure is inherited. However, any changes to the state remain in effect only until the called procedure returns. Because state information is preserved in this way, one source of undesirable side effects caused by actions of a subroutine is eliminated. For instance, you can use a TRACE instruction in a subroutine to initiate some form of tracing. Even if you don't subsequently turn tracing off, as soon as the subroutine returns, the previous state of tracing will be restored. Or a subroutine could turn tracing off after it has been debugged, while allowing tracing to proceed in the calling routine.

Some of the other state information that is preserved in this way across procedure calls includes:

The setting of the default command environment established by the ADDRESS instruction

All settings controlled by the NUMERIC instruction (DIGITS, FORM, FUZZ)

The status of condition traps enabled or disabled by SIGNAL ON and CALL ON

The value of an elapsed time clock started with a call to TIME('e')

Of course, the fact that program state is handled in this manner means that it is not possible to initialize such values in a subroutine for use elsewhere in the program. If any of these settings need to be done globally, they must be done in the top-level procedure of the program.

It should also be pointed out that such program state information, just like variable values, is not inherited by external procedures that are called. The theory is that all external REXX programs should begin with the same set of default state values, so that they may assume the defaults are in effect, and their behavior does not depend on conditions in the calling program, except for the values of arguments passed.

A related matter is the handling of exceptional conditions and the SIGNAL instruction in connection with the execution of procedures. Exceptional conditions are such things as program syntax errors or attempts to use undefined variables. The SIGNAL instruction, described in the preceding chapter, is a way of generating your own conditions of this sort. We will discuss the standard exceptional conditions at greater length later, but basically what happens is that when an enabled condition occurs, control is immediately transferred to a specific label in the program. Any DO loops or other control structures in the current procedure which were active at the time the condition was raised are deactivated. However, control structures, including DO loops, in higher-level procedures are not affected.

In fact, the procedure which was active remains active, regardless of where in the program the label to which control is transferred is located. You must still explicitly return from a subroutine after a condition is signaled. This can make it difficult to handle exceptional conditions which occur in deeply nested subroutines, since it can be difficult to determine exactly where you were in terms of the subroutine-calling hierarchy. Thus, you may not be able to do much useful processing in a single handler intended for use throughout an entire program.

There are certain features that mitigate this problem, such as the ability to handle a condition via a CALL ON instruction rather than SIGNAL ON. This allows the condition to be handled in a new procedure which can return to the point at which the condition was raised by a RETURN instruction. You can also designate alternate labels to handle the same condition, and thereby provide for alternate processing of a given condition dependent on where you are in the program.

Sometimes, when you can anticipate that certain serious exceptional conditions are possible, you can structure your program as one or more external procedures called from a separate main program. In the event of a serious problem, you would simply EXIT from the external subprocedure and allow the main program to restart from a known state.

6

Commands to External Environments

REXX is unique among general-purpose programming languages in that it has a fully-integrated capability for passing commands to *external environments*. That is, a REXX program can issue commands which are directed to and acted upon by some system or application software other than REXX itself. The most common example of an external environment is the operating system. The most common use of REXX, and the use for which it was originally designed, is to issue a sequence of commands to the operating system.

Operating system command languages, also known as *batch* or *procedure* languages, existed long before REXX, of course. The original purpose of command languages was to allow users to collect groups of system commands into a file, for submission to the operating system as a *batch*. This makes it possible to invoke a group of commands required for some task with a single new command and greatly reduces the effort required to perform common repetitive tasks. Even the earliest command languages made it possible for users to extend the operating system with new commands and to automate routine command sequences.

As system command languages evolved, they took on more of the characteristics of general-purpose programming languages. For instance, they added conditional execution and looping capabilities.

Sometimes they did this by adding new system commands which actually implemented control constructs with new system commands that could be used in procedures to provide conditionals and looping. (The MS-DOS IF and FOR commands are examples of this.) Usually, however, the trend was to add features to the language itself, as something separate and distinct from commands of the system.

REXX is a very advanced example of this latter trend. There is a very clear and distinct separation between REXX statements, as represented by REXX *instructions* and *assignments,* on one hand, and *commands* on the other. Nevertheless, commands are recognized as a third type of statement in REXX. Therefore, they are very naturally and easily incorporated into REXX programs, in a way that makes them appear to be almost an extension of the language itself, even though they are largely processed by some other software.

Commands in REXX are not limited to system commands, either. Another development that also began a long time ago was for application software such as databases and file editors to be driven by commands, and to allow for such commands to be processed in a *batch* just like system commands. Since the situation is so similar, it was only natural for such application macro languages to evolve very much like system command languages did.

Eventually, the logic of using the same language for both purposes became apparent. In the VM/CMS system, where REXX originated, this fact was recognized by the provision of application programming interfaces which made it possible for one language to serve easily as both a system command language and application macro language. Unfortunately, other operating systems did not appreciate the importance of this so quickly. Because of this and because applications often need to be portable, so that they cannot depend on operating system features for critical functions, most application software has tended to implement its own unique, proprietary language. This problem of a multiplicity of application-specific languages is only now starting to be addressed. Not surprisingly, REXX is one of the primary languages which may become used for both application and system command procedures, even across different computing platforms.

THE ADDRESS INSTRUCTION

As we've seen, any REXX statement that does not begin with a REXX keyword and which is not an assignment is automatically classified as a command and submitted to an *external environment* for processing. The main issue, then, is to identify which *environment* the command should be sent to. For every REXX program there is always a default external environment for handling commands. Exactly what the environment is depends very much on the particular implementation of REXX. But for any given implementation, the default environment usually depends on how the REXX program is started.

For instance, if the program is started by the operating system (usually because a user invoked it as a command from a system command line), the default environment is the operating system itself. If the program was started by an application, such as a communication program or text editor, the application is (very likely) the default environment. Usually, the application programming interface which permits an application to start a REXX program provides some means for giving a name to the default environment and for setting up the details of how the REXX processor actually passes the command to the environment. These details, of course, are system-dependent, and ordinarily not of concern to the REXX programmer.

In the simplest cases, the REXX program does not need to be aware of the name of the external environment. However, it may well be true that more than one possible external environment is available. For instance, if the REXX program was started from an application, the system command environment is probably still available as well. Some systems, like VM/CMS, even have more than one system command environment, with subtle differences in command handling between the alternatives. (In CMS, the alternatives are known as CMS and COM-MAND.) Many systems also make it possible for multiple application environments to be available simultaneously as well. In fact, this provision may place REXX in the position of being able to allow for easy communication between applications.

Any time a REXX program needs to send commands to more than one environment, some means of specifying which environment is obviously needed. That is the function of the ADDRESS instruction. There are basically two forms of this. The simplest is

```
ADDRESS environment
```

where environment is a symbol or literal string which is taken as the name of an external environment. The symbol is taken literally (so no substitution is performed), but case is ignored. Examples:

```
address command
address 'REXXTERM'
```

If the named environment exists, it becomes the new default environment to which subsequent commands will be passed for execution. If the named environment doesn't exist, the action of the instruction is undefined. Since some REXX implementations allow new environments to be created on the fly, it may be impossible to determine, until a command needs to be executed, that the proper environment doesn't exist. There is no language-defined method of determining what environment names are actually available.

It is also possible to compute the environment name at run-time by using an expression after the ADDRESS keyword. The first token of the expression must be something other than a symbol or literal, or else the expression must be preceded with the word VALUE:

```
ADDRESS (expression)
```

or

```
ADDRESS VALUE expression
```

This has exactly the same effect as before, except the value of expression (which could simply be a variable name) is used as the name of the new default environment. Examples:

```
address (editor_environment())
address value environment_of('pliopt')
```

The ADDRESS instruction can also be used all by itself with no name or expression in order to reinstate the last previous default environment. This allows you to toggle between two external environments, or to restore the previous environment without explicitly having to save its name.

There is an ADDRESS() built-in function which returns a character string containing the name of the current default environment. In addition to allowing you to save the name for later use, this can be helpful in cases where your program needs to behave differently if invoked in different circumstances.

The names of the last two default environments are included in the state information that is saved across procedure calls. A called procedure inherits these names, but may make arbitrary changes to the default environment without effect on the calling procedure.

The second form of the ADDRESS instruction allows you to specify both an environment name and a command to be executed. The form is

```
ADDRESS environment command-expression
```

As before, environment must be a symbol or literal string (but not an expression). It is the name of the external environment to which command-expression is to be sent for execution. This environment is used for only one command. The default environment is not affected. This form of ADDRESS executes a command exactly as if the command occurred by itself and the default environment was the one named. Examples:

```
address command "copy" file1 file2 ">nul"
address "REXXTERM" "match please log in:"
```

Whether or not you use the ADDRESS instruction explicitly to execute external commands, you should observe one simple rule for writing the command: it is always a good idea to enclose all nonvariable parts of the command in quotation marks, even if that is only the name of the command. For instance, always use

```
'copy' file1 file2
```

rather than

```
copy file1 file2
```

The reason for this is twofold. First, it is always possible that copy may have been used elsewhere in the program as a variable. Without the quotation marks, the value of copy would be substituted, producing an entirely different command. Second, future versions of the REXX language may conceivably introduce COPY as a new instruction keyword. The quotation marks, again, will prevent any misinterpretation.

If you do insist on living dangerously and don't put quotes around commands, you must at the very least avoid using a command name which is the same as a REXX keyword. The following are REXX keywords which must be quoted if used at the beginning of a command:

```
ADDRESS     ARG          CALL       DO
DROP        ELSE         END        EXIT
IF          INTERPRET    ITERATE    LEAVE
NOP         NUMERIC      OPTIONS    OTHERWISE
PARSE       PROCEDURE    PULL       PUSH
QUEUE       RETURN       SAY        SELECT
SIGNAL      THEN         TRACE      WHEN
```

This list includes all instruction keywords and a few others.

COMMAND RETURN CODES

In addition to performing some action, commands to an operating system or application program typically return a value, which is often numeric, but not necessarily so. The nature and meaning of this value is, of course, completely dependent on the particular command. Numeric values returned by commands are often called return codes, and they often give some clue as to the success or failure of a command. (For instance, in MS-DOS this value is called the *error level*.) Rules for the form of the value and how it is returned to REXX are implementation dependent. However, REXX does maintain a special variable, RC, to receive whatever is passed back as the *return code*.

The RC variable is similar to (but not to be confused with) the RESULT special variable which is set after any CALL to an internal, external, or built-in function. That is, you should not use RC for your own data as it will be changed after any command invocation. (It may possibly even become undefined if a command does not produce a return code.)

If you know the return codes which can be produced by the commands you issue, you may be able to determine whether the command did what you wanted it to. Return codes don't always indicate an error condition, however. Sometimes the return code provides system or application information. For instance, the SENTRIES command in VM/CMS places the number of lines in the external data queue into its return code.

A REXX program that is invoked by the operating system may be able to pass a return code back to the operating system, depending on the details of the interface provided. This is usually done by means of the RETURN or EXIT instruction that terminates the program. The treatment of this value by the interface depends on how the program was invoked. If the program was invoked as an external function, the value is simply the value of the function. But if the program was invoked as a system command, the value will be treated as a return code. If the value is to be a return code, it may be required to be numeric, with nonnumeric values being ignored.

Another way that a command issued from a REXX program can affect the program is by possibly raising an ERROR or FAILURE condition. These, in turn, may or may not be related to the command's return code. Of course, the details of how a command indicates such a condition, as well as the meaning of doing so, are highly implementation-dependent. The REXX language merely provides for such things to be used if desired.

An ERROR or FAILURE condition is one of a small number of exceptional conditions recognized by the language. Other conditions include HALT, NOVALUE, and SYNTAX. The recognition and handling of such conditions is under the control of the SIGNAL instruction, which will be discussed later in more detail. SIGNAL simply provides a way for such conditions to be enabled or disabled and to specify what should be done if one occurs.

The ERROR condition is intended to indicate that the command did not function entirely as expected, but at least a good attempt was made. This may or may not be reflected in the command's return code. In some operating systems, like VM/CMS, a positive return code is actually defined to mean that an ERROR condition should be raised. This can be a problem, as some commands (like the aforementioned SENTRIES) use the return code to pass back information unrelated to success or failure. The ERROR condition is usually not enabled by default. If you decide to enable and provide a handler for it, you should test very carefully that it does not get raised when you don't expect it. Ordinarily you would enable it only in circumstances where unanticipated command errors must not go unnoticed.

The FAILURE condition is considered to be more serious. It would indicate that a command could not be executed at all, for reasons external to the command. Possibly the command could not be found or there was not enough memory to run the command. This, too, may or may not be related to a return code. VM/CMS, for instance, tends to use a negative return code as an indication of FAILURE. The FAILURE condition is often enabled by default, which means that if you do not disable it or provide a handler for it, the entire REXX program may be terminated. Given that FAILURE is intended to indicate something seriously amiss, this is not unreasonable. However, if your programs have to be very robust and capable of handling any malfunction, you will need to provide a handler for the FAILURE condition. After all, you would need to detect and deal with the problem anyway. Unfortunately, the REXX language doesn't offer any further information to indicate the more precise nature of the difficulty.

7

Character String Handling

One of the key strengths of the REXX language is its character string handling abilities. These are inherent in the design of the language, since there are no explicit data types, and all data is represented internally as strings.

The most frequently used string operation—concatenation—is so common that REXX does it implicitly whenever two symbols or literals occur together in an expression and are not separated by an operator or special character. As we have seen many times, there are two forms of implicit concatenation: with and without an intervening blank.

Concatenation can also be represented by the "||" operator. This is necessary only when the syntax of the expression would otherwise be ambiguous. For instance, 'abc'x is a hexadecimal literal constant rather than a concatenation of the literal 'abc' with the value of the symbol x. To represent the latter you would have to use 'abc'||x. Similarly, 'abc'(x+3) is interpreted as a reference to a built-in or external function with the argument x+3. You have to use 'abc'||(x+3) to mean the concatenation of 'abc' with the value of x+3.

The other kind of elementary string operation that has its own operator symbol is comparison. The ordinary comparison operators ("=", ">", "<", "\=", "\>", "\<", etc.) operate on character strings using the standard collating sequence of the computer, but only after stripping off leading and trailing blanks. This is in keeping with the philosophy of REXX to do the most natural thing under the circumstances, because blanks are often nonsignificant. In case blanks are significant, or if the strings might be (incorrectly) interpreted as numbers, there are corresponding strict comparison operators ("==", ">>", "<<", "\==", "\>>", "\<<", etc.).

STRING HANDLING BUILT-IN FUNCTIONS

Perhaps the most powerful of all of REXX's character-string manipulation features are to be found in the built-in functions. There are many of them. Some perform very obvious operations, like SUBSTR( ), POS( ), and LENGTH( ). But there are a number of other functions that have some delightfully nonobvious uses. We're going to take a general overview of the string handling functions. Then we'll have a look at some of the more interesting and nonobvious uses.

A great deal is sometimes made of the power of the PARSE instruction for manipulating character strings. However, since one can deal with strings on a character-at-a-time basis, the built-in functions can in principle be used to do anything PARSE can do, and much more.

Well over half of the standard REXX built-in functions are for string handling. Within this group, several subgroups can be identified informally. We'll use this classification:

Character-oriented Functions

Abbrev	Center	Compare	Copies	Delstr
Insert	Laspos	Left	Length	Overlay
Pos	Reverse	Right	Space	Strip
Substr	Translate	Verify	Xrange	

Word-oriented Functions

Delword	Subword	Word	Wordindex	Wordlength
Wordpos	Words			

String Format Conversion

B2x	C2d	C2x	D2c	D2x
X2b	X2c	X2d		

Bitwise Operations

Bitand	Bitor	Bitxor

As we discuss these functions, we will observe some regularities in the use of built-in functions in general. Usually these are conventions and not formal parts of the language. However, it is a good idea to take note of them, since for consistency it is a good idea to use similar conventions in functions that you yourself write.

One of the standard conventions is that procedures may have both required and optional arguments. If a required argument is omitted, a syntax error will be generated. A syntax error will also occur if too many arguments are specified. User-written procedures can test for the presence or absence of specific arguments with the ARG() built-in function, but they are responsible for enforcing a particular argument to be required. In the standard built-in functions, it is always the case that all required arguments precede all optional arguments.

When describing built-in functions we will use notation like this:

```
STRIP(string, [option], [char])
```

This shows that the STRIP() built-in function takes up to three arguments. The first argument is required. The brackets around the second and third arguments indicate that they are optional and may be omitted. If one or both arguments are omitted, it is understood that the comma preceding them may also be omitted, provided no additional arguments follow (though it would not be an error to leave it in). Whenever an argument is optional and may be omitted, some specific default value will always be used.

Another convention is that many built-in functions have one or more arguments which are *options*. Such arguments are character strings which affect how the function operates in some way or another. For instance, the second argument of STRIP() is an option that indicates whether characters are to be stripped from a string in the Leading, Trailing, or Both positions. This option, if used, should be specified as a quoted string, but only the first character is significant, and it may be in either upper- or lowercase. So, the following statements all have the effect of stripping leading and trailing blanks from a string:

```
STRIP(string, 'b')
STRIP(string, 'B')
STRIP(string, 'blanks')
STRIP(string, 'Both')
STRIP(string, 'boing!')
```

A number of string handling functions take a particular sort of argument called a pad character. For instance, the COMPARE() function, which returns the number of the first position in which its first two argument strings differ, can optionally specify a pad character, which is considered to be appended to the shorter of the two strings before comparison, in case they are of different lengths. Whenever a pad character is used, it must always be exactly one character long. (It should also be quoted, so it is not misinterpreted as a symbol.)

Many of the string handling functions refer to relative positions in a string, either relative characters or relative words. Such positions are always numbered (from the left), starting with 1. A position number that is negative or zero is almost always invalid and will cause an error. A position number must also be a whole number in the sense that it may not contain a nonzero fractional part, nor may it be so large that it contains more digits than specified in the current NUMERIC DIGITS setting. String handling functions often take arguments which represent string lengths also. Such arguments must likewise be nonnegative whole numbers, though they may be zero.

STRING-ORIENTED FUNCTIONS

With these preliminaries out of the way, let's turn first to the character-oriented string functions. We have encountered a number of them already, such as SUBSTR(), RIGHT(), LEFT(), LENGTH(), POS() and STRIP(), because they are quite heavily used in REXX programs.

SUBSTR() and POS() are possibly the most frequently used string manipulation functions. The syntax of SUBSTR() is

```
SUBSTR(string, start, [length], [pad])
```

String is the string to be operated on. Start is the position of the first character to be extracted from string. This position could be beyond the end of the string, in which case only pad characters would be returned (or a null string). The result returned will be length characters long. If length is not specified, the default is the number of characters remaining in string (if any). Finally, if length is specified and start + length is beyond the end of the string, the result will be padded with the pad character to the specified length. The default for pad is a blank.

The syntax of POS() is

```
POS(target, string, [start])
```

Here, string is to be searched from left to right for a substring target. The search begins at the character position start (which defaults to 1). The match must be exact, in which case the function returns the position in string at which the first occurrence of target was found. If target is not found, the function returns 0.

For a simple illustration of these functions, we will consider a particular problem. The problem is analyzing the contents of electronic mail files. Typically a mail file begins with a header such as:

```
To: David Hilbert <hilbert@gottingen.edu>
From: Albert Einstein <einstein@berlin.edu>
Date: April 1, 1915
Subject: Need help with curvature tensors
```

In writing REXX programs to handle electronic mail, you will probably want to examine the mail files to extract the information contained in headers like this—who sent the mail, when, and what the subject is. Let's suppose the mail has already been read into a REXX compound variable with the stem MAIL., where MAIL.1 is the first line, MAIL.2 the second, etc., and MAIL.0 contains the total number of lines in the file. Assume that we cannot presuppose in what order the different lines of the mail header will appear. Then the following code fragment will set appropriate variables based on the information in the header:

```
/* initialize table of header tags */
istag. = 0
tag = 'TO'
istag.tag = 1
tag = 'FROM'
istag.tag = 1
tag = 'DATE'
istag.tag = 1
tag = 'SUBJECT'
istag.tag = 1
header. = ''

/* scan each line of mail for tags */
/* mail.0 contains the number of lines in the file */
do i = 1 to mail.0
    /* stop at first blank line */
    if mail.i = '' then
       leave
    /* upper case the line */
    line = translate(mail.i)
    /* stop on first line with no ":" in it */
    j = pos(':', line)
    if j = 0 then
       leave
    /* extract portion before ":" */
    possible_tag = substr(line, 1, j-1)
    /* check for tags to handle */
    if istag.possible_tag then
       header.possible_tag = strip(substr(mail.i, j+1))
    end
```

This example makes use of REXX associative arrays. The istag. array keeps track of the "tags" which are of interest to us in mail headers. It is initialized to 0, and subscripted elements which represent strings that are valid tags are set to 1. In this case, the affected variables are ISTAG.TO, ISTAG.FROM, ISTAG.DATE, and ISTAG.SUBJECT. Corresponding items in the header. array (HEADER.TO, HEADER.FROM, HEADER.DATE, and HEADER.SUBJECT) will contain the data extracted from the mail file.

The TRANSLATE( ) function, which has some possibly surprising applications, is used here to convert each file line to uppercase. (Standard REXX lacks both an UPPER( ) and a LOWER( ) function as such.) The POS( ) function is used to search for the occurrence of ':' in each line. If ':' is found, the part of the line preceding it is extracted with SUBSTR( ). This is tested for being a tag we are interested in. If it is one, then the remainder of the line following ':' is assigned to an appropriate element of the header. array.

Notice the use of the STRIP( ) function near the end of the example. This function is frequently used to remove extraneous blanks from the beginning and end of strings. Although ordinary REXX string comparisons ignore such blanks, they can be a nuisance in other contexts, as they can interfere with nicely formatted columns, appear inconveniently in the tails of a compound variable name, and so forth. The syntax of STRIP( ) is

```
STRIP(string, [option], [character])
```

The function removes all leading and trailing copies of character from string, if option is 'b' ("both"), or only leading or trailing copies if option is 'l' or 't'. The default for character is a blank.

The last example was somewhat contrived to illustrate POS( ) and SUBSTR( ). It is worth observing now that the PARSE instruction (discussed fully in the next chapter) would be a slightly more efficient and elegant way to do what we needed here. That is, we could have used

```
parse var line possible_tag ':' header.possible_tag
```

to search for ':', assign the part of line before it to possible_tag, and assign the rest of line to header.possible_tag—all in one statement! This demonstrates the power of the PARSE instruction. There are a couple of little problems, however. For one thing, PARSE doesn't care whether ':' is actually found in line. Since it doesn't, the whole line will be assigned to possible_tag, and header.possible_tag will be assigned a null string. Furthermore, there's no way to tell from PARSE, after the fact, whether the ':' was actually present or not. (It might have been the last character on the line.) In this case, it doesn't matter very much, except we may wind up assigning values of header.possible_tag when we didn't want to. If it's necessary to determine positively whether ':' was present, we'd have to use POS( ) anyway.

Another more awkward problem in this instance is that we want to work with the tag names in uppercase (so that "TO:" and "To:" are equivalent), yet keep the data following the tag the way it occurred. The first consideration dictates that we first uppercase line or use PARSE UPPER, but the second consideration dictates that we do not. The net result is that we are unable to use PARSE in its simplest form for this particular example.

A companion to the POS( ) function is LASTPOS( ). Its syntax is

```
LASTPOS(target, string, [start])
```

just like POS( ). However, in this case, string is searched from right to left for the substring target. The search begins at the last character of string, unless an optional start position is given.

An example of LASTPOS( ) is easily given that also deals with mail handling. There is a convention in specifying an address for sending mail through a network of Unix systems that the name of every intermediate system on the route can be given in succession, separated by "!". For instance,

```
uunet!apple!well!heisenberg
```

is a mail address that specifies routing to the node "well" through the nodes "uunet" and "apple." The last part of the address is the name of a mail box (essentially a user name) on "well." This method of including an explicit routing in a mail address is now losing favor, but is still frequently used. Anyway, suppose we want to pick out the final component of the path, i.e., the user name. It can be done with

```
user_name = substr(address, lastpos("!", address) + 1)
```

This even works if (as is possible) there is only one component in address, and no "!" is present. This is because LASTPOS( ), like POS( ), returns 0 if the target string is not found.

There is one other similarity between POS( ) and LASTPOS( ). This is the fact that if target is the null string, it is considered not to match any part of string. So both functions return 0 when their first argument is a null string.

It is often the case that one wants to work with a specific number of characters from the beginning of a string. REXX provides the LEFT( ) function as a useful special case of SUBSTR( ) to do this. Its syntax is

```
LEFT(string, length, [pad])
```

The arguments have the same meaning as they do for SUBSTR( ). In fact, it is defined to be the same as

```
SUBSTR(string, 1, length, [pad])
```

so in one sense it is just a convenience. It will usually be slightly faster than SUBSTR( ) when it can be used. You may also find it easy to remember if you want to take the leftmost length characters or to left-justify a string in a wider field, such as in a table. In this case, the length of the field will usually be wider than the length of the string, so it's not natural to think of the operation of taking a "substring".

Symmetrically, REXX provides the RIGHT() function, which has the syntax

```
RIGHT(string, length, [pad])
```

Although symmetric with LEFT(), RIGHT() isn't readily definable as a special case of SUBSTR(), because if length is greater than the length of string, then pad characters are added on the left, so that string is right-justified in the field of width length. This characteristic is useful when you format tables. However, when the string is longer than length, the function returns only the rightmost length characters. In this case, it is equivalent to

```
SUBSTR(string, 1 + LENGTH(string) - length)
```

but considerably easier to remember and write, and more efficient as well.

By the way, the purpose of the LENGTH() function is obvious—it returns the length of a string. Its syntax is simply

```
LENGTH(string)
```

Although LENGTH() is indispensable, if you find that you are using it heavily, this might be a clue that you are overlooking some alternative techniques that would be more efficient, such as use of LEFT() and RIGHT() in the examples above.

There are a couple of special cases when RIGHT() comes in quite handy. One is when you want to look at the last character of a string. This is simply

```
RIGHT(string, 1)
```

Another application is when you want to have leading zeros on a number, in a field of a certain fixed length. So you use

```
RIGHT(number, length, '0')
```

So far we have considered some of the most commonly used string handling functions. Next we are going to see a number of other more specialized functions by focusing on one of the most powerful—and unobviously useful—of the functions, TRANSLATE(). The simplicity of its

definition—to replace characters found in one table with the corresponding character from a second table—belies the variety of its
applications.

The definition of TRANSLATE( ) is

```
TRANSLATE(string, [output-table], [input-table],
    [pad])
```

where string is the data to be translated. TRANSLATE( ) looks up each
character of string in the input table. If the character doesn't occur in
the input table, it is not changed. Otherwise it is replaced by the corresponding character in the output table. The output table is extended by
the pad character if it is shorter than the input table. Some simple
examples:

```
translate('moon', 'bte', 'mno')
    /* result is 'beet' */
translate('lead', 'log', 'ael')
    /* result is 'gold' */
translate('Jaberwocky', '', 'aeiou', '*')
    /* result is 'J*b*rw*cky' */
```

Much of the elegance of TRANSLATE( ) results from a clever choice of
defaults. The default for the input table is XRANGE('00'x,'ff'x), i.e.,
all characters in the normal collating sequence. The default for the pad
character is a blank. Therefore

```
translate(string, copies(' ', c2d('0'))||'0123456789')
```

translates all nonnumeric characters in the string to blanks.

This example also introduces a couple of other useful functions.
First, COPIES( ), which has the syntax

```
COPIES(string, count)
```

performs the obvious function of returning count copies of string. In the
example, we make a certain number of copies of the blank character.

The number of copies of the blank is c2d('0'). This uses the C2D( )
function, whose nominal purpose is to convert the binary (*character*)
representation of a number to its decimal value. This operation can be
trickier than it might at first seem, due to oddities of binary representation. However, in this case, what we are doing is taking the binary
value of the character '0' (which happens to be '30'x in ASCII), and
converting it to decimal to get 48. That is, there are 48 characters before
'0' in the (ASCII) collating sequence. So COPIES( ) makes a string of

exactly 48 blanks, and concatenates those before `'0123456789'`. The result is the output table needed for this use of `TRANSLATE()`.

There is another function, `XRANGE()`, which is used frequently in conjunction with `TRANSLATE()`. Its syntax is

```
XRANGE([first], [last])
```

where `first` is the starting character of a range, and `last` is the end of the range. The default for first is `'00'x`, and the default for last is `'ff'x`. The function returns a string consisting of all characters of the collating sequence from `first` to `last`. Hence

```
xrange()
```

is all 256 characters of the collating sequence in order.

Other examples of `XRANGE()` are very dependent on the collating sequence in use. For instance, in ASCII

```
xrange('a', 'z')
   /* result is all lowercase letters */
```

but this doesn't work in EBCDIC, since the lowercase letters are not at contiguous code points. In EBCDIC we would have to use

```
xrange('a', 'i') || xrange('j', 'r') ||,
   xrange('s', 'z')
```

to get all lowercase letters.

Many practical instances of the use of `TRANSLATE()` use `XRANGE()` to generate the input or the output table, so uses of `TRANSLATE()` are frequently dependent on the collating sequence, too. As it happens, the preceding example of `TRANSLATE()` works equally well with either ASCII or EBCDIC. However, the corresponding expression

```
translate(string, copies(' ', c2d('a'))||,
   xrange('a','z'))
```

to translate all characters that aren't lowercase alphabetic to blanks doesn't work with EBCDIC, since in that system the lowercase letters aren't at contiguous code points.

To further make the point that REXX character string functions can have surprising uses, we note that there is an easier way than `COPIES()` to get a string of a certain number of blanks. `RIGHT()` or `LEFT()` can also be used, and even eliminate a concatenation in the process. Thus, the preceding example is equivalent to

```
translate(string, right(xrange('a','z'), c2d('z')+1))
```

Here are some further examples:

```
/* translate -, +, %, and * to blanks */
translate(string, , '-+%*')

/* another way to translate all non-numeric characters
   in string to blanks */
translate(string, ,delstr(xrange(), c2d('1'), 10))
```

The last example here is admittedly a little tricky. It uses the DELSTR( ) function, which has the syntax

```
DELSTR(string, start, length)
```

This function deletes length characters from string, beginning at position start, and returns the result. In the example, xrange() produces the string of all characters from '00'x to 'ff'x. c2d('1') is the relative position of '1' in the collating sequence, which is the same value as c2d('0')+1. So the call to DELSTR( ) yields a string which contains all characters except '0' through '9', i.e., all nonnumeric characters. And so TRANSLATE( ) then obligingly converts all nonnumeric characters to blanks (since there is no input table).

We just saw an example of translating to blanks all characters of a string which are contained in another string. Can we do the opposite and translate to blanks all characters which aren't in a given string? This is harder, but not much. Observe that the string

```
x = translate(xrange('00'x, 'ff'x), , '-+%*')
```

contains all the characters except -, +, %, and *. Therefore,

```
translate(string, , x)
```

translates everything in string to blanks except those four, solving the problem. In particular,

```
translate(string, , translate(xrange('00'x, 'ff'x), ,,
    '0123456789'))
```

translates all nonnumerics to blanks, providing yet another variation that makes no assumptions about the location of numeric characters in the collating sequence.

An amusing application of any of these expressions for translating nonnumbers to blanks is the problem of adding up all numbers contained within a string that may contain nonnumbers as well. For instance,

'January: 31, February: 28, March: 31, April: 30, ...'

Suppose that Y contains this string with all nonnumerics replaced by spaces. Then

```
interpret "say 'The sum is:'" space(y, 1, '+')
```

displays the result. SPACE() is used for the unobvious purpose of stripping out all blanks, leaving a '+' between each number.

SPACE() is an interesting function and worth remembering for various special purposes. Its syntax is

```
SPACE(string, [count], [pad])
```

Here, string is a character string viewed as a sequence of blank-delimited words. The function strips out all existing blanks (including leading and trailing blanks), and replaces them with exactly count pad characters between each word. The default of count is 1, and the default of pad is a blank. A count of 0 would remove all blanks. You might take advantage of this in conjunction with one of the previous examples. We have shown how to convert all characters in a specific set, or not in a specific set, to blanks using TRANSLATE(). Taking this a step further, they could be squeezed out entirely by using SPACE() with a count of 0.

It isn't very surprising that TRANSLATE() can be used to replace characters from one set with those from another. But TRANSLATE() can also do many other things. One important class of application involves formatting or rearranging a string based on a template or pattern.

Consider the problem of converting a date expressed as mm/dd/yy (REXX's USA format) to the REXX standard format yyyymmdd. Some implementations of REXX have a DATECONV() built-in function to do this special task, but it can also be done easily with TRANSLATE(). Suppose the variable X contains the unconverted date. Then

```
translate('19ghabde', x, 'abcdefgh')
```

does the conversion. Notice that some characters are deleted from the source string, while others are added. This class of examples can be confusing, because the string to be converted appears as the second argument to TRANSLATE() rather than the first. Instead, the first argument is a pattern describing what the result should look like. In this example, the lowercase letters are used, somewhat arbitrarily, as relative position markers. The output template string can be derived by writing the position markers next to a template for the input string, and putting the markers in the desired position in the output:

```
abcdefgh  <-- position markers
mm/dd/yy  <-- input template
```

It is worth studying this usage of TRANSLATE( ) a little more, as it comes in surprisingly handy. Another example is the problem of inserting commas every three digits in a number (the American convention). It can be done, for numbers of up to twelve digits, with

```
result = strip(space(translate("abc,def,ghi,jkl",,
    right(number, 12), "abcdefghijkl"), 0),, ",")
```

The call to TRANSLATE( ) inserts the digits of number into the corresponding location in the pattern. SPACE( ) squeezes out extra blanks. And STRIP( ) removes any leftover leading commas.

There remain a number of other character-oriented string manipulation functions we haven't examined yet. Some of them are quite powerful. One of these is ABBREV( ). It has the syntax

```
ABBREV(keyword, string, [length])
```

ABBREV( ) is often useful in working with interactive user input when it is desirable to recognize important keywords that may be abbreviated up to a certain minimum length. The value of the function is 1 if string is at least length characters long and it matches exactly the first length characters of keyword. Otherwise, ABBREV( ) has the value 0. The default for length is the length of string (in which case the minimum length test is irrelevant). So an equivalent expression would be

```
length(string) >= length & string == left(keyword,,
    length(string)
```

Of course, just because REXX provides a built-in function that seems to do just what you want, it does not follow that the obvious way is the most efficient or the easiest to maintain. Suppose that you want to test a user-entered command against a list of valid commands, allowing for abbreviation. Let's assume that the variable command is a verb entered by the user, has been lowercased, stripped of leading and trailing blanks, and isn't entirely blank. Then one way to identify it would be with a loop and ABBREV( ):

```
command.1 = 'copy'
command.2 = 'erase'
command.3 = 'rename'
command.4 = 'print'
full_command = ''
do i = 1 to 4
    if abbrev(command.i, input) then do
```

```
        full_command = command.i
        leave
        end
    end
```

But there are other ways, and they may be faster because they use the power of some built-in function to avoid an explicit loop. One trick which often comes in handy when working with relatively short lists of words is to keep them all in a single string, separated by blanks (or possibly other characters). For instance, the following code is equivalent to the above:

```
list = ' copy erase rename print'
j = pos(' 'command, list)
if j \= 0 then
    full_command = word(substr(list, j), 1)
```

In general, you will get best performance when you can find a way to do a given operation by taking advantage of an existing built-in function rather than by using a loop.

Another operation that needs to be performed frequently with user input is checking that the data entered is valid, i.e., belongs to an appropriate range of values. For example, if a user enters the name of a file to be created, you ought to check first that the name is legal. Rules for what constitute a legal file name vary from system to system, but there is usually a set of characters which are invalid in file names. You might put all these characters in a string and use the VERIFY() function to test for them:

```
invalid = '<>\,;"&|()'
if verify(filename, invalid, 'm') \= 0 then
    say filename 'is not a valid name!'
```

The syntax of VERIFY() is

```
VERIFY(string, search, [option], [start])
```

where string is to be searched for characters from search. If option is 'm' ("match"), the function returns the relative position in string of the first character occurring in search that is found. Otherwise, it returns 0. Start optionally specifies the position in string where the search is to begin.

Sometimes you may wish to limit input to a specific subset of characters. For instance, you might want to ensure that file names consist only of upper- and lowercase alphabetics, numerals, and a few special characters, even if the system would allow others. Then you might do

```
valid = xrange('a','z') || xrange('A','Z') ||,
    xrange('0','9') || '-_@#$'
if verify(filename, valid, 'n') \= 0 then
    say filename 'is not a valid name!'
```

This uses 'n' ("nomatch") option of VERIFY( ) (which is the default). It causes the function to return the position in string of the first character which is not in search, or 0 if all characters are in search.

We should mention at this point that for some sorts of input validation the DATATYPE( ) function can be very useful. It allows you to ensure that strings are of some required type, such as valid numbers, all alphanumeric, all lowercase, etc. DATATYPE( ) is fully described in Chap. 13.

Another common use of VERIFY( ) is in the processing of natural language text, where you want to process one word at a time. The word-oriented functions of REXX are not really applicable, since they recognize only blanks as delimiters. In real text, words are delimited with various punctuation characters as well. So a word processing loop might be constructed as follows:

```
/* process individual words in a file */
do while lines(file)
    line = linein(file)
    /* process each line */
    do while line \= ''
        /* search for word delimiters */
        i = verify(line, ' ,.;:"?!()', 'm')
        if i = 0 then do
            word = line
            line = ''
            end
        else do
            word = left(line, i-1)
            line = substr(line, i+1)
            end
        /* process "word" */
        ...
        end
    end
```

This program reads a file line by line. For each line, the VERIFY( ) function is used to identify individual words by searching for common punctuation characters.

There are five other character-oriented string functions we have not discussed. If you do much string handling, the usefulness of these functions will be obvious.

The CENTER( ) function (the spelling CENTRE( ) is also recognized) allows you to position one string in the middle of a field of a certain size, or to extract the central characters of a string. Its syntax is

    CENTER(string, length, [pad])

If length is greater than the length of string, then enough pad characters are added to the beginning and end to center string in the field. The default pad character is a blank. This is useful for formatting title lines on a page, for instance. If length is less than the length of string, the specified number of characters are extracted from the center of string.

The COMPARE( ) function can be used to find the position at which two strings first differ. Its syntax is

    COMPARE(string1, string2, [pad])

The function returns the index of the first difference. If one string is shorter than the other, it is extended on the right with pad characters (default: blank). If the two strings are identical (after padding), the function returns 0.

The INSERT( ) function inserts one string at a certain position in another. Its syntax is

    INSERT(string1, string2, [pos], [length], [pad])

String1 is the string to be inserted in string2. It is inserted after the position specified by pos. The default for pos is 0, which means to insert at the beginning of string2. String1 can optionally be truncated to length characters or extended by padding on the right with pad.

The OVERLAY( ) function is similar to INSERT( ), except that it replaces characters in one string starting at a certain position with characters from another string. Its syntax is

    OVERLAY(string1, string2, [pos], [length], [pad])

String1 replaces the characters of string2 starting at the position specified by pos, which has a default of 1. String1 can optionally be truncated to length characters or extended by padding on the right with pad.

Though it's not obvious at first, the REVERSE( ) function can come in quite handy at times. It simply reverses the order of characters in a given string. The function often helps when it is desirable to process the characters of a string from right to left instead of left to right. Its syntax is simply

    REVERSE(string)

WORD-ORIENTED FUNCTIONS

The next group of functions are the word-oriented string functions. These functions treat strings as a sequence of blank-delimited words. Any other punctuation characters are not treated as delimiters, and will be treated as part of "words." This includes even *white space* characters such as tabs and line feeds, which languages resembling C tend to count as equivalent to blanks. Multiple blanks are treated as a single blank. In general, the word-oriented functions are consistent with the PARSE instruction in the way they view strings as a sequence of words. When additional characters actually need to be treated as delimiters, the TRANSLATE( ) function can be used to convert them to blanks.

The two most important word-oriented functions are WORD( ) and WORDS( ). The first of these has the general form

    WORD(string, n)

where string is the string to be operated on. The function returns the nth blank-delimited word in string. The function WORDS( ), whose form is

    WORDS(string)

returns the total number of blank-delimited words in the string.

You may find the word-oriented functions of some utility if you write programs that interact with a user through command dialogs or in a pseudo-natural language manner. However, the character-oriented functions seem to be more generally useful than the word-oriented functions even though (or maybe because) they operate at a slightly lower level. Examples of the use of WORD( ) and WORDS( ) may be found in the program that displays the time in English, in Chap. 2, and in the program which searches through a file for lines containing one or more words from a list, in Chap. 3.

Let's look at one more example, which will illustrate a couple more of the word-oriented functions in a natural application. The example is an *Eliza* program. This is a program that simulates a natural language conversation by means of very simple tricks. The original Eliza program was written by Joseph Weizenbaum to show how the *Turing test* for computer intelligence could be misleading. The Turing test is the notion that if a person cannot detect that he or she is interacting with a computer in a conversation, then the computer must be in some sense "intelligent." What Weizenbaum's Eliza program showed was that a program could really be quite unintelligent and still carry on a credible conversation. (Did he get this idea at a faculty cocktail party?)

The original Eliza program simulated a Rogerian therapist in conversation with a patient. Though "unintelligent," it was quite elaborate in that it had a large number of possible conversational responses built in. The program demonstrated an ability to deceive some users, in a way that was disconcerting to Weizenbaum. (Little known fact: about the time he concocted Eliza, Weizenbaum was teaching beginning programming classes in a language called MAD.)

Our example is of necessity much less elaborate, since such a program draws its power to convince more from a large repertoire of conversational gambits than from programming subtlety. If you wish to experiment with it, you can make it much more interesting by adding new responses. It might be even more amusing if you choose a conversational paradigm other than psychoanalyst/patient—some singles' bar dialog, perhaps.

The program consists of three major parts. The first part is the main loop. It reads a response one line at a time from the "client." A double use of the TRANSLATE() function, similar to previous examples, is done to convert the input to lowercase and remove punctuation characters. The result is scanned using WORDPOS() for the occurrence of any of a number of certain trigger phrases. If one of the phrases is found, a plausible reply based on the input is constructed in the REPLY procedure. If no matching phrase is found, a random noncommittal response is generated.

```
/********************************************************/
/* Sample Eliza program in REXX                         */
/********************************************************/

call initialize
say "Hello, what's on your mind today?"
/* main processing loop */
do forever
   /* read user input */
   parse pull sentence
   if sentence = '' then
      leave
   /* translate to lower case & remove punctuation */
   lower_sentence = translate(translate(sentence,,
      xrange('a', 'z'), xrange('A', 'Z')), ,,
         ".,?!;:")
   /* search for trigger phrases */
   do i = 1 while phrase.i \= ''
      j = wordpos(phrase.i, lower_sentence)
      if j \= 0 then do
         say reply(i, j, sentence)
         leave
```

```
      end
    end
    /* if no trigger found, give a random response */
    if phrase.i = '' then do
      j = random(response_count-1) + 101
      say response.j
      end
    end
exit
```

The second part of the program is the subroutine that constructs randomly chosen responses to the client's last remark.

```
/*****************************************************/
/* Reply to current sentence                         */
/*    First argument: number of trigger phrase       */
/*    Second argument: word position of match        */
/*    Third argument: complete user input            */
/*****************************************************/

reply: procedure expose responses. response. phrase.
parse arg phrase_number, position, sentence
i = words(responses.phrase_number)
j = word(responses.phrase_number, random(1, i))
reply = response.j

/* if the prototype reply contains "_", substitute
   rest of input */
i = pos('_', reply)
if i \= 0 then
  return left(reply, i-1) || subword(sentence,,
    position + words(phrase.phrase_number)) ||,
    substr(reply, i+1)

/* if the prototype reply contains "$", substitute
   trigger word */
i = pos('$', reply)
if i \= 0 then
  return left(reply, i-1) || word(sentence,,
    position) || substr(reply, i+1)
/* if the prototype reply contains "#", substitute
   word after trigger. */
i = pos('#', reply)
if i \= 0 then
  return left(reply, i-1) || word(sentence,,
    position+1) || substr(reply, i+1)
/* prototype has no substitution symbols */
return reply
```

The third part of the program sets up the tables of trigger phrases and possible responses.

```
/*****************************************************/
/* Subroutine called to set up the vocabulary       */
/*****************************************************/

initialize:
phrase. = ""
phrase.1 = "i am"
responses.1 = '1 2 6'
phrase.2 = "i'm"
responses.2 = '1 2 6'
phrase.3 = "i have"
responses.3 = '3 5'
phrase.4 = "i hate"
responses.4 = '4 10'
phrase.5 = "i want"
responses.5 = '5 11'
phrase.6 = "i need"
responses.6 = '5 11'
phrase.7 = "i like"
responses.7 = '5 12'
phrase.8 = "mother"
responses.8 = '8'
phrase.9 = "father"
responses.9 = '8'
phrase.10 = "sister"
responses.10 = '8'
phrase.11 = "brother"
responses.11 = '8'
phrase.12 = "wife"
responses.12 = '8'
phrase.13 = "husband"
responses.13 = '8'
phrase.14 = "my"
responses.14 = '9'

/* "_" will be replaced by a phrase */
/* "$" will be replaced by first word of trigger */
/* "#" will be replaced by second word of trigger */
response.1 = "How long have you been _?"
response.2 = "Why do you say that you are _?"
response.3 = "How do you feel about having _?"
response.4 = "When did you first realize you hated _?"
response.5 = "What does having _ mean to you?"
response.6 = "Are you sure you are _?"
response.7 = "When did you start to _?"
```

```
response.8 = "Tell me more about your $."
response.9 = "Does your # bother you much?"
response.10 = "Why do you hate _?"
response.11 = "Why do you want _?"
response.12 = "Why do you like _?"

response.101 = "Do you feel any better now?"
response.102 = "Why do you say that?"
response.103 = "How long have you felt that way?"
response.104 = "Do you think that's really true?"
response.105 = "How do you feel about that?"
response.106 = "That's interesting."
response.107 = "Please go on."
response.108 = "Tell me more about that."
response_count = 8
return
```

The syntax of WORDPOS( ) is:

```
WORDPOS(phrase, string, [start])
```

Here phrase is a string that contains the words to be searched for, and string is the string of words to be searched. Blanks are the delimiters of individual words, and multiple blanks are treated as one. phrase matches a part of string, provided the words in phrase occur in string in the same order. The function is case-sensitive. If no match is found, a value of 0 is returned. Otherwise, the function returns the number of the word (not the character) at which the first match was found. Optionally, the word position at which to begin the search can be specified in start.

The REPLY procedure illustrates a number of string handling functions, such as POS( ), LEFT( ), and SUBSTR( ). It also introduces the SUB-WORD( ) function, which has the syntax:

```
SUBWORD(string, start, [length])
```

SUBWORD( ) is the exact analog of SUBSTR( ), operating on a string of words rather than a string of characters, just as WORDPOS( ) is the analog of POS( ). String is the string of words to be operated on, and start is the position of the first word to be selected. Length is the number of words to be selected. If it is omitted, the default is the rest of the words in the string. The function returns up to length words beginning at the start position. If start is greater than the number of words in the string, a null string is returned. Blanks within the string of subwords are retained, but leading and trailing blanks are omitted.

Some of the remaining word-oriented functions can also be understood as analogues of the character-oriented functions. For instance, WORDS() is analogous to LENGTH(), and DELWORD() is analogous to DELSTR().

OTHER STRING MANIPULATION FUNCTIONS

The remaining string manipulation built-in functions fall into two categories, both of which address somewhat lower-level concerns than we have dealt with so far. The first of these is string format conversion. Although in one sense all data in REXX consists of strings, the same strings can be regarded as representing different things, and different strings can represent the same thing. For instance, consider the string '299792'. It is just a way of representing a particular decimal number as a character string. For some purposes, it may be necessary to represent the same decimal number in different ways. Perhaps the number has to be written to a file so it can be read by another program. Then we have to know in what internal format the other program expects to find the number.

This is not a simple problem, because there are many possible equivalent formats, and it is not always easy to find out what format any given program is expecting to handle. Many programs written in languages other than REXX expect to deal with numbers in a computer-specific internal format, because this usually takes less space. To start with a simple example, the decimal number 255 is represented internally in most computers in exactly the same way as the REXX literal 'ff'x is. Specifically, this is a single *byte* of data in which all 8 bits of the byte are 1s. If you need to write this number into a file so that it can be read by a program which is expecting this internal format, you must write 'ff'x rather than 255, as could be done with the statement

```
call charout file, 'ff'x
```

Of course, this only works for a single value. So REXX provides a way to produce the internal representation of an arbitrary decimal number: the D2C() built-in function. Very confusingly, the internal representation is called the *character* representation of the number. (You may with much justice think that '255' ought to be called the character representation, but—sorry—that is just not the terminology adopted by REXX.) Accordingly, REXX uses D2C() as the name of the function that converts "Decimal to Character."

So, if you want to write a number to a file in the correct internal format, you would use something like

```
call charout file, d2c(number)
```

We say "something like" this, because there is another problem to deal with when we need to work with the internal form of numbers. The problem is that implicit assumptions are always made about the size of a number in internal form. Most computers are capable of dealing with numbers occupying 1, 2, or 4 bytes, and sometimes other sizes as well. All this ambiguity over what internal form to use for a number is precisely the kind of problem that REXX itself hides by consistently using a string representation. But when you have to exchange data with programs written in other languages, whether in memory or through external files, you simply have to face up to the difficulty.

Anyway, the D2C() function allows you to be explicit about the size of the number in internal form, by allowing this length to be specified as the second argument. Thus the full syntax of D2C() is

```
D2C(number, length)
```

Here, length is the length in bytes of the required internal form. Although the length argument is (sometimes) optional, you should always provide it with D2C(); otherwise, REXX produces a result which is just as long as it needs to be, but no longer. Thus d2c(255) is 'ff'x (1 byte), but d2c(256) is '0100'x (2 bytes). Most programs which process data will expect a certain definite size, so you should be careful to explicitly provide the right size, and accordingly write

```
call charout file, d2c(number, 2)
```

(for instance). Another reason for always including the length in D2C() is that it is required if number just happens to be negative.

D2C() always right-justifies the internal form. That is, if the requested length is longer than required, extra bytes of '00'x are added on the left for positive numbers, and extra bytes of 'ff'x are added on the left for negative numbers. (This is called *sign extension*, because the high-order bit of the most significant nonzero byte is propagated to the left as far as necessary.) If the requested length is too short, the result is truncated on the left.

Consistent with this behavior, D2C() always produces the internal form with the most significant bytes first, the way we normally think of them (numbers are written with the most significant digits first). This raises yet another problem, since many computers store numbers in an internal form with the most significant bytes last. So you are forced to be concerned with byte ordering as well when you use D2C(), and you must take proper steps if you are writing data that will be read by another program which counts on a particular byte ordering.

Fortunately, this happens to be very easy to do with the REVERSE() function, which swaps the order of characters in a string. If this were in fact necessary you would just change the example to

```
call charout file, reverse(d2c(number, 2))
```

One final thing to note about the D2C() function, and something that is true of other format conversion functions as well, is that the input must be in the proper form, or else an error will be generated. Just as you can only use valid numbers in numeric operations, you must provide only valid numbers as input to D2C() for conversion. In this case a valid number must be a *whole number* in the sense that it can actually be represented exactly as an integer given the current value of NUMERIC DIGITS.

We have dwelt on D2C() at such length because it seems to present the trickiest problems of all the format conversion functions; yet it is needed in many practical situations. Once you've understood the foregoing, the rest is pretty simple. In particular, there is an inverse function, C2D(), for converting from the internal *character* format to an (ASCII or EBCDIC) numeric character string. You would use C2D() in situations inverse from those where you would use D2C(), i.e., when you want to get data into a REXX program that has been produced externally. For instance,

```
number = c2d(charin(file, 2))

The syntax of C2D() is

C2D(data, [length])
```

Here, data is the internal form to be converted to a number. Length is the length of the internal form, and defaults to the length of data. As with D2C(), you may have to be careful of byte ordering: C2D() expects data to be ordered with the most significant bytes first. If this is not the case, you have to apply REVERSE() to the internal form before calling C2D(). Also, consistent with D2C(), the result must be expressible as a *whole number*, that is, an integer that does not have more digits than the current setting of NUMERIC DIGITS.

And as with D2C() there is a problem with the signs of numbers as well. This is similar to the mysteries in other languages of deciding whether to treat numbers as *signed* or *unsigned* integers. In this case, if length is not specified, the data is always assumed to be unsigned. Hence c2d('ff'x) is 255. However, if a length is specified, the sign of the result is determined from the sign bit of the internal form, i.e., from the leftmost bit. So c2d('ff'x, 1) is -1, but c2d('ff'x, 2) is 255, because when length is specified the input data is right-justified in a field of specified length, truncating on the left, or padding with '00'x as required.

All six of the remaining format conversion functions convert to or from hexadecimal representations, that is, to or from REXX strings that happen to be valid hexadecimal constants. Such strings can consist only of digits 0 through 9 and letters A through F (in upper- or lowercase), and possibly written in groups of even length separated by blanks. "01234 ABCD" is an example of such a string. Do not confuse hex strings like this with REXX hex literals like "01234 ABCD"x (which is a way of directly expressing a hex internal form).

These functions for converting to or from hex strings are actually of much less general utility than C2D( ) and D2C( ), unless you happen to be a professional programmer, since most real world data is not expressed in hex strings. Of course, if you are a programmer, you may find these functions useful for working with dumps or other kinds of program-generated debugging information.

The conversion functions come in pairs. For converting between hex strings and bit strings, there are X2B( ) and B2X( ). These are entirely straightforward, and merely effect a change in number base between base 2 and base 16. Thus, for instance, x2b('f0') is '11110000', and b2x('11110000') is 'F0' (note: not 'F0'x!). No length parameters are used with X2B( ) and B2X( )., because there are no ambiguities involving signs that have to be handled.

Likewise, there are no additional problems in understanding X2C( ) and C2X( ) for conversion between internal character format and hex strings, once you've mastered the terminology. For instance, c2x('313233'x) is '313233' and x2c('313233') is '313233'x. Again, no length parameters are used because none are necessary.

The only challenge presented by X2D( ) and D2X( ) is the handling of signs, just as with C2D( ) and D2C( ). So this pair of functions does have a length parameter. Once you've understood what D2C( ) does, D2X( ) is easy. For instance, d2c(255) is 'FF'x, while d2x(255) is 'FF'. C2d('ff'x) and x2d('ff') both have the value 255.

The length parameter in X2D( ) and D2X( ) performs just the same function as it does in C2D( ) and D2C( ), which is to handle ambiguous cases of signed numbers. In D2X( ), the length argument is the number of characters of the result, and it is required if the first argument of D2X( ) is negative. For instance, d2x(-1,1) is 'F', d2x(-1,2) is 'FF', d2x(-1,3) is 'FFF', and so on, while d2x(1,1) is '1', d2x(1,2) is '01', and d2x(1,3) is '001'. When the first argument of D2X( ) is nonnegative, the default length of the result is such that there are no leading 0s. Truncation or padding on the left with '0' or 'F' is done if necessary, according to the requested length.

Similarly, X2D() uses the length argument to determine whether to produce a positive or negative result. So x2d('ff',2) is -1, but x2d('ff',3) is 255, since 'ff' is padded on the left with '0' to produce '0ff' before conversion.

All of the functions that convert to hex string format, i.e., B2X(), C2X(), and D2X(), produce results that use uppercase values of A–F and contain no embedded blanks.

The functions BITAND(), BITOR(), and BITXOR() are also low-level string-manipulation functions, for a very different purpose—bitwise logical operations on strings. They are, like most other low-level functions, usually dependent on internal data formats.

The PARSE Instruction

PARSE is a complex and multifaceted instruction. Although many of its simpler uses include such diverse operations as identifying subroutine arguments and reading data from the user or a file, it also offers a flexible and moderately powerful character-string analysis capability. Many tedious string operations can be done with PARSE that could also be done with the string handling functions, though much less efficiently and elegantly.

Because PARSE is used for so much besides string handling, and at the same time introduces so many new ways of working with strings, it is fully deserving of a chapter by itself.

As a string handling facility, PARSE may be thought of as the inverse of the concatenation operation, since it takes strings apart rather than putting them together. Although PARSE can operate on strings as individual characters, in its simplest and most commonly used forms it is like the word-oriented character-string functions in that it views a string as a blank-delimited sequence of words. Indeed, the rules for separating out individual words are the same, since only blanks count as delimiters, and multiple blanks are (usually) equivalent to a single one.

PARSE is perhaps most frequently used disguised as the ARG and PULL instructions, which are short for PARSE UPPER ARG and PARSE UPPER PULL, respectively. ARG is normally used to receive arguments in subroutines, and PULL is used to read information from the user. Our discussion of PARSE therefore includes these very common instructions as special cases.

The high-level syntax of PARSE is

PARSE [UPPER] source [template]

UPPER is an optional flag that indicates the data taken from source is to be converted to uppercase before further use. (Curiously, there is currently no symmetric LOWER flag for PARSE.)

SOURCES OF INPUT TO PARSE

There are a variety of sources for the data string that PARSE is to operate on, corresponding to how source is specified:

ARG

In this case (and this case alone) there may be multiple strings handled by PARSE. The strings are the arguments to the current procedure. For the main procedure there is usually just one argument string. But for other procedures there may be an arbitrary number of arguments. If there are multiple arguments, they are separated from each other by commas in the procedure call. Commas are used in the template to indicate which part of the template applies to which argument.

LINEIN

The input string is the value of the LINEIN() function for the default input stream. Input streams, and I/O in general, are discussed in Chap. 9, but normally this means that the data is read directly from the user at the keyboard. If the default stream is the keyboard, this option will wait until the user enters a complete line and presses Return on the keyboard. LINEIN differs from PULL as a source in that it does not check the external data queue first. Unless it is specifically intended to pass data through the queue, it is preferable to use LINEIN rather than PULL to avoid confusion from data placed in the queue for other purposes.

PULL

The external data queue is checked first for the presence of any data. If it is not empty, the next line in the queue is used as the input line for parsing. Otherwise, the line is taken from the default input stream, as with the LINEIN option. PULL should be used rather than LINEIN if you anticipate that you will need to pass input data to the REXX program using the external data queue. Doing this offers an alternative to redirecting the default input stream to a file in order to run the program without manual intervention. Neither PULL nor LINEIN options will include delimiter characters such as carriage return (if any), regardless of whether the line comes from an input stream or the queue.

SOURCE

The data string is one specially constructed to provide information about how the current program was invoked. The first word of the string should be the name of the operating system, e.g., "PC-DOS" or "CMS". The second word should indicate how the program was invoked. It may be "COMMAND" if the program was run as command by the operating system or application, "SUBROUTINE" if the program was CALLed as an external procedure from another REXX program, or "FUNCTION" if the program was invoked as an external function. These alternatives will always refer to how the main procedure, rather than the currently active internal procedure, was invoked. The remainder of the data string is implementation dependent, but usually includes the actual name of the program file. Many operating systems allow blanks in file names, so extra care may be needed in separating the file name from any further information that may be present.

VALUE expression WITH

The string to be parsed is the value of expression. WITH is a reserved word in this context and cannot be used as a variable name in expression, since it marks the end of the expression. Be careful, also, not to use WITH in connection with any of the other types of source specification, as it will then be taken as part of the template.

VAR name

The data string is taken from the value of the variable name. The NOVALUE condition can be raised if it is enabled and name is not initialized.

VERSION

The data string is specially constructed to indicate the version of REXX and the language processor in use. It is therefore implementation-dependent. The first word will usually indicate which language processor is being used. The second word usually indicates the version of the REXX language; it may be used to test for the availability of certain language features (if you can figure out in which version a given feature was introduced). The next three words should contain the release date of the REXX processor, in the default format of the DATE() function (e.g., 21 May 1991).

PARSE TEMPLATES: SIMPLEST CASE

The remainder of the PARSE instruction, the template, is the most interesting part. It is optional. If the template is omitted, then all necessary steps are taken to construct the input string, but no parsing actually occurs. In practice, this means that input (or queue access) is performed for LINEIN and PULL, expression evaluation for VALUE, and data fetching for VAR. You might use PULL (or PARSE PULL) alone just to clear a line of input from the queue or standard input stream.

But the instruction is ordinarily worth doing only if there is a template. The simplest and most common form of template is a list of variable names. We shall need a standard string to parse in many of the following examples, so we shall assume the assignment

```
x = "'Twas brillig, and the slithy toves"
```

We could assign each word of this string to separate variables with the single instruction

```
parse var x x1 x2 x3 x4 x5 x6
```

and the effect would be the same as if we had said

```
x1 = "'Twas"
x2 = "brillig,"
x3 = "and"
x4 = "the"
x5 = "slithy"
x6 = "toves"
```

This is in fact a useful technique for setting a large number of variables quickly if each needs to be set to a single word without leading or trailing blanks. It is usually more efficient than the equivalent series of assignment statements.

The rule for parsing a string when the template contains a sequence of consecutive variable names is to start with the first word of the string (in the sense used with the word-oriented, built-in string functions) and assign it to the first variable, assign the second word to the second variable, and so forth. In other words, blanks (and only blanks) are treated as word delimiters and are stripped out before assignments are made.

A special rule applies in case there are fewer variable names in the template than words in the string. In that case, the remainder of the string is assigned to the final variable. So if we had

```
parse var x x1 x2 x3 x4 x5
```

then x1, x2, x3, and x4 would be assigned as before, but now

```
x5 = "slithy toves"
```

So the last variable in a list of variables in a template can be assigned more than one word. In fact, the last word can be assigned a string with both leading and trailing blanks. For instance, if we have

```
parse value copies(' xxx ', 3) with a b c
```

then we get

```
a = "xxx"
b = "xxx"
c = " xxx "
```

This is because of the rule (which is not claimed to be intuitive!) that for each variable assigned except for the last, all preceding blanks and one trailing blank in the PARSE string are consumed, but no preceding or trailing blanks are consumed in the assignment to the last variable.

In the simplest case,

```
parse var x y
```

we have exactly the same effect as the assignment

```
y = x
```

because no leading or trailing blanks will be stripped from x. Though this seems like a trivial example, it is essentially what happens with

```
pull answer
```

and you generally have to be careful to use the STRIP() function to remove surrounding blanks from answer before trying to match it with possible expected responses.

In the opposite circumstance, when there are fewer words in the PARSE string than variable names in the template, all "excess" variables are assigned the null string. In general, PARSE will make assignments to all variables named in a template, and will use a null value if nothing else is appropriate. So, with

```
parse value copies(" xxx ", 3) with a b c d
```

we would get

```
a = "xxx"
b = "xxx"
c = "xxx"
d = ""
```

Notice that here blanks were stripped from the last word before assignment to c, since c was not the last variable in the list.

To further get used to the rules for dealing with blanks at the end of a string, consider two cases. First:

```
parse value copies(' ', 2) with a
```

simply assigns a string of 2 blanks, the "remainder" of the string, to a. Second:

```
parse value copies(' ', 2) with a b
```

assigns a null string to both a and b. This is because the string is entirely consumed in trying to find a word to assign to a. So there is nothing to assign to a, and nothing left for b.

Sometimes you will want to simply ignore words in a string whose format is known. To do that, just use a period instead of a variable name at the corresponding location in the template. So, if we know x contains a string consisting of 6 words,

```
parse var x with first . . . . last
```

yields

```
first = "'Twas"
last = "toves"
```

and no other variables are affected. The period is a place holder which causes the same parsing as for a variable but without causing any assignment. It can be useful in avoiding some of the peculiarities which arise from the rules about the assignment to the last variable in a template. So, for instance, if you know that a string will contain a certain number of words but an unknown number of blanks between words, you can use

```
parse linein x y z .
```

to be sure that z does not contain leading and trailing blanks. Another common case is when you are interested in the first few words of a string. If all you care about is the first three words, then

```
parse linein x y z .
```

gets them for you, and you don't need to be concerned that z is assigned anything extraneous.

Because PARSE, in the simple cases we have been considering, views a string as a sequence of blank-delimited words, it can often be used in place of the word-oriented string functions—and frequently it is much more efficient. In particular, if you are concerned about performance, be careful when using WORD() to examine each word of a long string. In a loop like this,

```
do i = 1 to words(text)
  x = word(text, i)
  ...
  end
```

the text string has to be rescanned from the beginning every time through the loop. This will have a noticeable performance impact if text is even moderately long (even 80 characters or so). From a performance standpoint, a loop like

```
y = text
do while y \= ''
  parse var y x y
  ...
  end
```

will be significantly faster in most implementations. This example is in fact a frequently used REXX idiom for extracting successive words of a string, because of its efficiency. The key part is the line

```
parse var y x y
```

which places the first word of y into x and replaces y with the remainder of the string each time through the loop. (We first assigned text to a temporary variable because the string is entirely consumed in the parsing process and we might want to keep it around for some reason in its original form.)

PATTERN MATCHING IN TEMPLATES

PARSE templates can do much more than just break a string apart into blank-delimited words. By explicitly specifying string patterns to search for, you can use arbitrary strings as delimiters. We have already seen simple cases like

```
parse value time('l') with hours ':' minutes,
  ':' seconds '.' fraction
```

The time('l') call gives the current time in the form hh:mm:ss.uuuuuu (uuuuuu is a fraction of a second in microseconds).

PARSE scans the string looking for matches to literal strings given in the template. If all literals are found (in the order specified) in the string, then the string is broken into a number of substrings. Each substring is then parsed into words and assigned to any variables which are named in the template between pairs of literals. For instance, to use our original example,

```
parse var x "'Twas" a b c "toves"
```

we get the assignments

```
a = "brillig,"
b = "and"
c = "the slithy"
```

In other words, all of the rules for parsing strings into words and assigning the words to variables apply to the substring bounded by (but not including) pairs of literals in a template. You can even place two (or more) literals adjacent to each other in a template to bound a portion of a string which is to be ignored:

```
parse var x a "brillig" "slithy" b
```

yields

```
a = "'Twas "
b = " toves"
```

This example also illustrates another point, which is that a template is always assumed to start with a pattern that matches the beginning of the string, and to end with a pattern that matches the end of a string. Note, finally, the blanks at the end of a and the beginning of b. These are not stripped since a and b, being the only variables corresponding to their respective substrings, are assigned the entire remainder of the substring.

What if a literal pattern is not found in scanning a string? The answer is that this is not considered an error condition, and you cannot test directly for it. PARSE simply assigns the null string to all variables named after the literal string that was not found. The unfound literal pattern is treated as matching the end of the string. For example,

```
parse var x a "and" b "kumquat" c
```

yields

```
a = "'Twas brillig, "
b = " the slithy toves"
c = ""
```

Since "kumquat" was not found in the string, it matches the end of the string. Therefore, b is assigned the remainder (everything after "and"), while c is assigned a null string.

There is a special pattern-matching case which is handled in a way that may not seem intuitively obvious. This is the fact that a null string as a pattern in a template is considered not to match anything except the end of the string. Though perhaps surprising, this is consistent with other behavior of a null string in REXX, such as the fact that it doesn't match any part of the string in the POS() built-in function. It may be useful if you need a way to force a match at the end of the input string. Of course, this happens anyway if the template does not end with a pattern, but you might want to select use of this behavior by ending a template with a variable pattern (discussed later) which could possibly be a null string.

Because unfound patterns are considered to match the end of the input string, we can say that parsing is actually *driven* by the pattern matching. That is, the operation of parsing consists first of finding patterns in the string, and second of assigning the part of the string between two matched patterns to variables. When the template does not actually contain any patterns, as in the preceding section, it is assumed that the boundaries are the beginning and the end of the string. In the next section we shall see that pattern matches can be forced to occur at specific column locations in the input string.

POSITIONAL PATTERNS IN TEMPLATES

There is one additional kind of *pattern* which can occur in a template. It is called a positional pattern, because it allows you to specify explicit character positions in a string. You may think of a positional pattern as a pattern of zero length which matches the input string at a certain position.

The column position can be specified as either an absolute or a relative number. And absolute position is just an unsigned integer, while a relative position is an integer preceded (with zero or more intervening blanks) by a + or – sign. (For symmetry, you can use an = sign before an absolute position, if you like.) Obviously, counting character positions can be tedious in free-form text. The main purpose of positional patterns is for dealing with records that have fixed-field sizes, so that absolute or relative positions are easily calculated; but there are other surprising uses as well.

Let's consider absolute positional patterns first. Using the standard example,

```
parse var x x1 x2 16 x3 x4 23 x5
```

yields

```
x1 = "'Twas"
x2 = "brillig, "
x3 = "and"
x4 = "the"
x5 = " slithy toves"
```

since character position 16 is the "a" of "and" and position 23 is the blank after "the". What has happened is that the string was partitioned into three substrings: positions 1 to 15, 16 to 22, and 23 to the end. These were then parsed into variables as usual. Because positional patterns have zero length, all characters of the string wound up in one of the three substrings.

Since the string starts at position 1, we would get the same results from

```
parse var x 1 x1 x2 16 x3 x4 23 x5
```

and, in fact, all templates can be considered to begin with the absolute positional pattern 1, which matches the first position of the string.

To see the value of relative positional patterns, suppose we knew in advance that the string began with fields of widths 15 and 7. Then another equivalent way to write the same instruction would be

```
parse var x x1 x2 +15 x3 x4 +7 x5
```

since 1 + 15 is 16 and 16 + 7 is 23. This way of writing the template has the advantage that you can think of the relative positions as field widths. So if you know what the field widths should be, you don't have to compute absolute column positions yourself, and the program will be easier to maintain if any field widths have to change.

Although positional patterns appear reasonably straightforward from what we have seen so far, there are some special rules that make life more interesting. You may have noticed it was never said that absolute positions must be specified in a template in increasing order. The very fact that negative relative positions can be specified means backing up is allowed. The first rule comes into effect whenever a positional pattern, either absolute or relative, specifies a position at or before the last specified position in the string. The rule is that when this happens, the variable just before the positional pattern (if any) is assigned the entire remainder of the string.

Why? Well, ordinarily when a positional pattern is used, and it is to the right of the previous position, then the substring bounded by the two positions extends from the first up to (but not including) the second. Consequently, a variable which precedes the second positional pattern is assigned characters up to (but not including) the second position. For instance,

```
parse value '123456789' with 2 x 6 y
```

yields

```
x = '2345'
y = '6789'
```

But this way of looking at things breaks down when the second position is before the first position, since that would entail a result of negative length. The rule resolves this problem by making the end of the string, rather than the second position, be the right-hand limit of the substring. Thereafter, parsing resumes at the new position. Thus,

```
parse value '123456789' with 2 x 1 y
```

would be rather hard to make sense of if we didn't have the rule, which yields

```
x = '23456789'
y = '123456789'
```

Far from merely resolving a difficulty, this rule adds an interesting capability to PARSE. Since it specifically includes the case where the second positional pattern is the same as the preceding one, the rule means the same string can be parsed many times, each in a different way. For instance

```
parse value '123456789' with 1 x1 1 x2 6 x3 1 x4 4 x5,
   7 x6
```

yields

```
x1 = '123456789'
x2 = '12345'
x3 = '6789'
x4 = '123'
x5 = '456'
x6 = '789'
```

As a special case, this provides a way to initialize a number of variables to the same value with a single statement, e.g.,

```
parse value time() with 1 t1 1 t2 1 t3 1 t4 1 t5
```

sets each of t1, t2, t3, t4, t5 to the current time. This is more efficient than a series of assignment statements. And, as an added advantage, it is guaranteed that exactly the same value is assigned to each variable, since the function is evaluated only once.

But PARSE has still more surprises in store for us. The second special parsing rule we will consider is how positional and string patterns interact. Although we have avoided giving any examples yet, there are no rules that say positional and string patterns cannot be mixed in the same template. The fact is, they can be. Indeed, any mixture of variable names, string patterns, and positional patterns can be used in a template, in any order at all. The only question is how to interpret all the possible cases.

To begin with, REXX provides that every string pattern sets a position in the string which is equivalent to a positional pattern. That position is, specifically, the position of the first matching character of the string pattern. It could be the end of the string if the pattern is not found, since an unfound string pattern is considered to match the end of the string. This position is then the previous position used when the next pattern is positional. For example,

```
x = 'name: Fred    age: 35'
parse var x 'age:' age +7
```

yields

```
age = 'age: 35'
```

Note that the substring bounded by a string pattern followed by a relative positional pattern specifically includes the string pattern itself; the string pattern is not stripped out in this case. This is just part of the rule; it does not follow from anything else. What if you didn't want the string pattern to be included? Then use

```
parse var x 'age:' +4 age +3
```

Remember: there's nothing that says two patterns can't be adjacent in a template. Sometimes it's actually useful that they can be.

At this point, we have to note a minor inconsistency between the way that absolute and relative positional patterns work. It arises when a string pattern is followed by a positional pattern. Suppose we have a record format where a character string is followed by a field of fixed width. For instance,

```
x = "Invoice number: 012345"
```

The whole field, counting the tag it begins with, is 22 characters wide. Hence,

```
parse var x "Invoice number:" inv_no 23
```

will correctly set the variable inv_no with the number:

```
inv_no = " 012345"
```

The tag is stripped out because it matches part of the data. Yet the apparently equivalent

```
parse var x "Invoice number:" inv_no +22
```

causes the assignment

```
inv_no = "Invoice number: 012345"
```

because it is defined that the string pattern is included in what is assigned to the variable when followed by a relative positional pattern.

Though this is an inconsistency, it isn't very likely to occur in practice, because you aren't very likely to use an absolute positional pattern following a literal pattern—use of the string pattern generally implies a free-form data layout where absolute column numbers are not relevant.

If for some reason you wanted to do this and you wanted the literal not to be stripped out of the value assigned, you could do

```
parse var x "Invoice number" +0 inv_no 23
```

It is more likely that you would use another literal pattern in a case like this, perhaps

```
parse var x "Invoice number" +0 inv_no "Date:"
```

Either way, by inserting an extra relative positional pattern of +0 we have defeated the effect of stripping the matched string from the value assigned to the variable, so that we get

```
inv_no = "Invoice_number: 012345"
```

VARIABLE PATTERNS

Sometimes the literal or positional patterns needed in a template are not known in advance and must be computed at the time a program is run. It is even possible for strings to be self-defining in the sense that they contain information about the location or size of fields which they contain. In order to handle situations like this, REXX allows both literal and positional patterns to be specified by the values of variables. The variables can even be set in the same PARSE instruction where they will later be used to specify patterns.

Some syntactic device is necessary in order to distinguish variables which contain pattern information from those that are to be assigned values during the parsing process. That device is called a *variable reference,* and it consists of the variable name enclosed in parentheses. If this is to be used as a string pattern, that is all that is required. If it is to be used as a positional pattern, then the reference should be preceded by "=" (for an absolute position), or "+" or "–" (for a relative position).

For instance, we could parse dates written in any of the forms "mm/dd/yy", "mm-dd-yy", or "mm.dd.yy" with something like

```
datesep = "/"
parse var date month (datesep) day (datesep) year
```

Unfortunately, we can't handle all three alternatives at once. In other words, the program must decide in advance what will be used as the punctuation character. There is nothing in REXX that permits matching on any one pattern from a list of alternatives, nor is there any capability for using something like *regular expressions.* In this respect, the PARSE instruction is considerably weaker than other pattern-matching paradigms.

To see an example of variable positional patterns, let's consider the case of a record that consists of an arbitrary number of repeated data items. Each data item is of variable size. Suppose that the first three characters of each item contain the length of the remainder of the item. Then a loop like

```
do i = 1 by 1 while record \= ''
   parse var record length +3 data.i +(length) record
   end
```

would neatly break the whole record into individual items assigned to data.1, data.2, etc. Because of the + before (length), the variable reference is taken to be a relative positional pattern. The value assigned to length in the first part of the template must be numeric or an error will result. The end of the template specifies that everything left over replaces the original value of record.

Although this example is simple and elegant, it does not handle errors well. Since length must be a numeric value, the program will encounter a serious error if the input data inadvertently contains a nonnumeric value at the beginning of a field. It might be better in practice, therefore, to extract `length` first and test it for validity, so at least a sensible error message can be issued in case of a problem.

It is possible to get into trouble using variable patterns in which the variables are set during the PARSE instruction itself. For instance, suppose that you want to have a record where the first two items are the starting and ending column numbers of a third item. You might try to use

```
parse var x first second =(first) third =(second)
```

but that won't work. The problem is that, since parsing is driven by pattern matching, the variable first has to be referred to in order to determine a column number before it gets set. So it will have an undefined, or at best irrelevant, value. To handle this example correctly you would need something like

```
parse var x first ' ' second ' ' =(first) third,
   =(second)
```

to force a pattern match on the blanks following the first and second numbers. Then first and second get set properly, and the instruction works as expected.

One limitation with variable patterns is that only individual variable names can be used inside parentheses in a template. You cannot use any sort of expression. If computations are required, they must be done outside of the template and the results assigned to variables. However, you can use compound variables, and the tail may refer to variables which are set earlier in the template.

PARSING PROCEDURE ARGUMENTS

One of the most frequent uses of PARSE, though sometimes in a concealed form, is receiving the argument values in a procedure. The ARG instruction can be used for this, but it is really just shorthand for PARSE UPPER ARG. As a rule, it is better to use PARSE ARG explicitly (without UPPER), since it does not mangle the case of the arguments. Use ARG only if you definitely want to ignore case of the arguments.

When receiving passed arguments with PARSE ARG, and in this case alone, the template has a special form. Since multiple argument strings can be passed, some notation is needed to indicate which parts of a template apply to which strings. A comma is used for this. The part of the template before the first comma applies to the first argument, the part before the second comma to the second argument, and so forth. The commas used in the template are not patterns, and they are not quoted.

For instance, for a procedure called like this

```
call names 'Kellyn', 'Ashley', 'Shanna', 'Meghan'
```

we might have

```
names: procedure
parse arg name1, name2, name3, name4
```

so that

```
name1 = "Kellyn"
name2 = "Ashley"
name3 = "Shanna"
name4 = "Meghan"
```

This takes the four procedure arguments and assigns them to variables. One way to think of this is that the commas imply four distinct parsing operations, as if there were actually three templates used: one for each argument. The preceding example, in one sense, does no actual parsing or character string manipulation at all. Instead, for each argument in turn, the whole argument string is assigned to a variable without regard to the content of the string.

But each portion of the template could be more complex. We could have

```
call parse_poem,
    "'Twas brillig, and the slithy toves",,
    "Did gyre and gimble in the wabe:",,
    "All mimsy were the borogoves,",,
    "And the mome raths outgrabe."
...
parse_poem: procedure
parse arg first1 rest1, first2 rest2, first3 rest3,,
    first4 rest4
```

to extract the first word of each argument. The remainder of each line gets assigned to one variable, e.g.,

```
rest3 = "mimsy were the borogoves,"
```

because rest3 is the end of the template as far as the third argument is concerned.

In general, there should be as many commas in the template that parses arguments as there are commas between arguments in the procedure call (i.e., one less than the actual number of arguments). A frequent and easily made mistake would be to use (with reference to the earlier example)

```
parse arg name1 name2 name3 name4
```

This actually does something very different:

```
name1 = "Kellyn"
name2 = ""
name3 = ""
name4 = ""
```

Since there are no commas, this statement deals with only the first argument. It operates on one string (the first argument to the procedure) and searches for blank-delimited words, of which there is only one in the first argument.

So, if you have fewer *subtemplates* in an ARG instruction than you have arguments, some of the arguments will be ignored. On the other hand, if you have too many subtemplates, all variables in the excess subtemplates will be set to null strings, since in effect the excess subtemplates are parsing null strings. In particular, if you use templates with multiple subtemplates in any form of PARSE other than PARSE ARG, all variables in the subtemplates after the first will be set to null. This might even be useful:

```
parse value '' with x1, x2, x3, x4, x5, x6
```

is a quick way to set a number of variables to the null string, though

```
parse value '' with x1 x2 x3 x4 x5 x6
```

is even more straightforward.

You can use PARSE ARG anywhere in a subroutine. It does not have to be the first statement after the label or PROCEDURE instruction. You can also use it several times, with different templates each time.

PARSE IN RELATION TO OTHER FORMS
OF STRING MANIPULATION

In general, string manipulation chores that can be done with PARSE will be done more easily and more efficiently than the equivalent operations done with the word or character-oriented built-in functions. In addition to being easier to program (once you get the hang of it), you can gain execution speed since the whole operation can be done internally, without the need to constantly issue function calls. The use of

PARSE to separate one word at a time from a long string, instead of using the WORD() function, is a notable example of this.

However, there are trade-offs. Even when PARSE and the string functions can perform more or less equivalent operations, there may be reasons other than processing efficiency for choosing one over the other. One possible reason is that more detailed error-checking can be done if you work at a lower level with the string functions.

For instance, consider the problem of using PARSE to substitute one substring (contained in the variable x) for another (contained in y). You might be tempted to try something like

```
parse var string before (x) after
string = before || y || after
```

Although this is simple and elegant, it causes trouble if the substring x isn't contained in string. In that case, PARSE will merrily assign the whole string to before. Then the next statement will append the value of y. This is probably not what you want. The problem is that PARSE has made things (apparently) so easy that you can forget to test for exceptional cases. PARSE has no "smarts" and does not deal well with string match "failures." A more robust solution to the problem would be:

```
if pos(x,string) \= 0 then do
   parse var string before (x) after
   string = before || y || after
   end
```

This tests separately whether the value of x occurs in the given string, since PARSE doesn't do that for you.

String manipulation functions can always be used as an alternative to PARSE. Although they may be somewhat less efficient, they may be more flexible. For instance, INSERT() and DELSTR() can be used to do string substitution as in the previous example, and in order to use them you are almost forced to consider the possibility that the substring you want to replace isn't found:

```
i = pos(x,string)
if i \= 0 then
   string = insert(y, delstr(string,i,length(x)), i-1)
```

PRACTICAL EXAMPLES OF PARSING

One more example: in this we would like to show the symmetry which is revealed when you consider the handling of long records with many fields of specific lengths.

You might build up such a record for output with a statement like

```
record = right(val1, len1) || right(val2, len2) ||,
         right(val3, len3) || right(val4, len4) ||,
         right(val5, len5) || right(val6, len6)
```

Given this, the same record could be input with

```
record = linein(file)
parse var recordval1 +(len1) val2 +(len2),
                val3 +(len3) val4 +(len4),
                val5 +(len5) val6 +(len6)
```

Input and Output

Programming languages exhibit wide divergences in their input/output capabilities. Some languages like PL/I attempt to provide comprehensive I/O facilities within the language itself. Others like C leave I/O entirely to separate function libraries (though, in the case of C, the essential core functions have become standardized to the point of being a true part of the language). Still other languages, like Fortran, have opted to include basic I/O capabilities as part of the language, without attempting to address the full range of possibilities that PL/I (for instance) does.

REXX is in the middle. It is almost like C in that the language itself has no pure I/O constructs other than SAY. (The QUEUE, PULL, and PUSH instructions are halflings that sort of do I/O, some of the time.) REXX's I/O capabilities are embodied in a small number of built-in functions (mainly LINEIN(), LINEOUT(), CHARIN(), and CHAROUT()). These are, however, standard parts of the language, though their behavior is allowed a certain amount of latitude across implementations.

It is a good idea to distinguish two sorts of I/O which really place very different demands on a language. The first kind is I/O involving files and hardware devices like printers, where no human user or operator is directly involved. For this, the REXX built-in functions are fairly well-equipped to handle the most common basic tasks. They do not, however, offer any particular support for anything besides flat files, nor are they capable of dealing with idiosyncrasies of specific hardware devices.

The second kind of I/O involves interaction with a human user. For this, REXX satisfies the most rudimentary requirements by providing SAY and PARSE PULL. This assumes a hardware model that consists of a simple printer-keyboard combination. REXX has nothing to offer as part of the language for any more modern human interface styles such as windows or direct manipulation. But, then, neither do most other programming languages.

We stress this distinction, because REXX's file I/O facilities can also be employed for user interaction by means of the notion of treating a keyboard-screen combination as a virtual file on which a program can read and write. When this is done properly, it can add a certain kind of flexibility to a program, because the program may be able to operate equally well whether it is reading from and writing to a human operator, a file, a device, or even another program. Such device-independent programs offer a certain economy of effort, in that they may be used in a wider range of ways. In the best cases, such as the *filter* programs which are so common in Unix, this permits a powerful, building-block approach to writing utilities.

But, as everyone knows, though such programs are capable of interacting with people by treating the keyboard and screen as devices, the quality of the user interface leaves something to be desired. Furthermore, the intentional blurring of the distinction between human-oriented and computer-oriented forms of I/O capabilities can lead to certain confusions about specific REXX I/O features. Besides that, the two kinds of I/O often present different problems and possibilities in such things as *random access* and dealing with the *end of file*. And further confusion can arise because of the semi-incorporation in REXX of yet another kind of (pseudo-)device, the *external data queue*, to be discussed in the next chapter, which is (among other things) another paradigm for virtualizing a human operator.

In the first implementation of REXX, in IBM's VM/CMS operating system, the two kinds of I/O were completely separate, for better or worse. User interaction was done with SAY and PULL, but file I/O could be done only with external commands, such as EXECIO. This command was clever in that it could also work with the procedure language which preceded REXX, but it was ultimately a kludge. Nevertheless, it was necessary, as the earliest implementation of REXX in VM/CMS did not support the I/O built-in functions. (It still does not at the time of this writing.) Since this situation must inevitably change, we won't deal with EXECIO here, and it is not part of the REXX language in any case.

Like most of the rest of REXX, the I/O model was designed for simplicity of use. It was intended for handling what were expected to be the most common cases of I/O very easily. As far as user interaction was concerned, this meant a simple line-at-a-time, question-answer style of user interface. More sophisticated capabilities were consciously excluded.

Unfortunately, what is adequate for simple user interaction sometimes doesn't work quite so well for files. Furthermore, even the simple user interface model was falling from favor at the time REXX was designed. REXX emerged at the end of an era of computer technology in which it was still possible to take seriously the model of an interactive program which communicated with its user through a question-answer user interface. At the time (early 1980s), such line mode interfaces were already being rapidly supplanted by "full-screen" interfaces which exploited a two-dimensional surface for interacting with users. And these in turn rapidly gave way to even more elaborate systems of windows, pop-up or pull-down menus, dialog boxes, and the like.

At present, the complexity of programming adequate user interfaces, in either text or graphics mode, far outstrips the resources of any language in common use which does not have access to extensive (and unstandardized) interface libraries (or the equivalent *classes* of object-oriented languages). This makes any plain, unaugmented language, including REXX, not very suitable for building what are now considered to be "good" user interfaces. Fortunately for REXX (and other languages), not all programs require "good" interfaces. Some don't require a user interface at all. Because much use of REXX is for such things as system command procedures, application macros, and quick-and-dirty utilities, sophisticated interface tools are frequently not needed. But other common uses of REXX, such as prototyping and application building by combining tools, do suffer from the lack of good interface capabilities.

CHARACTER-ORIENTED VS. LINE-ORIENTED I/O

Let's leave such philosophical observations aside now, and begin to explore REXX's I/O capabilities by looking first at the file I/O functions. REXX provides two distinct sets of file I/O functions, corresponding to a distinction between two ways of regarding a file. From one point of view, a file is just a string of zero or more bytes. Every byte is just like any other byte in that the file system does not reserve special bytes to indicate the end of a line or a record. The other point of view is that a file is a sequence of zero or more lines or records. Each line is a sequence of zero or more bytes. Lines may all be of one fixed length, or they may be of varying length. Sometimes the end of a line is marked by one or more bytes actually contained in the file, and sometimes there are no such markers, with the file system itself keeping track of the location of line boundaries.

Most operating systems now support both of these views of what a file is, but they also generally favor one view or the other. Mainframe file systems, for instance, generally consider a file to be a sequence of lines, whereas most other systems treat a file as a sequence of bytes. These two views are not wholly incompatible, and any given file system may support both views of the same file, even simultaneously. This is obviously an area of much potential for incompatibility between systems.

REXX supports both views of file organization through its character-oriented and its line-oriented file I/O functions. They may even be used simultaneously on the same file, though this can be troublesome. The character-oriented functions are CHARIN(), which reads one or more characters; CHAROUT(), which writes one or more characters; and CHARS(), which returns the number of characters that remain to be read in a file. The corresponding line-oriented functions are LINEIN(), which reads a single line from a file; LINEOUT(), which writes a single line to a file; and LINES(), which returns the number of lines that remain to be read in a file.

OPENING A FILE

Most operating systems require that an operation called *opening* be performed on a file before it can be used. Correspondingly, most languages require files to be opened before using language I/O facilities. The open operation has several purposes. One of these is to identify by name the file or device that is to be used. Usually the open process associates the name with a *handle* or control block which is used in subsequent I/O operations rather than the name itself.

Another purpose of the open operation is to allow the user or programmer to make choices among various available options for file processing. The options that are available, of course, will vary greatly from system to system, but they often include:

whether the file is to be read, written, or both

whether writing (if any) should start at the beginning or end of the file

how the file may be shared by other programs that have concurrent access to it

what attributes the file should have if it is being created

how much space should be pre-allocated for the file if it is being created

Notice that all of these things are true options in the sense that they are not (ordinarily) characteristics of the file itself (if it already exists). Various other options deal with alternative ways of processing a file that may admit variation, yet must still be compatible with the true characteristics and organization of the file. This category of options includes:

whether the file is to be treated as *text* or *binary*. This distinction usually refers to whether there is to be special handling for control characters that indicate the end of a line.

what the logical length of a file record is, in case there is no internal indication in the file of record boundaries.

What this discussion is leading up to is the fact that there is no function in REXX, in contrast to most other languages, for opening a file. This is because, for most simple file operations, it is possible for REXX to open a file automatically the first time it is used. REXX does this in the spirit of "helping" the programmer by eliminating a frequently unnecessary and often confusing operation. This is akin to the REXX philosophy that it should not be necessary to declare variables before use. (It is not irrelevant, though, that in VM/CMS where REXX was first implemented the operating system did not require a file to be opened before being used.)

In languages where opening a file is required, the file is normally referred to by its name only at the time it is opened. Thereafter, the open file is referred to by either a *handle* (an object returned by the open routine) or by a control block. But in REXX a file is always referred to by its name. REXX internally keeps track of whatever handles or control blocks are needed by the operating system, automatically associating them with the name after the first time the file is used. Keeping such details out of the program itself can contribute to portability across systems.

Of course, the disadvantage of having no explicit open operation is that it is not possible in standard REXX to specify any of the options which are otherwise available when a file is opened. Standard REXX is able to handle some of the options by choices available in the file I/O functions. For instance, whether the file will be read or written is determined by whether both input and output functions are actually used. Since REXX can't know in advance whether you might want to update a file even if the first operation is to read it, a REXX implementation will typically open the file in read-write mode (if possible).

Thereafter, reads and writes can be intermixed in any order. If there is some reason why REXX cannot open the file in read-write mode, it may open it in read-only mode. Then REXX will signal an error condition if, and only if, an output operation is attempted. One side effect of this approach, which may or may not be a disadvantage, is that the file may be opened in a mode that prevents other programs from simultaneously reading or writing to it, even if the file is only going to be read.

The inability to choose at open time whether to start writing a file at the end (*append mode*) or at the beginning (*create mode*) is of lesser importance. Normally a REXX implementation will by default begin writing at the end of an existing file (to reduce the chance of unintentional destruction of data). But both the CHAROUT( ) and the LINEOUT( ) functions provide the ability to write at other positions in a file, including the beginning. (Though in some cases it may not be possible for an implementation to support writing at an arbitrary byte or line position in the middle of a file.)

Another common option in opening a file is whether to treat it as text (a sequence of lines) or binary (a sequence of bytes). In general, REXX's character-oriented functions, when fully implemented, deal with a file in binary mode as a sequence of bytes. That is, they read or write exactly what is contained in the file and do not make any transformations on the data or treat any characters as special (e.g., end of file characters). The line-oriented functions may, however, interpret certain control characters in special ways, usually to determine the end of a line. (But note that the distinction between text and binary is very situation- and system-dependent, and is not necessarily the same as the line vs. character distinction.)

Some operating systems like MVS permit certain file characteristics to be specified at open time, such as the length of logical records of a file. REXX's character-oriented functions (though not the line-oriented ones) handle this easily, since any number of characters can be read at a time.

There are several alternatives for handling those open options that can't be simulated in the REXX file I/O functions themselves. For one thing, there is a catchall built-in function called STREAM( ) which can be used by an implementation to provide any desired I/O capabilities above and beyond what can be done with the standard functions. Among other things, STREAM( ) may support an explicit open command which allows specification of necessary file open options. Unfortunately, the specific commands provided by STREAM( ), including the open command, are completely implementation-dependent and not standardized. You might just as well use the native file system facilities of your implementation of REXX.

An implementation can also add as many extra built-in functions as it likes to provide necessary I/O services. It may choose to offer a complete set of I/O functions more or less parallel to the standard ones but which correspond more closely to the I/O facilities of the underlying operating system.

The numerous possible file-handling options, and their lack of consistency among different systems, is one of the major reasons I/O has always been a difficult topic in learning a programming language. When treated in full generality, I/O remains difficult even in REXX. Yet a few of the most common requirements are handled cleanly and automatically by the language.

FILE READ/WRITE POINTERS

There is one concept which applies to most of the I/O functions, so we will discuss it first. This is the fact that REXX keeps track of its current position in the file at all times. This is done with something conceptually like a cursor or a pointer that always indicates the next character or line of the file that will be read or written. The current position is maintained independently for reading and writing with what we will refer to as a read pointer and a write pointer.

By definition, the read pointer is positioned just before the next character or line to be read from the file. When a file is opened, the read pointer is conceptually just before the first character of the file. As data is read by CHARIN( ), the read pointer is advanced by the number of characters read, so that it is positioned after the last one read. When LINEIN( ) is used, the read pointer is moved to a point right after the line just read, including any characters signifying the end of the line. If CHARIN( ) is used after LINEIN( ), the read pointer can be left pointing somewhere in the middle of a line. If LINEIN( ) is then used, it will return only a partial line, from the read pointer to the end of the line.

Similarly, the write pointer is always positioned at the point where the next output operation will add data to the file. When a file is opened, the write pointer will be right after the last existing character of the file, so that any newly written data will be appended to the file. As new data is written by CHAROUT( ), the write pointer is advanced to right after the last character written.

The read and write pointers can also be changed without actually performing I/O. All of the four principal file I/O functions are defined so that the read or write pointer can be moved to a specific location before the operation begins. This permits random access for reading and writing in a file. The functions also allow for requesting 0 characters or lines to be read or written. This allows for changing the read or write pointers without performing I/O. Additionally, the STREAM( ) function may provide another means of changing the pointers. This operation is sometimes called *seeking*.

When using the character-oriented functions to set the read or write pointer before an operation, the relative byte number in the file is specified. Bytes in a file are numbered starting from 1, which is consistent with how bytes in REXX strings are numbered. When the line-oriented functions are used to set the read or write pointer, the relative line number (starting with 1) is specified. There is no standard way of enquiring what the value of the current read or write pointer is, though it may be possible in some implementations through the STREAM( ) function. In cases where it can somehow be done, you need to understand clearly whether the numerical value used refers to a relative byte or line number.

We should point out that the behavior of the read and write pointers is as yet a somewhat unstandardized area of the language, as is true, in fact, for file I/O in general. Implementations definitely do differ. For instance, even though Cowlishaw explicitly states that the read and write pointers should be independent, at least one implementation (IBM's OS/2 REXX) forces them to be the same. This means that writing to a file can change the read pointer, and vice versa. Making the read and write pointers the same is, of course, extremely dangerous, since if a program reads randomly in a file and then does output, data may be inadvertently destroyed because the write pointer has been moved to the position of the last read. Be careful.

Anyway, the purpose of the read and write pointers is twofold. They make it possible, first of all, to have random access to a file, in order to read or write at arbitrary positions. This is done, as we said, when a position is specified explicitly in the file I/O functions.

The other purpose of keeping track of the current position (specifically, the read position) is to give a well-defined meaning to the CHARS( ) and LINES( ) functions. CHARS( ) returns the number of characters in the file that have not yet been read, i.e., the number of characters from the current read position to the end of the file. For instance, when a file is first opened, the value of CHARS( ) should be the size of the file. Similarly, LINES( ) returns the number of lines from the current read position to the end of the file.

It is worth noting at this point that these concepts are meaningful for files, but not for most of the other file-like things that may be accessed by the file I/O functions disguised as files. Such things include the user's keyboard and screen, devices like a printer, and *pipes* (which allow communication with another program as if it were a file). So our discussion here is essentially "file chauvinist." We speak as if the I/O functions always deal with files, and as if it is always possible to do something reasonable with a file. It must be recognized, however, that this point of view can't be maintained consistently when working with nonfiles. And what is even worse, there is no means in standard REXX of even detecting whether a name refers to an actual file, as opposed to a device, a pipe, or whatever. Indeed, many operating systems, in an effort to promote *device independence,* go out of their way to conceal this information from programs.

Cowlishaw's *The REXX Language* avoids most of these messy issues. It makes some attempt to distinguish between *persistent streams* and *transient streams*. However, these terms aren't defined, except by example. A persistent stream is, essentially, a file. The term implies that the object persists, so that one can reread it and get the same data, unless it has been explicitly changed. Such a thing also admits having a well-defined beginning and end, so that the notions of read and write pointers make sense. A transient stream, on the other hand, cannot be read or written at random and does not have a well-defined beginning and end.

You should also recognize that even in the case of a file, the underlying operating system may not permit random access. And even if random access is possible, it is often the case that such access can be done by byte number or by line number, but not both. Those file systems which view a file as a sequence of bytes generally allow random access by byte number. They do not usually allow random access by line number, nor can they report how many lines remain unread in a file. Similarly, if the file system views a file as a sequence of lines, it probably permits random read access by line number. It may or may not allow random write access by line number, and if it does, it may not allow change in the size of a given line, or it may delete all lines after a new one is written in the middle of a file. File systems of this sort rarely allow random access by byte number.

REXX does not provide any mechanism for indicating to a program what types of random file access are permitted. Your program is expected to know what is reasonable to do. If the program must be portable across systems, it should be aware of the environment it is running in, if only to provide warnings when it can't do something that would not be supported.

CLOSING A FILE

The operation that is the inverse of opening a file is *closing* a file. Several important purposes are served by this operation:

If new data has been written to the file, the operating system can be notified that the data is complete and should be *committed* to permanent storage. The system may assign a *last modification date* to the file at this time.

Restrictions on sharing the file which would inhibit access by other processes are removed.

File buffers (if any) may be released back to the operating system.

File *handles* (which may be a limited resource) can be released for reuse.

Because these functions, or close equivalents, are almost always needed, most operating systems support the concept of closing a file. In particular, you should never assume your data is safely written to disk so that it can be accessed by another program until the file has been closed.

Moreover, it is generally not possible to automatically or implicitly close a file when your program is done with it. The request to close a file is the way that the program says it is done with a file. Of course, most implementations will close all open files when a REXX program returns to the operating system, but it is very bad practice to depend on this. In a long-running program, quite a large amount of time may pass before a program terminates. During that time, an open file may be unavailable to other processes, and it may even be lost completely if the computer crashes. In the case of files destined for a printer, the operating system may wait until the file is closed until printing can begin. Yet another consideration is that REXX programs frequently invoke other programs or system commands. A file needed by such programs may be unavailable or incomplete unless it has been closed first, leading to mysterious errors and possible data loss. To avoid all this, just observe the simple rule: always close files as soon as you are finished with them.

REXX does have a means for explicitly closing a file, though it is unintuitive and a little obscure. Instead of simply having a function to close a file, REXX provides that when either the CHAROUT() or LINEOUT() function is used with only the file name as an argument, then the file will be closed. This applies even to files that have been used only for input, and even to files that are read-only. The STREAM() function may, in various implementations, also provide a way to close a file, but any such capability is not standardized.

LINE-ORIENTED FILE I/O FUNCTIONS

We'll take a closer look at the line-oriented functions first. They are, probably, the most commonly used, because they work well with the kind of text files one tends to deal with most often in REXX. There is no completely consistent definition of what a *text* file is which applies to all systems. In general, however, it is thought of as a file consisting of a sequence of lines of *text*. These lines usually (though not necessarily) will consist entirely of printable characters. Text files are usually created and maintained with a *text editor* (naturally enough). They are used for such things as program source code, electronic mail, and general program data input and output. On systems which internally store files as a sequence of bytes, the individual lines of a text file are generally delimited by specific control characters embedded in the file.

LINEIN() is the line-oriented input function. Its syntax is

```
LINEIN([name], [line-number], [line-count])
```

LINEIN() returns the next line of the file, starting at the current read position or the position specified by line-number. If the current read position is at the end of the file, LINEIN() returns a null string. When lines of a file are delimited by characters embedded in the file, the final delimiting characters are not included at the end of a line. Examples:

```
line = linein("PROFILE EXEC A")/* next line */
line = linein()/* read line from standard input */
```

All of LINEIN()'s arguments are optional. Name is the name of the file. Depending on capabilities of the operating system, name may actually refer to a device, such as a serial I/O port, which is being simulated as a file. If name is omitted or a null string, LINEIN() reads from the *default input stream*. The nature of the default input stream is system-dependent. In CMS it is always the keyboard. In MS-DOS, OS/2, and Unix, it is the *standard input* file, which might be the keyboard, a file, a device, or even another program (through pipes).

Line-number specifies the relative line number in the file at which the read should begin. REXX numbers file lines starting at 1. The default, if line-number is not specified, is to begin reading at the current read position. If calls to CHARIN() have been used, it is possible that the current read position may not be exactly at the beginning of a line, so that LINEIN() may not return a full line.

Furthermore, not all file systems are capable of supporting a read that starts at an arbitrary line number. In particular, when a file is organized as a sequence of characters and lines are delimited by a particular character sequence, the capability to begin reading at an arbitrary line number would be very inefficient to implement, so is not usually possible.

Line-count may be 0 or 1. It is 1 by default, and specifies that one line is to be read. A value of 0 indicates that no input is to be done, but the read pointer is to be moved to the line specified in line-number (if possible). In this case, LINEIN() returns a null string.

LINEIN() may behave differently with input sources other than files. A file has a definite location called the *end of file,* beyond which LINEIN() will return a null string. However, the end of file concept does not usually apply to devices, the keyboard, or other programs, though the operating system may provide a means of signaling end of file for some of these. In cases of this sort, LINEIN() may simply stop and wait until more input is available rather than returning a null string.

Positioning to a specific line number is also generally not possible for input sources other than files.

There are no standard REXX functions which can be used to determine whether a given name actually refers to a file, whether an *end of file* can be recognized, or whether random positioning by line number is possible.

Although LINEIN() returns a null string when the end of file is reached, this is not a reliable way of determining that there is no more input, since a file may very well contain null lines that are not at the end of the file. REXX provides the LINES() function to handle detection of the end of file. Its syntax is

```
LINES([name])
```

LINES() returns the number of complete or partial lines not yet read in the file specified by name. If name is omitted or a null string, the default input stream is assumed. LINES() determines the number of lines remaining in terms of the number of lines from the current read pointer to the end of the file. If the file has not yet been opened, LINES() will open the file and return the number of lines in it. If the end of file has been read, so that the read pointer is after the last line, LINES() returns 0.

Because not all file systems permit efficient counting of lines (as with files that are a sequence of bytes and lines separated by special control characters), LINES() may simply return 1 to indicate that there is more input to be read.

When LINES() is used with an input stream other than a file, such as a device, a pipe, or the keyboard, the result is harder to predict. Usually LINES() will return 0 if an input line isn't currently available. That is generally the same case in which LINEIN() would wait for input to become available.

LINEOUT() is the line-oriented output function. Its syntax is

```
LINEOUT([name], [data], [line-number])
```

LINEOUT() writes one line of data to the file, and returns 0 if it was successful. Otherwise it returns the number of lines not completely written (perhaps because the output disk was full or not ready). As usual, name is the name of the file (or device, etc.) to be written to. Data is the line of data to be written. Line delimiter characters, if used by the file system, should not normally be included in data, because they will be added automatically. Examples:

```
call lineout , 'Hello world!'/* standard output */
```

```
call lineout 'c:\autoexec.bat', 'set temp=d:\'
```

For file systems that support random file access by line number, line-number is the relative line number, starting with 1, where data is to be written. Even if a file system supports this kind of file access, it may cause loss of data beyond the new line being written, especially if the new line is not the same length as the one being replaced. Be sure you understand how your file system handles this situation.

If name is omitted or a null string LINEOUT( ) writes to the default output stream. The nature of the default output stream is system-dependent. In CMS it is always the terminal. In MS-DOS, OS/2, and Unix, it is the *standard output* file, which might be the screen, a file, a device, or even another program (through pipes).

If both data and line-number are omitted, the specified file is closed as described earlier. If data is omitted, but not line-number, the write pointer is set to the specified line (if the file system supports this). If line-number is omitted, which is by far the most common case, the new line is written at the current output position as specified by the write pointer, which is normally the end of the file.

The simplest type of file I/O that is done in REXX often involves reading a line, processing it in some way, and producing output. For instance, a simple program that copies one file to another might be no more than

```
parse arg input output
do while lines(input) > 0
   call lineout output, linein(input)
end
call lineout input
call lineout output
```

This is a just a read-process-output loop, where there is no processing to speak of. It can be elaborated upon to handle almost any situation that involves reading lines sequentially from an input file, processing each in some way, and writing to an output file. The processing might be searching for specific words (as in the WORDFIND program discussed in Chap. 3), reformatting the input lines, computing totals of input data, or whatever.

CHARACTER-ORIENTED FILE I/O FUNCTIONS

The character-oriented functions work equally well with *text* or *binary* files. Of course, if the file system does not permit character-level access to files, the character-oriented functions may be unsupported or only partially supported. These functions return the exact data which is in the file, without translation or interpretation. In particular, special control characters used to signify line end or end of file are returned along with ordinary data characters.

It should be possible to process any type of file with the character-oriented functions. This includes database files, executable programs, word processor files, or whatever. Your program is responsible for knowing the detailed low-level format of the file, however.

CHARIN() is the character-oriented input function. Its syntax is

```
CHARIN([name], [character-number], [character-count])
```

CHARIN() returns the next character-count characters of the file, starting at the current read position or the position specified by character-number. If the current read position is at the end of the file, CHARIN() returns a null string. Examples:

```
zip_code = charin('address.dat', pos, 5)
call charin file, 1000, 0 /* position at byte #1000 */
```

All of CHARIN()'s arguments are optional. Name is the name of the file. If name is omitted or a null string, it is assumed to be the default input stream.

Character-number specifies the relative character number in the file at which the read should begin. REXX numbers file characters starting at 1. The default, if character-number is not specified, is to begin reading at the current read position. Not all file systems are capable of supporting a read that starts at an arbitrary character number. This is frequently true with file systems that primarily regard a file as a sequence of lines.

Character-count may be any nonnegative whole number. It is 1 by default. A value of 0 indicates that no input is to be done, but the read pointer is to be moved to the line specified in character-number (if possible). In this case, CHARIN() returns a null string.

Like LINEIN(), CHARIN() may behave differently with input sources other than files. A file has a definite location called the *end of file,* beyond which CHARIN() will return a null string. In cases where end of file is undefined, CHARIN() may simply stop and wait until more input is available rather than returning with fewer characters than requested. Positioning to a specific character number is also generally not possible for input sources other than files.

CHARS() is the character-oriented analog of LINES(). It may be used to determine the number of characters left to read in a file. Ordinarily it is used simply to determine whether the end of file has been reached. The syntax is

```
CHARS([name])
```

`CHARS()` returns the number of characters not yet read in the file specified by name. If name is omitted or a null string, the default input stream is assumed. `CHARS()` determines the number of characters remaining in terms of the number of characters from the current read pointer to the end of the file. If the file has not yet been opened, `CHARS()` will open the file and return the number of characters in it. If the end of file has been reached, so that the read pointer is after the last character, `CHARS()` returns 0. `CHARS()` may return 1 if the end of file has not been reached on a file, but the exact number of characters to be read cannot be efficiently determined.

As with `LINES()`, when `CHARS()` is used with an input stream other than a file, such as a device, a pipe, or the keyboard, results are harder to predict. Usually `CHARS()` will return 0 if no characters are currently available, even though more may be added later to the end of the input stream.

It is not a good idea to use `CHARS()` to detect the end of file when input is being done with the `LINEIN()` function. The reason is that in some implementations `LINEIN()` may stop returning nonnull lines without actually reading past the end of file. (This can happen with files where certain control characters are used to indicate the end of file even though more data actually remains to be read.) As a rule of thumb, for reasons like this, it is a good idea not to mix the line-oriented and the character-oriented functions, unless you are sure of what you are doing.

`CHAROUT()` is the character-oriented output function. Its syntax is

```
CHAROUT([name], [data], [character-number])
```

`CHAROUT()` writes the specified data to the file, and returns either 0, if it was successful, or the number of characters which couldn't be written if not successful (perhaps because the output disk was full or not ready). As usual, name is the name of the file (or device, etc.) to be written to. Data is the string to be written. Examples:

```
call charout , 'Enter account code:'
     /* display prompt on standard output */
call charout 'image.dat', databits, location
```

For file systems that support random file access by character number, character-number is the relative character number, starting with 1, where data is to be written.

If name is omitted or a null string, `CHAROUT()` writes to the *default output stream*. The nature of the default output stream is system-dependent. In CMS it is always the terminal. In MS-DOS, OS/2, and Unix, it is the standard output file, which might be the screen, a file, a device, or even another program (through pipes).

If both data and character-number are omitted, the specified file is closed as described earlier. If data is omitted, but not character-number, the write pointer is set to the specified character position (if the file system supports this). If character-number is omitted, which is by far the most common case, the data is written at the current output position as specified by the write pointer, which is normally the end of the file.

COMMUNICATION WITH THE USER

There are no additional functions needed for communicating with the user of a program by means of simple dialogs. Everything that can be done along these lines in standard REXX can be done with the facilities already described. However, there are a few special considerations to be noted, and some instructions that provide a little cosmetic simplification.

Ordinarily, and by default, the standard input stream is the user's keyboard, and the standard output stream is the user's screen. The standard input and output streams can be specified in any of the file I/O functions simply by omitting the name argument or (on some systems) by making it a null string. It is not necessarily true that the default input and output streams are the user's terminal, since most environments permit streams to be redirected to files, pipes, or devices. (We will go into this a little further when we discuss *filters*.) But your program has no general means of determining whether its standard input and output have been redirected, so for the sake of generality it should assume that they have not been. That is, you should assume the standard I/O streams are connected to the user's terminal. To emphasize this, we will refer to these as the terminal I/O streams.

There are limitations on what can be done with the terminal streams. The main thing is, you cannot position randomly in them, so you should not specify character or line numbers in the I/O functions. There are no meaningful read or write pointers associated with the terminal input and output. However, as a special case, the CHARS() and LINES() functions will return a value of 1 for the standard input stream, to indicate that data may be available. Finally, you do not need to close the terminal streams. In fact, it is a good idea not to, since doing so may prevent other, independent parts of a program from doing terminal I/O.

REXX provides the SAY instruction as a shorthand form of LINEOUT(). In other words,

```
SAY expression
```

is almost fully equivalent to

```
CALL LINEOUT , expression
```

We say "almost," because `expression` in both cases is optional, but the results of omitting it are different in the two cases. If `SAY` is used by itself without an expression, it displays a null line on the terminal, as if the value of the expression were null. On the other hand, `LINEOUT()` with a null expression will display a blank line, but with an omitted expression it will close the terminal input stream.

It is customary in REXX programs to use `SAY` for terminal output. This saves typing a few characters and it makes the operation of the program a little easier for a reader to follow.

The `PULL` instruction is in some sense the analog of `SAY` in that it provides a simplified means of reading a line of input from the terminal. Unlike `SAY`, however, it is not equivalent to one single I/O function. In the first place, `PULL` is really a shorthand form of `PARSE`, so that

```
PULL template
```

is equivalent to

```
PARSE UPPER PULL template
```

In both cases, template is a `PARSE` template, which could perform elaborate input parsing. But when your program is doing terminal input, you probably don't want to make the user type things in a rigid format to match a complex template, so usually the template is just a variable name to which all input is assigned. So `PULL` saves a little typing over the equivalent `PARSE` form, but unfortunately it forces all input to uppercase. Not having to deal with mixed case can make it easier for a program to interpret user input, but it can also get in the way too.

There's another complication with `PULL`, in that before it reads from the terminal input stream, it will attempt to read a line from the external data queue. The external data queue is a separate REXX mechanism for storing data temporarily in a scratch area, and it will be discussed in detail in the next chapter. It is often used for communication between REXX programs (in the absence of any standard REXX means for sharing variables). And, in some implementations, the external data queue may be usable as a surrogate for terminal input. This usage of the queue is why `PULL` and `PARSE PULL` are defined to take input from the queue before they read from the terminal.

You can use the queue to prepare data in one REXX program that will be read as input by another REXX program called from the first, provided the called program uses PULL or PARSE PULL to read input. In this way the called program can be written so that it will accept input from the terminal if there is none in the queue. However, sometimes you will want to force a program to read input from the terminal, regardless of the contents of the queue. The way to do this is to use the I/O functions CHARIN() or LINEIN() directly, because they are defined to read only from a specified input stream (such as the terminal input stream), and never from the external data queue.

There is even a form of PARSE which recognizes this use of LINEIN() to bypass the data queue:

```
PARSE LINEIN template
```

is defined to be the same as

```
PARSE VALUE LINEIN() WITH template
```

EXAMPLE: BINARY SEARCH OF SORTED FILES

Our first extended example of file I/O to do something moderately interesting is an illustration of the binary search algorithm. This is a technique of searching certain sequential files that is much more efficient than a brute force search through the whole file. The technique depends on the assumption that the file has already been sorted (in ascending order, let's say) on the value of the key that we are searching for. It operates by first examining the record in the middle of the file. If that is not the record we want, we can then at least be sure that the record we're looking for must be either in the first half of the file or the second, if it is present at all, based on whether or not the desired key is lower or higher than the one in the record we examined. The process is repeated as many times as necessary, and each time the size of the portion of the file in which the desired record can be found is reduced by half. This is why it is called a *binary* search. It is a very fast process. A file of 1000 records can be fully searched for a record with a desired key in at most 10 steps, since $2^{10} = 1024$.

Here's a REXX program for doing a binary search:

```
/* do a binary search of file for specified key */
/* returns record number of line containing the key */
binsearch: procedure
parse arg file, key, lrecl
size = stream(file,'c','query size')
```

```
if size = '' then do
    say "File not found:" file
    return 0
    end
records = size % lrecl
high = records
low = 1
do while low <= high
    mid = (high + low) % 2
    call charin file, (mid - 1) * lrecl + 1, 0
    line = linein(file)
    test = word(line,1)
    if test < key then
        low = mid + 1
    else if test > key then
        high = mid - 1
    else
        leave
    end
call lineout file
if low > high then do
    say "Key '"key"' not found in" file
    return 0
    end
else
    return mid
```

The program is coded as an internal procedure which is meant to be called with three arguments. The first is the file name, the second is the key to be searched for, and the third is the *logical record length* of the file. To make the example interesting, we have assumed that the file system stores files as a stream of bytes, and record boundaries are marked by control characters contained within the file. It is further assumed that all lines have the same length. The logical record length is the length of each line plus the number of delimiters per line. (For instance, in MS-DOS or OS/2, there are two delimiters per line: a carriage return and a line feed.)

The example calls the STREAM( ) built-in function to determine the size (in characters) of the file. The arguments of the STREAM( ) function are not fully specified by the language. Here we have used arguments understood by Personal REXX and IBM's OS/2 REXX. Other implementations must use some other technique to obtain the size of the file. Since this is the size in characters, we have to divide by the logical record length to get the number of lines in the file. We used an integer divide here ("%") to be sure we have an integral number to work with. (This allows for the presence of overhead characters such as "end of file" that are not part of any line.)

Two variables, low and high, hold the top and bottom of the range of lines between which the desired record can be located. The loop is performed as long as low does not exceed high. It must terminate eventually, since the range is reduced by at least one line each time (and usually much more). The variable mid is the number of the record we will examine next. The call to CHARIN() positions the file in terms of a relative byte number, since we assume the file system does not support positioning by line number. Notice that we have to be careful with byte numbering, since REXX numbers files with the first character being 1 rather than 0. No data is actually read by CHARIN(), since the third argument is 0.

Having positioned the read pointer, the line we want to examine can be read with LINEIN(). For simplicity we have assumed that the first word of the line contains the key value on which the file has been sorted. A more general routine would allow the key to be located in any given position on the line. The loop terminates when the value in the line is neither higher nor lower than the key being searched for. If the key wasn't found, the loop will terminate because low became greater than high. In that case we return 0, which is not a valid line number, since we assume lines are numbered starting with 1. Otherwise we return the number of the line where the key was found.

EXAMPLE: MAKING A FILE INDEX

In a file system where a file is a sequence of bytes and records are separated by embedded control characters, there is a problem in representing a file as a sequence of items that can vary in size up to some large number if we want efficient access to each item. If we want to allow each item to be up to 64,000 characters long (for instance), the naive approach would be to create a file with logical records each 64,000 characters long. If the average item (record) is much shorter than this, we will have an exorbitant amount of overhead.

One simple way to deal with this situation is to store the data as two separate files. One file contains the actual data, and the second file is an index to it. Only the index file needs to have a fixed record length for efficient access. The length of each record in the index can be fairly short. Let us suppose the maximum size of the data file will be 1 gigabyte (1 billion bytes). For simplicity, let's suppose the limit is actually 999,999,999 bytes, so that a maximum of nine digits are needed to store the relative byte number with the default NUMERIC DIGITS 9. Five digits suffice to store the size of an item. The relative byte address and size of an item will be stored in an index record in character form, so each index record needs to be 14 bytes long (plus, say, two more bytes for delimiters).

We could use this index technique for other purposes as well. In fact, this is how databases are often implemented. The primary data records are stored in a main data file in the order they are added. The data records can be of either fixed or varying length. As many index files as desired can be built which represent the primary data sorted on different key values. Each index record would contain the key value and the relative byte address of the corresponding data record in the main file. Such index files can be searched by a binary search as discussed above, allowing fast random access to the primary data records based on various key values. About the only drawback to this technique as just outlined is that such index files have to be rebuilt entirely every time a new data record is added. It would be possible to go a step further and store the index files as *B+ trees* to allow for efficient modification of the indices. This would still be easy to implement in REXX, but a full discussion of this method would take us too far afield.

Instead, we'll look at one of the most elementary uses of an index file, where we just want an efficient way to access variable size data records by record number. The application is a "cookie" program that displays a random fortune cookie fortune each time it is invoked. Here it is:

```
/* display fortune cookies */

datafile = 'fortune.cookies'
indexfile = 'fortune.cookie.index'
lrecl = 16

count = stream(indexfile, 'c', 'query size') % lrecl
item = random(1, count)
call charin indexfile, (item - 1) * lrecl + 1, 0
index_record = linein(indexfile)
call lineout indexfile
parse var index_record rba 10 size

bytes_read = 0
call charin datafile, rba, 0
do while bytes_read < size
    line = linein(datafile)
    bytes_read = bytes_read + length(line) + 2
    say line
    end
call lineout datafile
```

That's all there is to it. Most of the details are similar to those of the previous example. Notice (again) that there are 14 bytes of information in each index record (a nine-digit and a five-digit number), but we have assumed two extra bytes per line for delimiters. Actually, we could dispense with the delimiter characters. It all depends on how the index file is maintained. As illustrated, the index file could be updated with a line-oriented text editor which will assume the line delimiters are present. In fact, editing the index would not make much sense, because it would be very tedious to put in file offsets and item sizes by hand. Instead, indexes should be created and maintained by a program, and we'll illustrate this shortly. The program can simply omit line delimiter characters. In that case, we would have to modify the above example by setting `lrecl` to 14, and replacing the line where we read an index record with

```
index_record = charin(indexfile, , lrecl)
```

We continue to assume that line delimiters are present in the data file, which requires us to account for them in the loop where we are reading a single item, by adding two to the length of each line.

Let's look at how to maintain the index. We shall assume that items to be added to the data file will be created with a text editor. Initially, each item is contained in its own file. We will have a REXX program that appends each item file to the main data file and updates the index. The main data file then winds up looking something like this:

```
A journey of 1000 miles must begin with a single step.
The moving finger writes; and, having writ,
Moves on: nor all thy piety nor wit
Shall lure it back to cancel half a line.
From listening comes wisdom, and from speaking
repentance.
...
```

Notice that there is no indication in the file where one item ends and the next begins. All that information is contained in the index.

More interesting as an example is the program that adds new fortune cookies to the file and the index. We suppose the new item is contained in a file by itself, whose name is to be supplied to the update program. We need to obtain the size of the data file in order to know the offset of the new item and the size of the item; these two pieces of information will be appended to the index. We are going to assume now that the index file does not contain embedded delimiter characters. This will help reduce its size a little, but preclude us from using an ordinary line editor to access it. Here is the update program:

```
/* add to fortune cookie database */

parse arg new_cookie .
```

```
datafile = 'fortune.cookies'
indexfile = 'fortune.cookie.index'
lrecl = 14

item_size = stream(new_cookie, 'c', 'query size')
item_offset = stream(datafile, 'c', 'query size') + 1
index_size = stream(indexfile, 'c', 'query size')
index_record = right(item_offset, 9) ||,
    right(item_size, 5)
call charout indexfile, index_record, index_size + 1
call charout indexfile

call charout datafile, , item_offset
do while lines(new_cookie) > 0
    call lineout datafile, linein(new_cookie)
    end
call lineout datafile
call lineout new_cookie
```

We had to use CHAROUT( ) in this example, instead of LINEOUT( ), to add the index record to the index file in order not to have line delimiter characters inserted. Also, we were very careful to use CHAROUT( ) to specify an offset in both the index and data files at which writing is to begin. This may be redundant, since any reasonable REXX implementation will set the write pointer initially to the end of an existing file. This is so that data will be appended to the end instead of overwriting the beginning of the file. But it's better to be safe than sorry.

There's another approach to handling this particular application we should mention. The main data file could be assumed to contain explicit separators between each item, perhaps a short string of asterisks. The data file could be maintained entirely with a text editor, and the person who maintains it would manually add a separator every time a new item is added. Then a REXX program could be written that reads the main data file and builds an entire index each time. Although this approach entails a great deal of extra processing every time an addition is made, it does have the advantage that the index can always be reconstructed easily if it gets damaged. The details of implementing this method are left as an exercise for the reader.

EXAMPLE: WRITING "FILTERS" IN REXX

To conclude this chapter, let's look at a different sort of example, a *filter*. The WORDFIND program in Chap. 3 was an example of a filter. We mentioned that this was a type of program which originated in Unix. A filter reads from a standard input file and writes to a standard output file. Of course, it can read and write any number of other files, too. Such programs are called filters, because in Unix and other operating systems that support the concept of pipes, a filter program can be inserted between two other programs. The filter reads its input from the output of the first program, and it writes its output to the input of the second program. How this is expressed depends on the specific operating system. In Unix, MS-DOS, and OS/2, "|" is the symbol for a pipe from one program to another, so a composite command might be written

```
first | filter | second
```

(Note that this use of "|" has nothing to do with the REXX use of "|" as the logical or operation. If the composite command were used in a REXX program, the whole thing should be enclosed in quotation marks.)

A very common example of a filter is a sort program. If the program called second expects its input to be sorted in some way, but the first program does not sort its output, then inserting sort between them solves the problem:

```
first | sort | second
```

The philosophy of using filters is that each filter program should be as simple as possible. A filter program should read from standard input, perform one elementary operation, and write results to standard output. Filters can then be combined in a large number of ways to perform a wide variety of more complex processing tasks.

Filters are easy to write in REXX. We'll take a very simple example here just to illustrate the mechanics. The example just deletes all blank lines from an input file:

```
/* DELBLANK - Delete all blank lines in a file. */
arg infile outfile
do while lines(infile)
   line = linein(infile)
   if line \= '' then
     call lineout outfile, line
   end
call lineout outfile
call lineout infile
```

If this program is invoked with pipes for both input and output, then it will not actually have any arguments. Therefore, infile and outfile will be null strings. So, when they are used elsewhere in the program, they will refer to the standard input and output files respectively, which is just what we want.

That's really all there is to writing a filter. The nice thing about how this works in REXX is that we could supply actual file names if we wanted, instead of using pipes. A command line like

```
delblank original_file deblanked_file
```

would work just as well. (The file names should be different, of course. And if the second file already exists, it will be appended with the results rather than being overwritten.) And just for a little more redundancy, we could have used operating system *redirection* notation to accomplish the same thing:

```
delblank <original_file >deblanked_file
```

This notation, as used in OS/2, MS-DOS, and Unix, means that `original_file` is to be the standard input and `deblanked_file` is to be the standard output. Again, the REXX program will work with null strings rather than the actual file names, but the result will be the same.

The External Data Queue

The external data queue is a curious hybrid. It is a concept that belongs partly to REXX and partly to the operating system. Its function is partly I/O, partly interprocess communication, and partly "other."

Conceptually, you may think of the queue (as we'll call it for short) as a temporary string storage area. Even the metaphors used to describe operations to the queue are a bit mixed. In the horizontal queue metaphor, strings can be added at the front or the back of the queue, but they can be removed only from the front. Sometimes a vertical metaphor is employed, and the queue is called a *stack*. In these terms, it is like a *pushdown stack,* and strings can be added at the top or at the bottom, but they can be removed only from the top.

The command names for queue operations are derived from both metaphors. A string is added to the top (front) of the queue with the PUSH instruction and to the end (bottom) with the QUEUE instruction. Don't let the mixing of metaphors throw you. It's the same thing either way you look at it. Strings can be removed from the top (front) of the queue with the PULL instruction. (Since there's only one removal operation, REXX decided to be noncommittal as to metaphors, so it is not called either POP or DEQUEUE.)

PULL is really shorthand for the instruction PARSE UPPER PULL. Therefore it can use a general PARSE template to parse the retrieved string into separate variables. Unfortunately, because of the UPPER option, it mangles strings into uppercase, so you may wind up using the more verbose form PARSE PULL most of the time, unless you don't care whether strings come out of the queue in the same form they went in.

QUEUE is a first-in, first-out operation (FIFO), in the sense that if you repeatedly QUEUE strings at the end of the queue, they will be removed by PULL in the same order as they were added by QUEUE. PUSH, on the other hand, is a last-in, first-out operation (LIFO), in that if you repeatedly PUSH strings on the top of the queue, then they will be retrieved in the exact reverse order in which they were added by PUSH. If you mix QUEUE and PUSH, it's a little harder to keep track, but not too bad, since in either case new strings are added only at either one end of the queue or the other, never in the middle.

Strings in the queue generally retain their identity. That is, regardless of the lengths of the strings or their contents, they are removed from the queue one at a time in exactly the same form in which they were added. They are not combined or concatenated as a result of being added to the queue.

To complete the roster of REXX facilities for working with the queue there is one built-in function, QUEUED(), which takes no arguments and returns the numbers of strings currently in the queue.

USAGE OF THE QUEUE

The queue can be employed for a wide variety of purposes. It is very commonly used as a way to pass data to and from subroutines. Although data is usually passed to a subroutine through the arguments of the routine, there may be implementation limits on how much data can be passed this way. For instance, REXX in CMS allows only 10 arguments to any subroutine. Other implementations may not have such draconian limits, but still impose some because of limits on the size of single clauses. The stack, on the other hand, is usually limited only by the amount of available memory. So, if you want to pass all the text stored in lines of the array text. to a subroutine, you might use

```
do i = 1 to n
   queue text.i
   end
call text_routine n
...
text_routine: procedure
do i = 1 to arg(1)
   parse pull line
   /* process "line" */
```

```
       . . .
       end
   return
```

This avoids limitations on how much can be passed through arguments to a procedure, since only the number of strings needs to be passed. But it also saves a lot of typing. Imagine the effort involved in typing out all the arguments you would need if there were 100 lines of text.:

```
   call text_routine text.1, text.2, text.3, text.4,,
       /* etc.! */
```

Also, there isn't any way in REXX to code a single subroutine call with a varying number of arguments—you would have to pass the maximum number every time.

The stack is at least as useful for returning data from subroutines. REXX definitely limits a subroutine to at most one return value. If you need to provide more, whether two or a very large number, the queue is a good way to do it. For instance, suppose you want to have a subroutine that returns a list of file names. Perhaps it is a list of all file names which match some name pattern involving *wildcard* characters. Then a routine like

```
   get_file_names: procedure
   parse arg pattern
   name = get_first_name(pattern)
   do i = 1 by 1 while name \= ''
       queue name
       name = get_next_name()
       end
   return i - 1
```

might do it. The subroutine returns the number of names found as its value, but the names themselves are returned in the queue. (Get_first_name() and get_next_name() are hypothetical, lower-level procedures for reading the file directory and retrieving one name at a time that matches the pattern.)

We should note that there is one obvious alternative to the use of the queue for passing a large number of strings into and out of subroutines. That alternative is a compound variable array. In this approach, you assign all inputs or outputs to successive elements of the array. You can pass the array name (or names) to the subroutine, but there is a little awkwardness in that you need to use the VALUE() function to read and write elements of the array when the name of the stem is passed as an argument. This is avoided if you can use some conventional names for the input and output stems, perhaps ARGS. and RESULTS..

Indeed, compound variable arrays have a lot in common with the queue for handling simple lists of strings. Compound variables actually provide a more powerful tool, since they permit random access rather than just access to the front element in the queue. A queue could be fully simulated with a compound variable, but it would be extra work to keep track of the indices of the front and back elements of the queue. So the queue is more easily used when just a simple access pattern is required and you don't want to bother making up a new array name. Also, when the subroutines being called are external, the queue must be used for passing data, since external REXX procedures can't share variables.

This comparison of the relative merits of compound variables and the queue points up one aspect you need to be careful about when using the queue. That is, there is only one queue. Indeed, it is called the *external* data queue in part because it is external to any single REXX program. Within a nested set of external REXX procedures that call each other, there is just one queue which is the same for all of them. This is a great advantage in that the queue can be used, as above, to pass data into and out of subroutines (an advantage not shared by compound variables). But there is the potential disadvantage that the queue already contains data placed there by one routine at the time another routine needs to use the queue for a different purpose.

Dealing with this problem is one of the reasons you might use the queue in a LIFO manner with PUSH instead of QUEUE. Using PUSH is somewhat harder, because it often requires you to do processing backwards. But it provides a way to share the one external data queue for several purposes. The earlier example of passing strings to a subroutine could easily be rewritten as follows to use PUSH instead of QUEUE:

```
do i = n to 1 by -1
   push text.i
   end
call text_routine n
...
text_routine: procedure
do i = 1 to arg(1)
   parse pull line
   /* process "line" */
   ...
   end
return
```

All that needed to change was to run the loop index backwards. The subroutine retrieves the strings in the same order as before. (We presume that the order was important.) The difference here is that data is added only to the front of the queue, so that any strings already present will not be disturbed—as long as we are careful to read no more than were added.

This problem of having to be careful about data already present in the queue is one reason for not using the QUEUED( ) function to take a certain shortcut. You might be tempted to think that it is not necessary to pass separately the number of strings passed into or out of a subroutine via the queue. After all, the subroutine could simply call QUEUED( ) to determine how many strings there were. But this approach gets into trouble if unrelated data has already been placed in the queue.

Nevertheless, QUEUED( ) can be used to let you program defensively in using the queue. Consider the case of a subroutine which places information in the queue (LIFO), and the subroutine must return some value other than the number of strings added to the queue, a return code perhaps. You can still determine how many strings were added this way:

```
old_count = queued( )
if queue_sub( ) = 0 then do/* success */
   count = queued( ) - old_count
   do i = 1 to count
     /* process queue items */
     ...
     end
   end
```

RELATION OF THE EXTERNAL DATA QUEUE AND THE STANDARD INPUT STREAM

PULL and PARSE PULL are not purely queue access instructions. They are defined so that if the queue happens to be empty, then they will take a line from the standard input stream—and they will wait if none is available (e.g., when reading from the keyboard). The reason for this is that the queue can be viewed as a surrogate for the standard input stream, if you think of PULL as primarily an I/O instruction rather than a queue instruction.

In fact, if you consistently write REXX programs so that they use PULL or PARSE PULL for input, then you can at any time decide to call the same program from another REXX program, and provide through the queue some or all of the input it requires.

Perhaps, for instance, you have an external program called MOVE-FILES which asks interactively for a list of file names and a destination.

It might start like this:

```
/* file mover */
say "Enter names to move, end with null line."
do i=1 by 1
  parse pull name.i
  if name.i = '' then
    leave
  end
say "Enter destination of move."
parse pull destination
...
```

Then you could run this from the system command line, and it would prompt you for the information it needs. Or you could call it from another REXX program and supply all the information ahead of time:

```
push new_directory_name
push
do i = n to 1 by -1
  push file_name.i
  end
call movefiles
```

Notice that we have added to the queue LIFO with PUSH, as a precaution against the possibility that the queue already contains data. PUSH with no string specified put a null line into the queue at the appropriate place to end the list of file names.

In this case, the way MOVEFILES was written allows it to be called from another REXX program without having to disturb data already in the queue. If you regularly write REXX programs that use PULL or PARSE PULL to do input, you should be cautious about calling such programs from others that may use the stack for something else.

PULL and PARSE PULL are the only REXX input facilities that use the queue and the standard input stream together in this way. Everything else that does input (CHARIN( ), LINEIN( ), PARSE LINEIN, and interactive tracing) reads only from the standard input stream and ignores the queue.

RELATION OF THE EXTERNAL DATA QUEUE AND THE OPERATING SYSTEM

In the VM/CMS operating system, where REXX originated, the external data queue is an integral part of the operating system rather than exclusively a REXX feature. This means that it is possible for programs written in any language to read and write to the queue in the same way that REXX does. Furthermore, the standard system input

function behaves like PARSE PULL in that it will take a line from the
front of the queue, if there is any, before reading from the keyboard. As
a result, when most CMS programs are run from REXX they can have
their input supplied through the queue without any special action on
the program's part. Any program can also add to the queue in the way
PUSH and QUEUE do, but this requires explicit programming.

Many CMS utilities have command-line options to tell them to place
their output into the stack instead of writing it to the screen. These
utilities can then be used from REXX and their output interpreted by
the REXX program in order to automate many procedures. However,
because of the kind of confusion that can arise when the queue is used
for several purposes simultaneously, CMS utilities have gradually
added the ability to write their output directly to REXX variables.

In addition, CMS provides extra capabilities in the queue that help
alleviate such contention problems. Primarily it adds the concepts of
separate *buffers* in the stack. When a new buffer is created, strings
added by PUSH and QUEUE go only into that buffer, as if it were the entire
queue. This solves an error-handling problem that arises frequently
with the queue. Namely, if a program wants to terminate prematurely
because it has encountered some error condition, it is a very highly recommended practice to remove any data that may have been placed in
the queue. A command is provided specifically for the purpose of delet-
ing only the most recently created buffer in the queue, instead of the
whole thing (which would also be an antisocial form of program behavior). This is most important in systems like CMS which funnel most terminal input through the queue. Otherwise, orphan lines left in the
queue when a program terminates unexpectedly can be read by the
operating system and treated erroneously as system commands.

Some implementations of REXX take the queue idea even further.
Personal REXX for MS-DOS allows arbitrary keystrokes and time
delays to be inserted into the queue, in addition to whole lines. This
caters to the MS-DOS environment, since many programs make heavy
use of special keystrokes rather than verbose commands. Personal
REXX also allows the queue to be treated as a write-only device to
which command output can be written by redirection. This permits
retrieval of program output even from programs which have not been
designed to write to the queue.

A similar concept is used in OS/2, where there is a command
(RXQUEUE) which copies its standard input stream to the queue (FIFO or
LIFO). Piping output to RXQUEUE from another command then allows
REXX programs to process it out of the queue. On the other hand,
OS/2 does not have a general implementation of the queue that per-
mits it to be a form of surrogate keyboard input to programs written in
languages other than REXX.

Chapter

11

Exception Handling

We generally think of a program as a sequence of instructions which flow smoothly and sequentially from one to the next, unless the sequence is explicitly altered in accordance with the rules of one of a small number of well-defined control structures (IF, DO, SELECT, CALL, etc.). However, it has been found that this simple model is somewhat lacking when we think about error handling. And we should think about error handling. REXX is often used for small, one-shot, "quick and dirty" programs with a limited purpose. But in all cases except these, we want our programs to be as robust as possible—and the more we use them, the more robust we expect them to be. Robustness means ideally that a program never fails to produce the desired results. Short of the ideal, however, we still should expect that a program will not fail without at least a comprehensible error message, and that a failure will never cause irreversible damage.

So we have to think about error handling in order to build robust programs. Because errors do occur, for reasons completely outside of a program's control, as well as for errors in the logic of a program itself (*bugs*). In fact, we may well prefer to employ the euphemism *exceptional conditions* rather than errors—meaning any conditions not foreseen in detail by the program. Such conditions are often not really errors, but they do need to be allowed for by a robust program. It is often observed that in good quality robust software, 90 percent or more of the code may actually be concerned with handling exceptional conditions in some way or another.

Error handling often calls for nonsequential flow of control. The primary reason for this is that errors can occur in such a wide variety of places in a program. If a program were to check for errors every place they could occur, the program itself would be overwhelmed by error-checking. In order to overcome this problem without sacrificing robustness, REXX has adopted the position of treating errors as if they were actually *asynchronous* events, that is, events generated by unpredictable causes outside of a program. Such events are called *conditions*, and REXX allows code to be executed out of the normal sequence when particular conditions occur.

Let's consider briefly the sorts of errors we need to contend with. I/O errors are among the most typical. Many kinds of errors can occur with I/O. External devices like disk drives can fail or simply be *not ready* (have no disk loaded). Printers can run out of paper. Magnetic media can be defective. Disk space may become filled, and so forth. But clearly it is very tedious to test every I/O operation within a program for any error at all, let alone each error that can possibly occur.

Another common source of errors which is fairly unique to REXX is that external programs invoked from REXX can malfunction or fail for a wide variety of reasons. The reasons are often operational in nature, such as failure to find a required file or insufficient memory. Or the operating system may have been unable to find or run the external program. Again, the locations where such errors can occur are numerous, and checking for each possible problem becomes prohibitively expensive.

Finally, errors can occur because of bad data input to the program— data that is out of the expected range or simply invalid. And all of these possible error sources are in addition to programming logic errors in a narrow sense such as misspelled variable names or invalid syntax. (Since REXX has an INTERPRET instruction, syntactic errors can result from incorrect input and be impossible to detect before run-time.)

Now, even though most of these errors can occur only at certain specific locations within a program, the number of such locations may be very large. And the same sorts of tests need to be performed in each appropriate location. So a great deal of duplicated code can be eliminated if we simply provide one place to handle each type of error and have that code invoked out of sequence whenever the corresponding error occurs.

This same mechanism can handle genuine asynchronous events as well, of course. The one case where REXX does this is where an interactive user of a program chooses to terminate it while it is running, perhaps because it is in an infinite loop. (Just how this decision is indicated by the user depends on the particular operating system involved.) Even though the program should be ended as soon as possible, it is often desirable to perform some cleanup functions before stopping.

REXX formally recognizes six types of events as conditions:

ERROR

When a command to an external environment terminates with an indication that it encountered an error, the ERROR condition is raised. The command may have been issued either directly or with the ADDRESS instruction. Command errors are usually indicated by means of return codes, as discussed in Chap. 6.

FAILURE

When a command to an external environment cannot be executed at all, the FAILURE condition is raised. The command may not be executable for a variety of reasons, such as it could not be found or there was not enough memory to start it. The command may have been issued either directly or with the ADDRESS instruction.

HALT

The HALT condition is raised when an interactive user of the program requests the operating system to stop the program. Depending on capabilities of the operating system, this request may also be made by the operating system itself or another running program.

NOVALUE

The NOVALUE condition is raised when a symbol that is a valid variable name is used in certain contexts but the variable it names has not been initialized. The contexts in which this can occur are expressions, in PARSE VAR, or in a variable reference. (A variable reference is a variable name enclosed in parentheses, as can be used in a PARSE template, the PROCEDURE instruction, and the DROP instruction.) An uninitialized variable named in the VALUE( ) built-in function or used in the tail of a compound symbol does not, by itself, raise the NOVALUE condition.

NOTREADY

An I/O error that occurs in an I/O built-in function or the SAY, PARSE LINEIN, or PARSE PULL instruction will raise the NOTREADY condition. Attempts to read beyond the end of a file also raise NOTREADY.

SYNTAX

The SYNTAX condition can be raised by a wide variety of errors in the processing of a program. There are specific error numbers and (usually) standard messages which are associated with each such error. Many of these errors are truly syntactic, such as invalid expressions. But many others are nonsyntactic in nature, such as a variable with a nonnumeric value used in an arithmetic expression or the inability to find an external procedure.

ENABLING AND DISABLING CONDITION HANDLING

When a REXX program begins, all conditions have no program-defined handlers for them. Such conditions are said to be *disabled*. This doesn't mean they cannot occur, only that condition handlers other than the REXX defaults will not be invoked. The default handlers for ERROR, NOTREADY, and NOVALUE simply ignore the condition. In effect, these conditions are by default treated as if they do not occur. The default handler for FAILURE immediately raises the ERROR condition (which is then ignored if it is disabled).

By contrast, however, the default handlers for HALT and SYNTAX immediately terminate the program, issue a message, and cause a return to the caller with a return code that indicates which error occurred.

Program-defined handlers for each condition may be one of two possible types. For simplicity we will refer to them as Type 1 and Type 2:

Type 1 condition handlers

Can be specified for any type of condition.

Are enabled with a SIGNAL ON instruction.

Are disabled as soon as the condition occurs. They must be re-enabled in order to be used again.

Automatically terminate any active DO, IF, SELECT, or INTERPRET instruction. They do *not* terminate the active procedure.

Permanently alter the sequence of execution. It is not possible to return to the point where the condition was raised.

Type 2 condition handlers

Can be specified for ERROR, FAILURE, HALT, and NOTREADY conditions, but not NOVALUE and SYNTAX.

Are enabled with a CALL ON instruction.

Are not disabled when the condition occurs, but are placed in a special *delayed* state. The precise handling that occurs when another condition of the same type is raised while the condition is in the delayed state depends on the condition.

Do not terminate active instructions or the current procedure.

Do not permanently alter the sequence of execution. A RETURN instruction executed in the condition handler causes execution to resume at the point where the condition was raised.

A Type 1 condition handler corresponds to the SIGNAL instruction, and a Type 2 condition handler corresponds to the CALL instruction. For instance, a Type 1 handler for the ERROR condition is invoked as if the instruction

```
signal error
```

were issued at the point ERROR is raised. A Type 2 handler is invoked, instead, as if the instruction

```
call error
```

were issued. Notice that the type of the condition handler depends on how it has been enabled, which controls how the handler is invoked.

The start of the condition handler is the first clause after a label which corresponds either to the name specified on the CALL ON or SIGNAL ON instruction or else to the name of the condition. For example, the handler for the ERROR condition would normally follow the (first occurrence of the) label ERROR:.

Notice that it is quite possible for a condition handler to be enabled, but not actually defined. That is you could have

```
signal on novalue
```

in your program but no NOVALUE: label anywhere. If the NOVALUE condition is ever actually raised, the SYNTAX condition will be raised immediately afterwards because the label is not found. If the SYNTAX condition has not been enabled, the program will then be terminated, since that is what the default REXX handler does. But if SYNTAX has been enabled and if there is actually a handler for it in the program, any appropriate action can be taken. In practice, one usually uses signal on novalue simply to catch the use of uninitialized variables quickly, and termination of the program with an error message that indicates the line where the error occurred is all that is wanted.

If you wish to explicitly disable a condition handler, you can do so with either the SIGNAL OFF or the CALL OFF instruction. It does not matter which type of condition handler is involved. So

```
signal off novalue
```

disables any program-defined handling of the NOVALUE condition within the current procedure. It restores handling of the NOVALUE condition to the REXX default, which is to ignore the condition.

If you read the description of signal handling in *The REXX Language,* you may find it a little confusing. The reason is that certain terms are used somewhat loosely and certain facts about the sequence of events in the handling of a condition are not made clear. For instance, when the term *trapped* is used, it seems to mean variously that a handler has been defined for a condition, that the events defining the condition have occurred, or that the handler for the condition has been invoked. We will try to be a little more precise.

When we say that a condition has been *enabled* we shall mean that a user-defined handler for the condition has been specified with the SIGNAL ON or CALL ON instruction. As has already been pointed out, a condition can still occur even if it has not been enabled, because REXX default handlers are always defined.

When the circumstances which define the condition are first noticed by the REXX run-time system, we shall say that the condition has been *raised*. Finally, when the condition handler is actually invoked, we shall say that the condition has been *trapped*. Most of the time, a condition is trapped immediately after it has been raised. In particular, the language specifies that this is the case when a Type 1 condition handler has been enabled, as long as the label identifying the handler exists in the program.

On the other hand, when a Type 2 handler has been enabled, REXX specifies that the condition may not be trapped until the end of a clause, which could be some time after when it is raised. We shall say that a condition is *pending* during the time between when it is raised and the time it is trapped. Later, in the discussion of Type 2 handlers, we shall mention some problems that arise with pending conditions.

USING TYPE 1 CONDITION HANDLERS

A Type 1 condition handler is enabled with the SIGNAL ON command, which has the form:

```
SIGNAL ON condition [NAME handler]
```

Condition is the name of the condition to be trapped. Handler is a symbol which specifies the label to which control will be passed if the condition is raised. By default, handler is the same as the condition name. But it could be any other symbol. So, though you cannot have more than one handler active for a given condition at any one time, you can switch easily among a number of different handlers as required.

The label that actually identifies the handler may occur anywhere a label is allowed. As with labels on procedures, only the first occurrence of the label within the program can be used for a condition handler. If the condition is raised and the label is not found, the SYNTAX condition will be raised.

The state of a condition's being enabled or not and the name of the handler (if any) are inherited by any internal procedures that are called. A procedure may change the handling of any condition, but the state of the condition is returned to what it was when the procedure returns to its caller, just as REXX treats other state information when internal procedures are called.

In particular, any time it is important to handle some condition in a special way when a certain procedure is invoked, the procedure should give a SIGNAL ON instruction that specifies its own preferred handler. Then, regardless of where the handler is actually located, it will be invoked when the condition is raised while the procedure is active.

It is very important to note that a Type 1 condition handler is invoked by the SIGNAL instruction, so it does not terminate the active procedure. (Though it does terminate all active DO, SELECT, IF, and INTERPRET instructions.) This means that if the condition is trapped in a deeply nested subroutine, especially one that has been called recursively, it can be tricky to get back to a predetermined location higher up in the calling sequence.

The most common use of a Type 1 signal handler is probably to provide diagnostics in the event of a SYNTAX error. Here is an example of a simple handler for the SYNTAX condition:

```
syntax:
say 'REXX error' rc '('errortext(rc)||,
    ') occurred in line' sigl'.'
if sourceline() > 0 then
    say '=====>' sourceline(sigl)
signal on syntax
signal restart
```

This example illustrates several REXX features that are useful in dealing with conditions. The first line after the label provides an error message which is much like the one REXX would issue if there were no SYNTAX condition handler. REXX sets the special variable RC to the number of the error which occurred. Error numbers are more or less standardized in REXX, so that you can usually depend on being able to tell fairly well what sort of error occurred based on the value placed in RC. For instance, error number 5 is associated with the message "Machine resources exhausted", which means that the REXX language processor ran out of memory. This might be because the program had an error and was in a loop creating new variables. But in other circumstances, it might not indicate an error, but merely a normal (though annoying) operational difficulty with a program that has large memory requirements.

At the same time, the SIGL special variable is displayed, because REXX has set it to the number of the line in the source program that was being executed when the SYNTAX condition was raised. (SIGL is always set when a SIGNAL or CALL instruction is executed.) This value is used later in order to display the actual line of source code involved. Another feature, the ERRORTEXT() built-in function, has been used in the first line of the handler. This function displays the error message associated with the number of the error that occurred.

The second line of the handler contains a call to SOURCELINE() with no arguments. This returns the number of lines of source code in the program. It illustrates another case of defensive programming. Some implementations of REXX (usually compilers) do not have access to the program source code in order to display them with SOURCELINE(). In this case, the function called with no arguments should return 0 to indicate that source code is not available. If source is available, the example displays the line of code that caused the condition to be raised.

At this point, the handler has done only what REXX's default SYNTAX condition handler would do. Presumably a special handler was used to add some additional capability. Usually this is simply to afford an opportunity for the program to continue execution if it chooses to do so, instead of being terminated, which is the default action. Since REXX programs may use the INTERPRET instruction to execute other instructions, which might be based on expressions or data supplied interactively by a user, it can make sense for the program to wish to continue even when a seemingly severe error has occurred.

If the program is in fact going to continue, the next step should be, as in the next to last line of the example, to issue another SIGNAL ON SYNTAX instruction. This is because REXX has automatically disabled handling the SYNTAX condition at the time it was raised. This is always done for Type 1 condition handlers, in order to reduce the possibility of an infinite loop should the handler itself do something to raise the condition again. The final step is to use an ordinary SIGNAL instruction to transfer control back to some known location in the program so that it can proceed.

We want to stress again that a condition handler like this is most easily used for conditions that are raised in the top-level (main) procedure of a program. Otherwise, it is necessary to provide additional logic (perhaps in the form of variables which indicate what the program was doing) in order to restart in a procedure somewhere above the one which was active when the condition was raised.

USING TYPE 2 CONDITION HANDLERS

A Type 2 condition handler is enabled with the CALL ON command, which has the form:

```
CALL ON condition [NAME handler]
```

Condition is the name of the condition to be trapped. Handler is a symbol which specifies the label to which control will be passed if the condition is raised. By default, handler is the same as the condition name. But it could be any other symbol.

The SYNTAX and NOVALUE conditions cannot be handled with a Type 2 handler. This is because they can occur in the middle of expressions and it is probably not meaningful to continue after the point of failure for these conditions.

As with a Type 1 handler, the first label in the program that matches the name of the handler (i.e., usually the name of the condition) is invoked when the condition is trapped. It is invoked with a CALL instruction rather than a SIGNAL, so that the handler can return to the point at which the condition was raised. In fact, the handler generally must use the RETURN instruction when it is done (if it doesn't use EXIT). This is because since the handler is executed as a subroutine, use of SIGNAL does not terminate the subroutine.

The handler should not specify a value on the RETURN instruction, since it will be ignored and not assigned to the RESULT variable. However, all other conventions of subroutine invocation are observed when a Type 2 handler is called. In particular, the state of the program is saved on entry to the subroutine and inherited by it. But any changes that the subroutine makes to the state persist only until the subroutine returns. (See Chap. 5 for a full explanation.) Therefore, the handler cannot make permanent changes to the state of the condition it is handling, or to any other for that matter. Consequently, after the handler returns the condition is still enabled, which is unlike the situation with a Type 1 handler where the condition has to be explicitly enabled again.

Another difference from a Type 1 handler is that a Type 2 handler does not terminate active DO, IF, SELECT, or INTERPRET instructions. When a Type 2 handler returns, execution is resumed at the point immediately after the condition was raised. This means that it is not possible to retry the operation that failed. For instance, in the case of an ERROR or FAILURE condition, execution will resume with the statement following the command. If your program wants to reissue the command, it must do so in the handler itself.

A subtle point about all of the conditions that may be handled with a Type 2 handler is that they can be trapped only at a clause boundary. This is obvious for ERROR and FAILURE, since a command to an external environment is a clause by itself. It is less obvious for HALT and NOTREADY. Nevertheless, in order to permit orderly resumption after a Type 2 handler is invoked and returns, REXX specifically provides that the HALT and NOTREADY conditions can be trapped only at clause boundaries.

In the case of I/O functions, in which the NOTREADY condition can be raised, it should be noted that the function will always return a well-defined result even if an error is encountered. For instance, CHAROUT( ) will return the number of characters that were not successfully written. In this way, expressions involving the I/O built-in functions will still have well-defined values even if an error occurs. REXX will trap the NOTREADY condition only after the expression is fully evaluated and the end of the clause is reached. This is a consideration mainly in DO, IF, and SELECT instructions which may involve multiple expressions in a single clause, or multiple clauses in the instruction.

Here is a simple example:

```
call on notready
...
if charout (output_file, output_string) > 0 then do
    say 'Attempted to write' output_string
    say 'Unable to continue output.'
    return
    end
...
notready:
say 'Error writing' condition('d')
return
```

In this example, if an error occurs in the call to CHAROUT( ) the function returns with a nonzero value, which is compared to 0. The end of the clause is just before THEN. Only at that point will the NOTREADY handler be invoked. The handler will display a simple message, using the CONDITION( ) built-in function to determine the name of the file that was in use. (This function is described in the next section.) Upon return from the handler, execution continues with the DO group, which issues additional messages and returns.

It turns out that only the HALT and NOTREADY conditions may possibly be trapped at a later time than they are actually raised, if a Type 2 handler has been enabled. So the question arises as to what happens if one of these conditions occurs again while one is pending. In principle, any number of NOTREADY conditions could occur during the execution of one clause. For instance, the clause might contain an expression involving a number of I/O functions. REXX guarantees that only the first NOTREADY condition that is raised will actually be trapped at the end of the clause. This is because the condition is put in a special delayed state while it is pending, and any other NOTREADY conditions that may subsequently occur in the clause are simply ignored. Though this may seem like a fine point, you should be aware of it if you write a program that depends on trapping NOTREADY conditions.

You can use Type 2 handlers for purposes other than error handling per se. For instance, most operating systems permit a user to generate some sort of a signal to interrupt a program. Normally this signal is used to terminate the program (if it seems to be in a loop, for example). REXX recognizes this signal as a HALT condition and allows it to be trapped. You can then use the signal simply as an opportunity to provide information about the progress of a long-running computation, and (perhaps) allow the user to decide whether or not to continue. Here is a HALT condition handler to do that:

```
halt:
say cases 'cases out of' total 'have been processed.'
say 'Do you wish to continue?'
pull reply
if \abbrev('NO', reply, 1) then
    return
else do
    say 'Processing terminated.'
    exit
    end
```

In this example, the variable cases is assumed to be maintained as the number of cases completely processed. Unless the user types n or no, the program can continue as if nothing had happened, because the handler returns to the exact location at which the HALT condition was raised and no program state information has been changed.

After a condition occurs and before or during the execution of a Type 2 handler, the condition is in a delayed state, which is between enabled and disabled. This additional state is provided to minimize the chances of an infinite loop of errors. The provision of a delayed state for conditions means that REXX does not have to go so far as to completely disable the condition in order to prevent possible loops.

A condition normally occurs while it is in a delayed state only if it occurs in a Type 2 handler for the condition. This is because the delayed state reverts to the normal enabled state when the condition handler returns. If the condition does occur while it is in a delayed state, then it will simply be ignored if it is an ERROR, FAILURE, or NOTREADY condition. In effect, the condition is disabled from the time it occurs until the Type 2 handler returns.

If a user causes a second HALT signal to be generated while the HALT condition is in the delayed state, then raising of the condition will simply remain pending until the handler returns. It is relatively safe to do this, since HALT conditions arise from circumstances outside the program and are unlikely to lead to an infinite loop.

The delayed state of a condition can also be changed if a CALL ON or SIGNAL ON instruction is executed in the handler. If this is done while a second interrupt happens to be pending, the condition is raised immediately, and control returns to the beginning of the handler, via CALL or SIGNAL, as appropriate. Also, if CALL OFF or SIGNAL OFF is used in the handler, the state of the condition changes from delayed to disabled. Therefore, should another condition of the same type occur, the default REXX action for the condition will be taken. (For HALT, the only condition for which this can occur, that action is to terminate the program.)

THE CONDITION() FUNCTION

Additional information about trapped conditions is available to both types of condition handlers with the CONDITION() built-in function. It can identify the name of the current trapped condition, the instruction that invoked the condition handler (SIGNAL or CALL), the state of the condition (enabled, disabled, or delayed), and also provide a short descriptive string providing further details about the condition.

Note that the CONDITION() function reports information only for the current trapped condition. If no conditions have been raised within the program, CONDITION() will return a null string. Also, it cannot tell you the state (on, off, or delayed) for conditions other than the one currently pending or trapped.

After a condition has been trapped by a Type 1 handler, CONDITION() will continue to report information about the condition until the next one occurs or the active procedure returns to its caller. In the case of a Type 2 handler, however, CONDITION() is applicable only until the handler issues a RETURN instruction to return to the place where the condition was raised. The syntax of CONDITION() is:

```
CONDITION([option])
```

If option is not specified, it defaults to 'I'. Otherwise it should be one of the following, to specify what sort of information is needed:

'C' indicates the name of the trapped Condition.

'D' indicates the Description of the trapped condition. This may be a null string if no description is available. Otherwise it varies depending on the type of condition:

ERROR: the command string which was issued and caused the condition

FAILURE: the command string which was issued and caused the condition

HALT: extra information provided with the request to terminate the program (if any)

NOVALUE: the derived name of the uninitialized variable that caused the condition to be raised

NOTREADY: the name of the I/O stream in which an error occurred

SYNTAX: additional implementation-dependent information (if any) regarding the error.

'I'   indicates the *Instruction* that invoked the condition handler (either CALL or SIGNAL).

'S'   indicates the *State* of handling for the condition: ON (enabled), OFF (disabled), or DELAYED.

Of course, most of this information can be deduced by the program on its own. Usually a given handler is specified for only one possible condition and as either a Type 1 or Type 2 handler. And the state of handling for the condition can be deduced from the type of the handler. But some interesting things may be done with the condition description.

In the case of ERROR and FAILURE conditions, the handler can examine the actual command that was issued. It may be determined, for instance, that the operating system simply did not have the right *search path* for the command, and a new, more appropriate one, may be established. The program could even ask the user for help in finding the command or in otherwise correcting the error. This might be useful in REXX programs that are packaged with other software and are used to install the software. Such programs need to be run in very diverse environments and may not always be able to find the commands they need to run.

For the NOTREADY condition, having the name of the file that caused the error makes it possible to process a long list of files and keep a log of any in which errors were encountered. This is more easily done in a condition handler than in the main line of the program if the file is referred to in a large number of places, so that testing each I/O operation is cumbersome.

Here's a final example that uses CONDITION() in a FAILURE handler to attempt reexecution of a command that could not be found:

```
failure:
command = condition('d')
say 'Error' rc 'occurred running' command
if rc \= -3 then do
    'Please notify a systems programmer.'
    exit
    end
parse var command name tail
do forever
    say 'The' name 'program was not found.'
    say 'Enter name of directory for' name,
        'or a null string to quit.'
    pull directory
    if directory = '' then
        exit
```

```
/* try to re-execute command with new directory */
directory||name tail
if rc = 0 then
  return
end
```

This example assumes that a return code (RC) of –3 means that the command could not be found. This is the convention used on various systems, including CMS and MS-DOS.

The INTERPRET Instruction

In this chapter, more than any other in this book, it would be well to recall the remark of the anonymous sage: "A language is not worth knowing unless it teaches you to think differently." Efficient and advantageous use of the INTERPRET instruction requires a very new mindset towards programming. Yet, in the appropriate circumstances, and once you get it, many otherwise difficult problems can be solved quickly and efficiently with INTERPRET.

INTERPRET offers a capability in REXX that can be found in few other languages. It allows a program to create REXX instructions and execute them dynamically. That is, it permits programs whose instructions are not fully determined until execution time—they can vary as the program is run.

The following example is one without which no book on REXX is complete. It is usually called REXXTRY, because it allows you to type in one or more REXX instructions at the keyboard and have them executed immediately. Though it is mainly of interest as a quick way of learning REXX interactively by trying out actual REXX code, it can be of use in allowing you to invoke REXX utility services without going to the trouble of creating a program.

```
/* test individual rexx commands */
say 'Enter REXX statements:'

restart:
```

```
signal on syntax
do forever
    _ = charout( , 'Rexx>')/* display prompt */
    _command = linein()  /* read input */
    interpret _command
    end
return

syntax:
say 'REXX error' rc '('errortext(rc)||,
    ') occurred.'
say '=====>' _command
signal restart
```

All of the real action here occurs inside the loop. It simply puts up a prompt, reads a line of input, and uses INTERPRET to execute it. The remainder of the program is a handler for SYNTAX errors, much like the one discussed in Chap. 11. Since typing errors as well as language usage errors are all too easy to make, this is a handy safety net that allows REXXTRY to keep running regardless (almost) of what is entered.

A couple remarks about some of the programming decisions made in this example may be helpful. First, CHAROUT() is invoked as a function rather than with the CALL instruction, since we wanted to avoid setting the RESULT variable as a side effect. This way, RESULT is affected only by the command that is interpreted. Second, and more importantly, we used LINEIN() to read input instead of PARSE PULL. This prevents any confusion due to reading data that might get put on the queue with PUSH or QUEUE instructions.

You are strongly encouraged to type in this program and try it out. It is an excellent way of seeing exactly what REXX instructions and built-in functions do. This includes, in particular, the INTERPRET instruction itself—there is no restriction on using INTERPRET recursively (though it can be hard to follow what is going on!).

The syntax of INTERPRET is

```
INTERPRET expression
```

Expression is any REXX expression, which is first evaluated according to all the normal rules of REXX: substitution of values for symbols, evaluation of string and arithmetic operators, etc. Then the result of that evaluation is executed just as if it were part of the program, so that another level of expression evaluation can occur. For instance, in the sequence

```
x = 'a + b'
a = 1
```

```
b = 2
interpret 'say' x
```

the expression after interpret evaluates to

```
say a + b
```

and when this itself is executed, substitution and expression evaluation occur again so that the result 3 is finally displayed.

Although REXXTRY uses INTERPRET, it is set up so that what you type in is executed just as if it appeared in the program. So, suppose you typed the following lines into REXXTRY:

```
command = 'say'
varname = 'x'
x = 'Hello world!'
```

Then you can try some experiments. If you type

```
say x
```

the program displays

```
Hello world!
```

just as it would have if the line had occurred in the program.

To see how INTERPRET itself works, you can type either

```
interpret "say x"
```

or

```
interpret command varname
```

and the program again displays

```
Hello world!
```

because the expression command varname evaluates to say x, which is then executed normally. That is, it was subjected to a second level of interpretation, in which say was recognized as a keyword and x as a variable, whose value was substituted into the final result. But if you type

```
command varname
```

then the program will try to pass the command say x to the external environment (where it will probably be rejected as an unknown command). Why? Because the string command varname will be processed just as if it were a line in the program. Since the first token isn't a REXX keyword and the instruction isn't an assignment, the instruction is assumed to be a command. Then substitution of the values of command and varname occurs and an attempt is made to execute the command.

If you find this a little confusing (quite possible!), it is suggested again that you experiment with REXXTRY a little. Or, read further to see some additional examples.

RULES FOR INTERPRET

Almost any valid REXX statement can be the object of an INTERPRET instruction. In fact, almost any sequence of statements separated by semicolons can be INTERPRETed, even an entire DO ... END loop. It is, however, required that any complex statements (IF, DO, or SELECT) be complete. Also, LEAVE and ITERATE can only refer to DO loops contained within the interpreted sequence of statements. But you could very well have a CALL to a subroutine or a RETURN from one. Labels are also not allowed. So if you do use CALL, it must be to a label existing elsewhere in the program.

Execution of the interpreted statements occurs within the current program context. That is, all variables are available and have whatever value was last assigned to them. Variable values can be changed and new variables created. Any such changes persist after the conclusion of INTERPRET.

SIGNAL can be used within INTERPRET. It causes a transfer of control just as it normally would, and it also immediately terminates the INTERPRET instruction. The same is true when SIGNAL is used to invoke an enabled condition handler. Handlers can be enabled by the instructions that are interpreted. Indeed, all other instructions that change the state of program execution can be used (ADDRESS, NUMERIC, etc.), and their effects persist after INTERPRET finishes.

Implementation of the INTERPRET instruction obviously requires the full capabilities of a REXX interpreter at execution time. Therefore, the instruction is often unavailable in *compiled* implementations of REXX. Because of this, it is a good idea to use INTERPRET sparingly if there is any chance your program will ever have to run in other environments. Use of alternatives like the VALUE() function (when possible) will probably run faster, in addition to being more portable. If use of INTERPRET is unavoidable, it may still be a good idea to test at the beginning of the program whether it is available. You can use code like this to test:

```
signal on syntax name interpret_check
x = 0
interpret 'x = 1'
interpret_check:
if x = 0 then do
    say "INTERPRET instruction unavailable!"
    exit
    end
signal off syntax
```

EXAMPLES OF INTERPRET USAGE

In earlier versions of the REXX language INTERPRET was needed for certain things that can now be done with the VALUE() function. In particular, if you wanted to pass a stem name to a subroutine and be able to read and write compound variables using that stem, it was convenient—or necessary—to use INTERPRET.

For instance, a bubble sort typically has something like

```
if x.i >> x.j then do
    temp = x.j
    x.j = x.i
    x.i = temp
    end
```

to exchange adjacent items if they are out of order. But if we want this to work for an arbitrary stem whose name is passed to the routine, then we need something like

```
bubble_sort:
parse arg stem, size
do n = size to 2 by -1
    do i = 1 to n-1
        j = i + 1
        interpret "if" stem".i >>" stem".j then do;",
            "temp =" stem".j;",
            stem".j =" stem".i;",
            stem".i = temp;",
            "end"
        end
    end
return
```

This is a complete sort subroutine which takes two arguments: the name of the array to be sorted and the number of elements.

This sort of thing can be confusing to read. The main trick in reading examples like this is to see what is inside a quoted string and what is outside. In this case, all references to stem are outside of quotation marks, so that its value, which was passed as an argument, can be substituted for it.

Notice that this example is written with a single INTERPRET instruction rather than one per line. This was necessary in order to have the entire DO . . . END sequence in the same instruction. It is also more efficient, even if the DO group had not been a consideration. It was necessary to separate clauses with semicolons, since there are no line-ends within the string that is interpreted. But by writing the expression across several continued lines (which causes concatenation), a similar appearance results.

Since the VALUE() function can be used to assign values as well as retrieve them, this could be rewritten:

```
bubble_sort:
parse arg stem, size
do n = size to 2 by -1
   do i = 1 to n-1
      j = i + 1
      if value(stem'.i') >> value(stem'.j') then
         call value stem'.i',,
            value(stem'.j', stem'.i')
         end
      end
   end
return
```

Here we have used the fact that VALUE() returns the current value of its first argument before reassigning it. This approach is more efficient, and works even with a REXX compiler that doesn't support INTERPRET. However, if you have a version of REXX in which VALUE() can't do this, INTERPRET is the only alternative.

Probably the most common circumstance in which INTERPRET is hard to avoid involves using variable subroutine names. Taking the sorting example a little further, it is common to want to sort elements of an array on some basis other than simple string comparison. For instance, the array might consist of indices into another array which is really the thing that is to be sorted. That is, we wish to say $x.i$ is "less than" $x.j$ just in case

```
ii = x.i
jj = x.j
real_array.ii << real_array.jj
```

The way this is handled in full generality is to pass to the sorting routine the name of another routine which will perform the comparison any way it likes. This routine, in other words, defines the ordering relation. In other languages, like C, it is very common to pass the names of functions (i.e., pointers to them) to other routines so that the programmer has control over which function is to be called at any particular time. This idea is used even more heavily in object-oriented languages like C++ which use *methods* or *member functions* associated with objects in order to provide customized object behavior.

The only way to do this kind of thing in REXX is to use INTERPRET, because the CALL instruction (or function reference) treats the procedure name to be called as a literal. So, let's assume a third argument is passed to the sorting routine and gives the name of the comparison function. The comparison function in turn takes two arguments. It returns –1 if the first argument is less than the second, 1 if the first is greater, and 0 if the two arguments are the same. Then our sorting example could be written

```
bubble_sort:
parse arg stem, size, compare
do n = size to 2 by -1
   do i = 1 to n-1
      j = i + 1
      interpret,
       "if" compare"("stem".i,"stem".j) > 0 then do;",
         "temp =" stem".j;",
         stem".j =" stem".i;",
         stem".i = temp;",
         "end"
   end
 end
return
```

which is really just a very simple change. Notice that the reference to compare is outside of quotation marks, as is stem, so that proper substitution occurs.

INTERPRET is usually an expensive instruction to use, in terms of time. It is slow because it has to perform all the tokenization and syntactic analysis REXX needs every time it is invoked, whereas most REXX implementations are optimized to do that sort of thing on any given instruction only once, when the program is first loaded. This can be a problem especially in a sorting routine, which performs the same operation many times. (And even more especially with an inefficient sorting algorithm like the bubble sort.)

One way to minimize the impact of this is to take INTERPRET outside of any loops, if possible. In other words, make most of the body of the subroutine into the object of INTERPRET:

```
bubble_sort:
parse arg stem, size, compare
interpret, /* begin interpreted code */
"do n = size to 2 by -1;",
    "do i = 1 to n-1;",
      "j = i + 1;",
      "if" compare"("stem".i,"stem".j) > 0 then do;",
          "temp =" stem".j;",
          stem".j =" stem".i;",
          stem".i = temp;",
          "end",
      "end;",
    "end;" /* end of interpreted code */
return
```

This admittedly is tricky: you have to remember the semicolons and continuation characters. And make sure the right things are outside of quoted strings.

In Chap. 5 we saw that one of the problems with passing arrays to subprocedures was that of exposing the array so that it is accessible, in case the subprocedure begins with a PROCEDURE instruction. The recommended solution involved something like this:

```
argname = 'array.'
call function
...
function: procedure expose (argname)
/* all references to arguments use value() function */
...
```

It was noted that this is a little clumsy, in part because function could not be invoked with normal CALL or function reference syntax. This is a serious problem if we want to use references to the function in an expression. INTERPRET provides a way around the problem.

Let's define a new function called APPLY that will take a function name and arguments as its arguments and return the value of the function applied to the given arguments, so that we could get the desired result with

```
x = apply('function', 'array.')
```

Here's a first cut:

```
apply:
argname = arg(2)
interpret "return" arg(1)"()"
```

If it helps, you can think of this as something like a *macro*. That is, it's an expression with function-like syntax that expands into a number of REXX instructions. We can generalize this in several directions.

Obviously we may want to work with functions of any number of arguments, some of which need to be passed *by reference* and some *by value*. Passing an argument by value is the normal way, and passing by reference is what we are trying to simulate. Let's assume we want all arguments being passed by value to be named in a string which will be the second argument of APPLY. That is, we want to be able to say

```
x = apply('function', 'arg1. arg2.', 'x', '3', 'a+b')
```

in order to pass arg1 and arg2 by reference, and the rest as ordinary arguments. Also, we would like each function called this way to have its own private name for its by-reference argument list, to avoid conflicts. That is, rather than use argname all the time, we would adopt the convention that the name of the function with the suffix _args is the name of the list of by-reference arguments. Then we might have:

```
apply:
call value arg(1)"_args", arg(2)
arglist = ''
do i = 3 to arg()
    if i>3 then arglist = arglist','
    arglist = arglist||arg(i)
    end
interpret "return" arg(1)"("arglist")"
```

We wanted to avoid double evaluation, and so we also passed the actual arguments to be used as quoted strings. The loop builds a valid function argument list. Notice in the last line that evaluation of arg(1) and substitution of the value of arglist occur before INTERPRET is actually executed. Then, when the resulting expression is interpreted, further substitutions and expression evaluations can occur. When this is all executed it is as if, in the present instance, we had

```
apply:
function_args = "arg1. arg2."
return function(x,3,a+b)
```

in the program.

A completely different direction in which to pursue generalization of this example is to pick up on the remark that INTERPRET can add capabilities to REXX that are much like the macro feature of languages such as PL/I, C, and most assemblers. That is, you can write code which has a function call syntax but which actually expands into code customized for some specific purpose.

For example, suppose we want a tidy way to assign to all elements of one array the value of an arbitrary function applied to the corresponding elements of another. It could be done with inline code like:

```
drop target.
do i = 1 to n
   target.i = function(source.i)
   end
```

The problem here is that this only works for one specific function. But we want this to work for any function we wish to name. Except for this condition, we could do this with an ordinary REXX procedure. So let's make a macro to do it. We'll call it ASSIGN, and specify that we want to invoke it with a call like

```
call assign 'target.', 'source.', 'function', n
```

We could do this as follows:

```
assign:
_assign_args = arg(1) arg(2)
call _assign arg(3), arg(4)
return
_assign: procedure expose (_assign_args)
stem1 = word(_assign_args, 1)
stem2 = word(_assign_args, 2)
interpret,
"drop" stem1";",
"do i = 1 to arg(2);",
   stem1".i =" arg(1)"("stem2".i);",
   "end"
return
```

We have taken the extra step in this example of adding an extra lower-level procedure (called _assign) which uses a PROCEDURE instruction to avoid any trouble from use of i as a private index variable. The rest of the details are much the same as preceding examples.

Of course, this macro is not terribly different from an ordinary REXX subroutine. It merely does things not possible without INTERPRET, in that it allows the name of a function as an argument.

It might seem so far that INTERPRET doesn't add much to REXX besides an ability to perform indirect function calls. But this is far from the truth. Another whole class of applications for INTERPRET is the handling of expressions read from a file or the user at a terminal.

An obvious example is a calculator program, which is just a slight variation of the REXXTRY program:

```
/* expression calculator */
restart:
signal on syntax
do forever
   say "Enter expression:"
   _expr = linein()
   if _expr = '' then
     leave
   parse var _expr variable '=' value
   if value \= '' then
     interpret _expr
   else
     interpret 'say' _expr
   end
return

syntax:
say 'REXX error' rc '('errortext(rc)||,
   ') occurred.'
say '=====>' _expr
signal restart
```

The modification we've made to REXXTRY is to examine each line of input. If it looks like an assignment statement, it is executed. This allows the calculator to have memory by storing numbers in variables. Any input other than an assignment is assumed to be an expression, and its value is displayed. We still rely on the SYNTAX error handler to inform us of any errors, instead of allowing them to terminate the program. We also test for a null input line as a way to get out of the calculator (since we can't simply enter the EXIT instruction).

Endless elaborations are possible on this simple example. For instance, REXX does not have a wealth of built-in mathematical functions such as the trigonometric, exponential, logarithmic, or other transcendental functions. But if you need them, they can easily be included in the calculator program itself. In another direction, this kind of program could be extended to plot graphs of any desired expressions. This would be especially nice if a decent graphics library is available. Without such a library, or alternatively, the program could produce output on Postscript printers by generating the appropriate Postscript code.

Our final example of INTERPRET may be somewhat surprising. We noted earlier that INTERPRET can be a slow instruction to use. Nevertheless, there may be situations in which it can be used to speed up a program. One situation involves the use of large SELECT statements that involve many conditions to be tested. For instance, a program that is command-driven may consist of a main loop that reads commands, parses them, and then uses a large SELECT statement to invoke appropriate code for processing the command, something like this:

```
do forever
   parse linein verb rest
   verb = translate('verb')/* upper case */
   select
     when verb = 'ANALYZE' then
         call analyze rest
     when verb = 'BUILD' then
         call build rest
     /* etc., etc. */
     otherwise
         say "Invalid command."
     end
   end
```

While this is satisfactory for a dozen or so commands, it could be very slow if there are several dozen or more different commands, because the SELECT statement would have to make on average a number of comparisons equal to half the number of commands (unless the statement were carefully constructed to put the most likely commands first). Moreover, many REXX implementations are not smart enough to skip efficiently to the end of a long SELECT statement after finding the first condition that is true.

Even if the performance were acceptable, with many commands you would have a single SELECT statement sprawling over hundreds of lines of code, which would make the program hard to read. And, if nothing else, think of all the boilerplate WHENs and THENs that would need to be typed.

Then think how much easier it would be to do something as simple as:

```
do forever
   parse linein verb rest
   interpret "call" verb "rest"
   end
```

This assumes that each command is handled by a subroutine having the same name. If this is not the case, you could use a compound variable that provides the dictionary telling which subroutine to call for each command. Or, to be fully general, the compound variable could contain the actual code to execute for each command, e.g.,

```
code.analyze = "call prepare; call analyze rest"
code.build = "call build rest; say 'Done!'"
code.collate = "say 'Not implemented yet!'"
...
```

and the corresponding line to do the right thing for each command is just

```
interpret code.verb
```

13

REXX Arithmetic

One significant aspect of REXX that has not been given special prominence in this book is the way numbers and arithmetic are handled. We have emphasized REXX as a language for personal programming, for writing command procedures, for working with character string data, and so forth. Numerically intensive computation does not ordinarily play a large part in this kind of programming. And the fact that REXX is interpretive and treats numbers as character strings tends to make it slow for numeric computing.

However, REXX does have a very distinctive way of dealing with numbers, which can be very important in some cases. For instance, REXX handles high-precision arithmetic very naturally and easily. This can be quite useful when one needs to deal with very large numbers or many digits of precision.

REXX is very unusual among programming languages in that it never works (as far as the user is concerned) with numbers using the standard arithmetic instructions of the computer. Instead, REXX works entirely with a general, abstract definition of numbers and arithmetic. Thus the word length of the host computer and the various sizes of its different types of internal representations of numbers are irrelevant. *Underflow* and *overflow* of quantities, as understood by the computer, cannot occur. Intricacies of binary representation of floating point numbers may be ignored.

The result is that REXX programs can be much more portable as far as their numeric computations are concerned, since the programmer needs to understand only REXX's rules for arithmetic, not the rules of every computer on which the program might run. If a program is written correctly according to the rules of REXX, it should produce exactly the same numeric results regardless of where it is run.

REXX is able to do this because, as we have observed, numbers are always represented as character strings. Numbers may be used as character strings and vice versa. The way in which a number is expressed as a character string is important only when arithmetic operations are to be performed, or when using certain instructions and built-in functions which require numeric arguments of a certain type.

Strings that represent numbers can be created in a number of ways. They may be literals in the program, and they may be either unquoted literals, or quoted strings, including hexadecimal or bit strings. Thus 1, '1', '31'x, and '0011 0001'b are all valid representations of the number 1 (in ASCII). Notice that these are machine-independent representations. The machine-specific binary representation of a number, such as '01'x, is not a valid representation of the number 1. Valid numeric strings can also be created by character operations, read from a file, etc. Thus

```
'1'||'1'
copies('1',2)
```

and so forth create valid representations of the number 11.

A character string is a valid number if:

1. It is a sequence of 0 or more digits ("0" through "9") followed by a period, followed by another sequence or 0 or more digits, except that a period by itself isn't a valid number.

2. It is a number as in 1. preceded by a + or − sign and 0 or more spaces, e.g., '+1', '+ 1', '− 1'.

3. It is a number as in 1. or 2. with 0 or more leading or trailing blanks, e.g., ' 1 ', ' + 1 '.

Valid numbers may also use *exponential notation*. This means a number more or less as just described, followed by e or E, optionally followed by a + or − sign, and ending with 1 or more digits. Examples:

```
1e9
' + 3E+4 '
' 666.000e-10 '
```

The part of the number before the E or e is called the mantissa and the part after is called the exponent. The meaning of the notation is that the number represented is the mantissa times ten to the power of the exponent. (If the exponent is negative the mantissa is multiplied by one over ten to the absolute value of the exponent.) No blanks are allowed between the mantissa, the E or e, the sign of the exponent, and the exponent itself.

Although strings as described above may be used as numbers, when REXX produces a numeric result in the form of a character string, a certain standard form is used. For instance, such strings will never contain embedded blanks. They will have a sign only for negative numbers, and E is used in exponential notation rather than e. In addition, when a result is not given in exponential notation, it will always begin with a zero before the decimal point, for numbers less than one in absolute value, but otherwise will have no leading zeros. If the result is given in exponential notation, numbers in standard form will always have just one nonzero digit before the decimal point. The determination of whether to present the result in exponential form or not depends on the value of NUMERIC DIGITS, which we discuss below.

Zero itself will always be represented simply as 0, without decimal point or fractional part. You can always force a valid numeric string into the standard form by adding 0. These details are important when dealing with numeric results as character strings—for instance when you are concerned with how numbers appear in a report.

PRECISION OF ARITHMETIC

One other very important fact about the way REXX handles numbers and arithmetic is that at any one time it works with, at most, some maximum number of *significant digits*. This affects not only arithmetic, but also numbers used directly by REXX, such as positional parameters in PARSE templates.

This is because it is inefficient to do arithmetic with truly unlimited precision numbers. For most ordinary purposes, all that is required is to work with a sufficient number of significant digits, rather than exact values. Why suffer the expense of computing with hundreds of digits when all you care about (perhaps) is only 10 or so? Most fractional quantities cannot be expressed exactly in decimal notation anyway. There isn't any way to represent $1/3$ precisely as a decimal, and .333333333 is usually more than close enough. Even disregarding the inefficiency of computing with many digits, just think how annoying it would be to see reports filled with quantities that look like

.333333333333333333333333333333333333333333333333333333333333

To avoid such excess, REXX always has some specific limit on the number of digits it will work with. The default is nine digits, but it can be changed at any time with the NUMERIC DIGITS instruction. This has the form

```
NUMERIC DIGITS [expression]
```

where expression evaluates to a whole number greater than 0.

The current value of NUMERIC DIGITS may always be obtained with the DIGITS() built-in function.

A very important fact about REXX is that it does not cause a program failure or even an error when a computation exceeds the specified maximum precision. Nor does REXX silently just produce completely invalid results by discarding the most significant digits of a result, as occurs with most other programming languages. Instead, it discards the least significant digits of a result, to stay within the specified number of digits of precision.

The concept of NUMERIC DIGITS is actually quite hard to define precisely. It is best understood in terms of the effects it has on REXX handling of numbers, as described below. There are a large number of such effects. They include rounding which may occur to numbers used in arithmetic, the default way in which arithmetic results are represented, and whether a given number is regarded as a valid *whole number*.

ARITHMETIC OPERATIONS

First and foremost, NUMERIC DIGITS affects how each of the arithmetic operations is performed and how the results are represented. To begin with, both operands are truncated (not rounded) to NUMERIC DIGITS + 1 significant digits (in the REXX sense). This provides one extra *guard digit* to help preserve accuracy. After the operation has been performed on the numbers, the result is rounded to NUMERIC DIGITS places, starting from the high-order nonzero digit. It is quite common for a result to have more than NUMERIC DIGITS of precision before this rounding. For instance, the product of two three-digit numbers can easily have six digits. And the quotient $1/3$ has an infinite number of digits.

The rules for arithmetic in REXX are mostly the same as in pencil-and-paper arithmetic. However, the common rules are not always precise or unambiguous enough, so REXX has made a few arbitrary rules which in some cases are not intuitively natural. Addition and subtraction present some of the more unusual cases. Subtraction, in particular, because it may involve a great deal of cancellation, provides some interesting examples.

First of all, addition or subtraction when one of the operands is zero is a special case. The result is simply the value of the nonzero operand rounded according to NUMERIC DIGITS and with the sign adjusted.

Adding zero to a number is sometimes a useful way of putting it in the standard form.

The general rule for addition and subtraction is first to *normalize* both operands (after both have been truncated to NUMERIC DIGITS + 1 digits). This is done by expressing in exponential notation the operand which has the largest absolute value. Then express the other operand in exponential notation using the same exponent as the first. This process may result in expressing the second operand in a form with more than NUMERIC DIGITS + 1 digits. If so, it should be truncated to NUMERIC DIGITS + 1. This truncation prevents the inclusion of illusory precision in the result.

The addition and subtraction can then be performed on the mantissas of the operands. The result, finally, is rounded to NUMERIC DIGITS— counting from the leftmost nonzero digit (if there is at least one to the left of the decimal point), otherwise from the digit just to the left of the decimal point, even if it is zero. Again, this prevents keeping apparent precision that really isn't there (if subtraction has led to significant cancellation).

These rules are fairly complex and sometimes produce surprising results, but they are designed to properly represent the precision of a result. For example, suppose NUMERIC DIGITS is 2. A simple case is

```
100 - 95
```

In exponential form this is 1E2 - 0.95E2, which is 0.05E2. This has to be rounded to just two significant digits, so it is 0.1E2—i.e., 10! Even more surprisingly, 100 - 96 becomes 0.04E2, which rounds to a result of 0.

Clearly, choosing a small number like 2 for NUMERIC DIGITS can have a drastic effect on arithmetic. Of course, the same effect occurs with NUMERIC DIGITS 9. It's just easier to ignore it because of the much smaller relative size of the rounding effect. Notice also that REXX does not round off the numbers before operating on them. If that were the case, 95 would round to 100, and 100 - 95 would be 0.

For a more complicated example, let's figure out the value of

```
0.00445 - 0.004505
```

In exponential form the first operand is 4.45E-3, so it does not need to be truncated, but the second is 4.505E-3, so it is truncated (not rounded) to 4.50E-3 to have three significant digits. Then we compute

```
4.45E-3 - 4.50E-3
```

which is -0.05E-3. Now we have to round this result since there are more than two digits, including the one to the left of the decimal point. Rounding is done in the usual way: if the digit to be rounded off is 5 or more, add 1 to the digit to its left, otherwise just drop it. (The sign of the number is not considered.) So we have $-0.1E-3$. In nonexponential form this is -0.0001, and this is the way the result is finally expressed. This follows from the rules below about the use of exponential representation because there are not more than four digits to the right of the decimal point.

If we had computed instead

```
0.00446 - 0.004505
```

we would get $-0.04E-3$. We are still obliged to round this to two digits, but now the result is 0 after rounding. So the final result is 0.

To some extent, cases like this may seem paradoxical. Why, after all, should one expect $.00446 - .004505$ to be 0? The answer is the somewhat artificial nature of the example. We have been illustrating how the setting of NUMERIC DIGITS (just 2 in this example) affects arithmetic operations. In practice, most programs will hardly ever use anything other than the default NUMERIC DIGITS 9. There is almost no performance penalty for doing so, since the number of digits of precision in most numbers used in typical REXX programs is usually much less anyway. When doing scientific or engineering calculations where the quantities involved approach nine digits of precision, you might well raise NUMERIC DIGITS somewhat higher, to avoid unnecessary loss of precision.

Whether you actually need great precision or only a little, it's easy in REXX to compute with a lot more than you really need. Then, for saving or reporting final results, you can use the TRUNC() or FORMAT() built-in functions to express your answers.

These considerations of how NUMERIC DIGITS affects arithmetic operations, subtraction in particular, are also relevant to comparison of numbers. When both operands are numbers, the normal REXX comparison operators (<, <=, =, >, >=) become numeric comparisons. That is, they are based on the actual numbers rather than on the exact string representations, which may be misleading. (For instance, the string representation of a number can have leading blanks without affecting the number. The strict comparison operators (<<, ==, etc.) should be used when the character representation is the important thing.)

Numeric comparisons in REXX are defined in terms of the subtraction and comparison to 0. That is, A < B just in case A − B < 0, A = B just in case A − B = 0, and so forth. REXX uses this slightly roundabout definition because, as we have just seen, it is quite possible for two "different" numbers to have a difference of 0. In this case, REXX stipulates that the numbers are equal. Thus the expressions

```
0.00445 < 0.004505
0.00446 = 0.004505
```

both have the value 1, by the preceding calculations, if NUMERIC DIGITS is 2. Of course, if NUMERIC DIGITS is 9, as usual, then

```
0.00446 < 0.004505
```

as you would expect. This is true even if NUMERIC DIGITS is 3. The point is, use a small value for NUMERIC DIGITS only if you find this way of looking at numeric comparisons useful for your purposes.

EXPONENTIAL REPRESENTATION

Even when a number produced as an arithmetic result does not require rounding to stay within NUMERIC DIGITS of precision, REXX may still change its representation to the exponential form. For instance, if NUMERIC DIGITS is 3, then an arithmetic result of 1000 will be expressed as 1.00E+3. The rule is that a result will be expressed in exponential notation if the number of digits before the decimal point is more than NUMERIC DIGITS or if the number of digits after the decimal point (disregarding any trailing zeros) is more than twice NUMERIC DIGITS. Otherwise, a result will be expressed in nonexponential notation.

Note that this does not apply to the results of built-in functions. For instance (still with NUMERIC DIGITS 3),

```
pos('1', copies('0',1000)'1')
```

has 1001 as a result.

WHOLE NUMBERS

Many instructions and built-in functions in REXX, as well as certain other circumstances, require argument values which are whole numbers. This is a number which is an integer, i.e., has no fractional part, or nothing but zeros after the decimal point when expressed in nonexponential form. And in addition there is a limit on how large the number can be: a whole number must have no more than NUMERIC DIGITS to the left of the decimal point (excluding leading zeros). In other words, a whole number is an integer which would not need to be expressed in exponential form according to the preceding rule.

This isn't to say that a number in exponential form can't be a valid whole number. For instance, if NUMERIC DIGITS is 9, 1.1E2, 1E1, and 1E8 are all whole numbers, though 1E9 is not.

The following are circumstances in which REXX requires whole numbers:

positional patterns in PARSE templates.

the right operand of the exponentiation operator (**) (but not necessarily the exponent of a number represented in exponential form: e.g., 1E9999 is acceptable even if NUMERIC DIGITS is 3).

the repetition count in a DO instruction.

values specified in NUMERIC DIGITS or FUZZ.

trace counts specified in the TRACE instruction.

certain arguments of some built-in functions: ARG(), D2C(), D2X(), and SOURCELINE(). Also, string functions which take length or position arguments require them to be whole numbers. In general, such functions require whole numbers because their arguments must be exact values which cannot admit rounding to NUMERIC DIGITS of precision.

the string arguments to C2D() and X2D() must be such that the function result is a whole number.

results of the operations of integer division and remainder must be whole numbers.

There is currently some variability in how different REXX implementations deal with these rules. The problem occurs with values less than 9 of NUMERIC DIGITS. Many implementations allow integers up to nine digits to be used as valid whole numbers for most purposes even though, strictly speaking, they are not when NUMERIC DIGITS is less than 9. This is a sensible policy, but it points up another good reason not to set NUMERIC DIGITS less than 9, because you can't be sure of portability.

The DATATYPE() built-in function can always be used to check whether a given string represents a valid whole number. That is

```
datatype(string, 'w')
```

has a value of 1 if string is a valid whole number, and 0 otherwise.

ARGUMENTS TO BUILT-IN FUNCTIONS

Many built-in functions do not require that their arguments be whole numbers but do round off the arguments before using them. These are primarily the mathematical functions ABS(), FORMAT(), MAX(), MIN(), SIGN(), and TRUNC(). This is appropriate, since such functions are really arithmetic operators in function form.

BUILT-IN FUNCTIONS FOR NUMERIC FORMATTING AND ARITHMETIC

REXX arithmetic often produces results with quite a few digits after the decimal point, particularly in calculations that involve any division. Unless you use integer division, or happen to get results that have an exact decimal representation, this is more or less guaranteed: $1/3$ becomes 0.33333333. This is usually more digits than you ordinarily want to bother with when displaying results. REXX doesn't require you to use arcane *format* statements to display output as do most other languages. But if you care about the appearance of reports you will usually want to change some of the REXX formatting defaults.

The simplest way to do this is with the TRUNC() built-in function. Its format is

```
TRUNC(number, [digits])
```

where number is the number to be truncated, and digits is the number of digits to be included to the right of the decimal point. The default for digits is 0, which causes the function to return the integer part of the number. Although the function is called *truncate,* extra zeros will be added if necessary. If zero digits are requested, the decimal point itself will be omitted. The result is never affected by the NUMERIC DIGITS setting. Also, exponential form will never be used, so TRUNC() provides a convenient way to convert to nonexponential form.

Sometimes, more control is needed over the representation of a number, particularly for numbers used in tabular reports. The FORMAT() built-in function can handle this problem. Its form is

```
FORMAT(number, [m], [n], [exp1], [exp2])
```

Number is the number to be formatted. M is the number of digits allowed before the decimal point, and n is the number after the decimal point. The number will be represented in exponential or nonexponential form according to the usual rule: exponential form is used just in case more than NUMERIC DIGITS are required before the decimal point or twice NUMERIC DIGITS are required after the decimal point. The exp2 argument can be used to change this *trigger point:* if specified, it is the number used instead of NUMERIC DIGITS to determine whether to use exponential form. Exp1 determines how many digits should be used for the exponent (if required), excluding E and the sign. All arguments except number must be nonnegative whole numbers.

If the number of places before the decimal point isn't specified, only as many as required will be used, with any blanks before or after the sign of the number being removed. A + sign, if any, is also removed. But if the number is negative, m must allow room for the – sign. An error results if not enough room is allowed. The number will be padded on the left with blanks if m is specified and there are fewer digits than that before the decimal point. Extra zeros are added after the decimal point if n is larger than the number of existing digits. If there are more digits after the decimal point than will fit, the number is rounded. (Note that this differs slightly from the TRUNC() function, which truncates instead of rounds.) Examples:

```
FORMAT(' + 1.2 ', 2, 2)    " 1.20"
FORMAT(' – 1.2 ', 2, 2)    "-1.20"
FORMAT('1.23456', 2, 3)    " 1.235"
FORMAT('1.23E1', 2, 3)     "12.300"
FORMAT('1.567', 2, 0)      " 2"
```

You can force a number into exponential form by using a value of 0 for exp2. However, if the exponent is 0, then the exponent is simply omitted (if exp1 isn't specified), or replaced by exp1+2 blanks, to keep the field width right (if exp1 is specified). Examples:

```
FORMAT(-12.3, 3, 3, , 0)   " -1.230E+1"
FORMAT(-12.3, 3, 3, 2, 0)  " -1.230E+01"
FORMAT(-1.23, 3, 3, 1, 0)  " -1.230   "
FORMAT(-1.23, 3, 3, , 0)   " -1.230"
```

You can force a number into nonexponential form by using a value of 0 for exp1. If exp1 is specified but is not large enough, an error will result. Examples:

```
FORMAT(1.23456789E9, , 1, 0)   "1234567890.0"
FORMAT(1.23456789E8)           "123456789"
```

The last example is converted to nonexponential form, because when FORMAT() is used with no arguments other than the number, its result is the same as the expression number + 0.

If you are using FORMAT() to present numbers in tables or in other ways where the exact total field width occupied by the number matters, you should use the exp1 and exp2 arguments to ensure either that all possible numbers are in exponential form or nonexponential form. There is no way to specify the total field width except by m, n, and exp1 individually. The total field width will be m+n+1 (nonexponential form) or m+n+exp1+3 (exponential form).

ADDITIONAL MATHEMATICAL FUNCTIONS

REXX does not have standard built-in functions for the transcendental functions such as LOG, EXP, SIN, COS, TAN, etc. It does, however, support a few useful arithmetic functions: ABS( ), SIGN( ), MIN( ), and MAX( ). They work more or less as would be expected:

ABS(number)
> Returns the absolute value of number. It is the same as number + 0, without the sign.

SIGN(number)
> Returns –1 if number is less than 0, 0 if it is equal to 0, and 1 if it is greater than 0.

MIN(number, [number], ...)
> Returns the smallest argument. Remember that comparison in REXX is done by subtracting and comparing the result to zero. Arguments that are actually different may be considered to be equal, especially if NUMERIC DIGITS is small. For instance, if NUMERIC DIGITS is 2, 96 is *equal* to 100, i.e., their difference is zero. In a case like this, MIN( ) will always return the value of the first argument which is less than or equal to all the others. Thus min(96,100) is 96, but min(100,96) is 1.0E+2.

MAX(number, [number], ...)
> Returns the largest argument. More precisely, it returns the first argument which is greater than or equal to all of the others in the special sense that REXX uses.

There is just one other purely mathematical function, which is useful in games or simulations: RANDOM( ). It generates pseudo-random numbers according to an algorithm which is not specified and may vary from implementation to implementation.

A *seed* value can optionally be specified. The random number algorithm uses the seed to determine the first number in the sequence. No number by itself, strictly speaking is *random*. It is, rather, the sequence that is random. Each seed determines the whole sequence (which is why it is not really random), and different seeds almost always produce different sequences. Consequently, you should supply a seed only on the first call to RANDOM( ) in each program. This causes the same sequence to be generated each time, so the program is repeatable. If you don't supply a seed on the first call, one is chosen automatically, typically based on the time of day. This is better for games, since you will generally get different sequences each time.

You can also specify the range of numbers to be produced by RANDOM(). If you simply want a whole number between 0 and some maximum value (inclusive) you can use

```
RANDOM(max)
```

where max is the maximum possible value. This form does not allow you to specify the seed. More generally you can use

```
RANDOM([min], [max], [seed])
```

where min is the minimum possible value and max is the maximum. Min, max, and seed must be nonnegative whole numbers. In addition, the range between the minimum and maximum cannot exceed 100,000.

There is one other function which is partly mathematical, but which has other uses as well: DATATYPE(). Its syntax is:

```
DATATYPE(string, [type])
```

String is always the character string whose type is to be determined. If type is omitted, the function returns NUM if the string is a valid number, otherwise CHAR. A string is a valid number or not depending on whether it can be used in arithmetic without error, according to the rules listed at the beginning of this chapter. DATATYPE() can be used to validate any data before using it in calculations if you want to bullet-proof your program against unexpected termination due to bad data.

Finer discriminations of the type of a string can be made by supplying the type argument. If it is present, the function returns 1 or 0, according as string is or is not a valid instance of the specified type. The possible values are:

'A' Alphanumeric—all characters in the string are upper- or lowercase alphabetic characters or a digit from 0 to 9.

'B' Bit—all characters in the string are either 0 or 1. Blanks are not permitted, so this is slightly different from the format that is permitted for a bit string literal.

'L' Lowercase—all characters in the string are lowercase alphabetic characters.

'M' Mixed case—all characters in the string are upper- or lowercase alphabetic characters.

'N' Numeric—the string is a valid number. This is 1 just in case DATATYPE() with only one argument would return NUM.

'S'   Symbol—the string consists only of characters which are valid in REXX symbols. This is not quite the same thing as saying the string is actually a valid REXX symbol. It might, for example, be longer than the implementation allows.

'U'   Upper case—all characters in the string are uppercase alphabetic characters.

'W'   Whole number—the string is a valid whole number, as discussed earlier, according to the current value of NUMERIC DIGITS. Remember that a number may not be *whole* if it is too large, as well as if it is not integral.

'X'   Hexadecimal—the string represents a valid hexadecimal number. This means that it may contain blanks, digits 0 through 9, "a" through "f", or "A" through "F". If spaces are used, the string must follow the rules for hexadecimal literals. A null string is specifically included.

Except for the 'X' type, null strings are not included in any of the types, and DATATYPE() will return 0 if the first argument is a null string.

14

Tracing and Debugging

Debugging probably ranks near the bottom of the list of the aspects of programming that programmers most enjoy, right along with documentation. Unfortunately, it is even more unavoidable.

Few programming languages have debugging facilities of any kind as part of the language definition, but REXX is an exception. The TRACE instruction has been provided to enable a number of useful tracing and debugging capabilities.

On the other hand, most modern implementations of popular languages, such as C, now come with very powerful debugging tools external to the language itself. These tools include features like full-screen displays, sophisticated breakpoint capabilities, and automatic display of program data as it changes.

Though REXX's debugging capabilities are relatively primitive in comparison with the current state of the art, being part of the language definition confers on them the advantage that one can work with a complete REXX implementation on any platform and be able to use familiar, standardized tools for debugging.

THE TRACE INSTRUCTION

All REXX debugging services are enabled and controlled with the TRACE instruction. Its syntax is

```
TRACE setting
```

where setting is a code that selects a tracing option. Occasionally it is useful to have this setting determined dynamically, so it is also possible to use the form

```
TRACE VALUE expression
```

where expression is a REXX expression that evaluates to one of the allowable settings. One might do this, for instance, in order to be able to control tracing centrally with a program command or option. The TRACE instructions could then be left in the code but rendered inoperative unless requested.

One thing to remember is that TRACE is just a normal, executable REXX instruction. So its use can also be governed with ordinary REXX conditional statements like IF and SELECT. In particular, it does not take effect until encountered in the normal flow of program execution. Therefore, you can place it only where tracing is actually needed within a program to examine a particular problem.

Like other REXX state information, the TRACE setting is saved before calling a subroutine and restored afterwards. Though the current setting is in effect when the subroutine is entered, you can change it in the subroutine. Then when the subroutine returns, the original setting will be restored.

In many REXX implementations it is also possible to control tracing externally with system *environment* variables or with options on the command line that starts a REXX program. Although this is often very useful in debugging, there's not much we can say about it here since the actual usage varies among implementations. Once enabled by whatever means, however, specific trace settings should behave the same on any implementation.

REXX tracing occurs in one of two modes: passive or interactive. In the passive mode, certain program data is traced through messages written to the standard output stream, but the program does not pause and its operation is not otherwise affected. In the interactive tracing mode, program execution actually stops after most clauses are traced to allow the user to enter any desired REXX statement. One may invoke SAY statements to display the values of variables, call subroutines to perform more complex tasks, or use assignment statements to change the values of variables. Many clauses can actually be reexecuted after such a pause, to test the effect of any changes made.

PASSIVE TRACING

We'll consider passive tracing first. This is invoked by choosing appropriate TRACE settings. For general debugging you will primarily want to see exactly which statements of a program are executed, and possibly the results of expressions used in those statements. The setting to use may be one of the following:

A—trace all clauses

R—trace all clauses and all expression results

I—trace all clauses and all intermediate evaluation results

0—turn off tracing

Only one setting may be used at a time; they cannot be combined. The difference among the first three settings is the level of detail presented on the evaluation of REXX expressions. The instruction

```
trace a
```

simply enables the display of each clause as it is executed. To get more detail, use

```
trace r
```

In addition to displaying each clause as it is executed, REXX will also display the final results of the evaluation of any expression in the clause. For instance, when the following instruction is executed:

```
x = '***' copies('-', 10) '***'
```

then REXX displays on the screen:

```
3 *-* x = '***' copies('-', 10) '***'
  >>>    "*** _____ ***"
```

The first line here is the trace of the clause before it is executed. It begins with the line number of the clause in the source file (3). This is followed by *-*, which is an eye-catcher used by REXX to indicate the trace of a source line. After that is the actual clause being traced. The following line contains the result of evaluating the expression in the assignment. The >>> is an eye-catcher that indicates an expression result.

A third level of trace detail is enabled with the instruction

```
trace i
```

which traces all intermediate results in expression evaluation. If this is in effect, then for the previous example REXX would display

```
3 *-* x = '***' copies('-', 10) '***'
  >L>    "***"
```

```
>L>    "_"
>L>    "10"
>F>    "_ _ _ _ _ _ _ _ _ _"
>O>    "*** _ _ _ _ _ _ _ _ _ _"
>L>    "***"
>O>    "*** _ _ _ _ _ _ _ _ _ _ ***"
```

This is obviously very detailed, probably too detailed for general use.
Here, after tracing the source line, REXX displays the results of every
intermediate step in the evaluation. Each line begins with an eye-
catcher that indicates what is going on. The possible values for this
three-character prefix are

>L> indicates a literal value

>F> indicates the result of a function call

>O> indicates the result of a binary operation

>V> indicates the value of a variable

>C> indicates the fully substituted name of a compound variable

>P> indicates the result of a unary (prefix) operation

The example above illustrates only the first three of these. As you can
see, the trace gives you very explicit information about what is hap-
pening as REXX evaluates an expression. In particular, it can help you
understand better how REXX works, because it indicates the precise
sequence in which operations take place. This can be very instructive
as you are learning REXX. It is also very helpful during debugging in
cases where you don't understand why a given expression results in a
particular value.

Here's another example that illustrates some of the other information that can be presented as a result of using TRACE I:

```
/* trace compound variables */
trace i
i = 1
x.1 = -3 + i
y = x.i
```

And here is the output:

```
3 *-* i = 1
   >L>    "1"
4 *-* x.1 = -3 + i
   >L>    "3"
   >P>    "-3"
   >V>    "1"
```

```
   >O>    "-2"
5  *-*  y = x.i
   >C>    "X.1"
   >V>    "-2"
```

This example shows tracing of variables, prefix operations, and compound variable substitution. You may find this useful while learning REXX to help understand just how compound variables work.

TRACE R is also useful for understanding how the PARSE instruction works. It will show exactly what is assigned to each variable. For instance, the statement

```
parse value 'The Wrath of Khan' with a b .
```

would produce the trace

```
3  *-*  parse value 'The Wrath of Khan' with a b .
   >>>    "The Wrath of Khan"
   >>>    "The"
   >>>    "Wrath"
   >.>    "of Khan"
```

The first line after the trace of the instruction is the value of the literal expression. The next three lines are the assignments to a, b, and the period used as a placeholder.

A general debugging strategy using the passive tracing facilities would be to use TRACE A first to get an overview of how the program is behaving. Very often when a program under development is tested for the first time you will find it does something strange, like exiting mysteriously, going into a loop, or producing completely unreasonable results. Usually this is because DO loops or conditional instructions like IF do not work as expected. TRACE A is the easiest way to understand the overall flow of control. It will tell you exactly what statements of the program were executed.

Generally, you will find that a conditional instruction did not work as you expected, causing the program to take an unexpected path of execution, because some expression did not evaluate the way it should have. Once you have identified where things went wrong, TRACE R is a good way to try to find out why they went wrong. Sometimes, in dealing with particularly complicated expressions, you will need to use TRACE I to see how they are actually evaluated. But because of the volume of information these tracing directives cause, it is best to place them in your code as near as possible to the location where the problem occurs.

There are several other kinds of passive tracing settings that can be used to handle a different class of problems. Many REXX programs have as their primary purpose the issuing of commands to an external environment such as the operating system. Errors occur when the program issues commands which are not exactly what you intended. To deal with problems like this, you can use one of the following settings:

F—trace commands that end with a "failure" error code

E—trace commands that end with any abnormal error code

C—trace all commands

When you use TRACE C, all commands are traced before they are executed. The trace includes the original source code statement in the program, as well as the evaluated result which is passed to the external environent. For instance,

```
trace c
file = 'payroll.dat'
'listfile' file
```

might produce

```
3 *-* 'listfile' file
   >>>    "listfile payroll.dat"
LISTFILE Error 135: File(s) not found.
   +++ RC(28) +++
```

This begins with the instruction as it appeared in the program, followed by the result of evaluation. This occurs before the program is actually executed. The third line of output is an error message from the program. The fourth line is trace output that is generated because an abnormal (nonzero) return code was produced by the program. The number (28) is the actual return code, which is assigned to the RC variable.

Usually you do not want this much detail. TRACE C will generate output for all external commands executed. Normally you only need to know about commands that do not work properly. As discussed in the chapter on commands to external environments, this is usually indicated by a nonzero return code from the command. However, the specific details vary quite a bit from one environment to another, and sometimes commands will place information in return codes even when they have not encountered an error condition.

REXX provides the TRACE E instruction to trace only those commands which end with an error. If we had used this instead of TRACE C in the last example, we would get the output

```
LISTFILE Error 135: File(s) not found.
3 *-* 'listfile' file
```

```
>>>    "listfile payroll.dat"
+++ RC(28) +++
```

This is different only in that the program error message comes first, because the trace output occurs after the command has run, when REXX knows that it ended with an error. If it had produced a return code of 0, no trace would have occurred at all.

TRACE E is a useful instruction in programs that depend on the execution of external commands, because it alerts you when the commands do not work correctly. Sometimes even this produces extraneous trace information, for instance if your program already tests the RC variable to detect errors. One further alternative is TRACE F, which traces instructions only when they end in a *failure*. This condition is usually defined as the production of a negative return code by the command. Normally this means a more severe type of error, such as an inability of the operating system to even run the command, perhaps because it could not be found or there was not enough memory to run it. These are still just debugging tools. If you want to write your program so that it responds appropriately to error conditions, you need to test return codes explicitly, or else use the CALL ON ERROR or SIGNAL ON ERROR instructions to handle the situation.

INTERACTIVE TRACING

Passive tracing can illuminate many problems, but for serious debugging work it is much more effective to be able to interact directly with the program. The way interactive tracing works is that, when it is active, REXX will pause after executing most statements that have been traced. The user is prompted for input. The input can be either a null line, to proceed with the program, or an = sign, to reexecute the clause that was just traced. Any other input is assumed to be one or more REXX statements, which will be handled generally as they would by the INTERPRET instruction.

Interactive tracing is requested by prefixing the trace setting in the TRACE instruction with a question mark. For instance,

```
trace ?a
```

causes tracing of all clauses with the addition of the interaction as just described.

```
trace ?c
```

similarly traces only external commands, and pauses for interaction only after such commands have been executed.

There are several cases in which REXX will not pause after executing a clause even if it has been traced. Clauses consisting of END, THEN, ELSE, OTHERWISE, RETURN, EXIT, SIGNAL, and CALL are in this category. The reason is that REXX would be unable to safely reexecute such clauses since they have already altered the flow of control within the program. Similarly, clauses that raise a condition for which there is an enabled condition handler or that cause a SYNTAX error cannot be reexecuted, and REXX will not pause for them.

When REXX does stop during interactive tracing, you can issue just about any valid REXX statement or group of statements (separated by semicolons). Typically you would use one or more SAY statements in order to examine the contents of variables or the values of expressions. If you need to examine a large number of variables you might even provide special purpose subroutines in your program to display the data. These routines can be invoked from a trace prompt with a CALL instruction.

You can change any of the current generation of variables with one or more assignment statements. You can also invoke procedures that make changes to variables. Such changes are persistent, just as if the statements had been executed normally as part of the program. If you then resume program execution by entering an = sign, the statement that caused the pause is reexecuted with the new variables. In this way you can, for example, change the outcome of an IF or WHEN test.

Another thing you can do at a trace prompt is to issue commands to external environments. You might, for instance, view or modify files used by the program to examine their current state. Of course, this could be tricky if the file is currently open in the REXX program, so it should be done only with some caution.

If things look really hopeless, you can simply enter

```
exit
```

and the program will immediately terminate.

Lastly, you can modify the operation of tracing itself from the interactive trace prompt. For instance, if you use the instruction

```
trace o
```

tracing will be turned off and the program will resume execution immediately. You might do this if you have been tracing all statements, but you enter a subroutine you don't care to trace. Tracing will then resume when the subroutine returns. You can also use

```
trace ?
```

to turn off interactive tracing, but continue to trace instructions pas-

sively. Any other form of the trace instruction may also be used interactively to change the type of tracing in effect.

There is another form of the TRACE instruction which is particularly
useful during interactive tracing. If you specify a positive number as
the TRACE operand, then tracing will proceed for that number of traced
clauses without pausing in a case where REXX ordinarily would pause.
That is, exactly the same statements are traced, but REXX does not
pause until the specified number have been traced. You can also turn
off tracing completely for a given number of statements by specifying
the number as a negative quantity.

The tricky part is estimating the correct number of statements to
specify. Normally you would do this in a loop, because you want to let
it run to a certain point and you know fairly well how many statements
to go. Unfortunately, REXX has no more advanced debugging capabilities, such as executing until a particular variable is changed or
reaches a certain value, or until an expression has a certain value.

Another thing that REXX tracing cannot do is to execute until a particular routine is called. It can, however, trace *labels,* that is, trace
whenever a label is encountered. This is done by using L as the TRACE
setting:

```
trace l
```

So if you have a loop which contains only one subroutine call, and
you want to skip over the first 50 calls, you could use

```
trace ?l
trace 50
```

to stop at the 51st subroutine call.

When you enable interactive tracing with a TRACE instruction like

```
trace ?c
```

(and especially in a case such as this, where not all subsequent instructions will be traced), then further TRACE instructions in the program
will be ignored. This is to avoid prematurely terminating interactive
tracing mode. However, if you want to be sure that trace directives are
always effective, there is a TRACE() built-in function. Its syntax is

```
TRACE([setting])
```

where setting is the trace setting to use. The function returns the current trace setting and changes to the new one (if any). Numeric values
for setting are not allowed in this case.

When you enter one or more statements at the interactive trace prompt, there are certain subtle differences in the way they are executed:

TRACE instructions in the input (but not in other code which might be called from an instruction in the input) are honored. Moreover, they cause REXX to resume program execution until the next statement (if any) traced according to the new setting is executed. So if you want to alter the trace setting and then reexecute the current clause, you must use the TRACE() built-in function.

No tracing of clauses is performed except for the display of return codes from commands (if appropriate).

Commands to external environments do not cause the RC variable to be set.

Enabled condition handlers are ignored, even in code called from input statements. If a SYNTAX or HALT condition is raised during execution, a message is displayed, execution stops, and REXX returns to the interactive trace prompt.

REXX Instructions

Several conventions are used in the following instruction syntax summaries. REXX keywords are in uppercase. These must be spelled as shown, though any mixture of lower- and uppercase may actually be used. Elements in lowercase represent user-supplied information. Anything enclosed in brackets ([ ]) is optional. Alternative forms of the instruction are listed on separate lines. Ellipses (. . .) indicate that the preceding element may be repeated. Semicolons may be included at the end of any clause. They are included below only when required in a context that is not the end of a line.

```
ADDRESS [environment [command]]
ADDRESS VALUE [environment]
```

Summary: changes the current default external command environment or issues a command to a specified external environment.

Arguments:

environment: name of a command environment.

command: command to issue to a command environment.

Notes: When ADDRESS is used by itself, it makes the previous command environment the current environment. If VALUE is not used, the specified environment is taken literally as a name without evaluation. If no command is specified, the environment named becomes the current command environment. If a command is included, it is issued to the specified environment.

```
ARG [template]
```

Summary: converts program or procedure arguments to uppercase and parses them according to a supplied parse template.

Arguments:

template: a parse template.

Notes: The template may contain one or more subtemplates, separated by commas. Each subtemplate is used to parse the corresponding argument. If there are more subtemplates than arguments, variables named in the subtemplate are set to a null string. ARG is equivalent to PARSE UPPER ARG.

```
CALL name [expression] [,expressionn] . . .
CALL ON condition [NAME handler]
CALL OFF condition
```

Summary: either calls a subroutine with specified expression values as arguments or enables or disables a handler for a specified condition.

Arguments:

name: the name of a subroutine, which may be a label in the program, the name of a built-in function, or the name of an external function.

expression: argument to the subroutine.

condition: one of the following condition names: ERROR, FAILURE, HALT, or NOTREADY.

handler: the name of a handler for the specified condition.

Notes: The first form of CALL is a normal subroutine call. The second form enables a handler for a particular condition. If no handler name is specified, it is the same as the condition name. The third form disables any existing handler for the specified condition.

```
DO [repetitor] [conditional]; [statement-list] END [symbol]
```

Summary: delimits a group of statements which may be treated as a single statement and optionally controls repetitive execution.

Arguments:

repetitor: either an expression, the keyword FOREVER, or a phrase of the form assignment [TO expt] [BY expb] [FOR expf], where expt, expb, and expf are expressions.

conditional: either WHILE expression or UNTIL expression.

statement-list: zero or more statements separated (if on the same line) by semicolons.

symbol: the symbol which is the target of an assignment when the assignment form of repetitor is used.

Notes: TO, BY, and FOR may be used in any order in an assignment repetitor. The expressions following TO, BY, or FOR may not contain the keywords WHILE or UNTIL.

DROP name [name] . . .

Summary: resets simple and compound variables to an uninitialized state.

Arguments:

name: a symbol that names a variable or a stem, or a symbol enclosed in parentheses.

Notes: When a stem is dropped, all variables having that stem become uninitialized. When a name is enclosed in parentheses, it is assumed to be a string consisting of names of other variables. All variables named in the list (but not the list variable itself) become uninitialized.

EXIT [expression]

Summary: terminates execution of a REXX program and passes a return value to the caller.

Arguments:

expression: value to be returned to caller.

Notes: Only the current REXX program is terminated. A calling REXX program (if any) will resume execution at the point the current program was invoked.

IF expression THEN statement1; [ELSE statement2]

Summary: conditionally executes a statement based on the value of an expression.

Arguments:

expression: a REXX expression that evaluates to 0 or 1.

statement1: statement that is executed if the expression value is 1.

statement2: statement that is executed if the expression value is 0.

Notes: THEN is a reserved word and may not be used in the expression. Either statement may be a DO group, consisting of a list of statements contained between DO and END.

INTERPRET expression

Summary: executes one or more REXX statements that are generated as the value of an expression.

Arguments:

expression: an arbitrary REXX expression.

Notes: The value of the expression should be a list of REXX statements separated by semicolons. DO, IF, and SELECT statements (if any) must be complete. The statements are executed as if they were a part of the program at that point.

ITERATE [symbol]

Summary: causes control to pass to the top of an iterative DO group.

Arguments:

symbol: the name of the control variable of an active DO group.

Notes: The control variable (if any) will be incremented appropriately and the terminating conditions will be tested as if the END statement closing the DO group had been encountered. A symbol may be specified to identify the DO group.

LEAVE [symbol]

Summary: causes control to pass to the statement following the END of an iterative DO group.

Arguments:

symbol: the name of the control variable of an active DO group.

Notes: A symbol may be specified to identify the DO group.

NOP

Summary: instruction that does nothing.

Notes: NOP can be used as the instruction required after THEN in an IF or SELECT instruction.

```
NUMERIC DIGITS [expression]
NUMERIC FORM [form]
NUMERIC FUZZ [expression]
```

Summary: defines certain parameters of REXX numeric representation and arithmetic.

Arguments:

expression: REXX expression that evaluates to a positive integer.

form: either a literal SCIENTIFIC or ENGINEERING, or an expression that evaluates to SCIENTIFIC or ENGINEERING.

Notes: NUMERIC DIGITS is (roughly) the number of significant digits retained in a numeric value. NUMERIC FUZZ is the number of least significant digits ignored when doing numeric comparisons. NUMERIC FORM specifies whether the exponent of a number in exponential form should be a multiple of three.

```
PARSE [UPPER] source [template]
```

Summary: parses an input string into REXX variables according to rules specified in a template.

Arguments:

source: defines the source of the input string, which can be:

ARG	program or subroutine arguments.
LINEIN	line read from standard input stream.
PULL	line read from external data queue.
SOURCE	information about the program.
VALUE	the value of an expression.
VAR	the value of a variable.
VERSION	information about the REXX language processor.

template: a parse template.

Notes: When the source is VALUE it must be followed by an expression and then the reserved word WITH (which cannot occur in the expression). When the source is VAR it must be followed by the name of a variable.

```
PROCEDURE [EXPOSE name [name] . . . ]
```

Summary: creates a new generation of variables for a subroutine.

Arguments:

name: a symbol that names a variable or a stem, or a symbol enclosed in parentheses.

Notes: When a stem is exposed, all variables having that stem are exposed. When a name is enclosed in parentheses, it is assumed to be a string consisting of names of other variables. All variables named in the list and the list variable are exposed.

PULL [template]

Summary: converts to uppercase and parses a line of input read from the external data queue or the standard input stream.

Arguments:

template: a parse template.

Notes: PULL is equivalent to PARSE UPPER PULL.

PUSH [expression]

Summary: places a line of data in the external data queue.

Arguments:

expression: data to be placed in the queue.

Notes: The data is placed in the queue LIFO (*last-in-first-out*). A null string is placed in the queue if the expression is omitted.

QUEUE [expression]

Summary: places a line of data in the external data queue.

Arguments:

expression: data to be placed in the queue.

Notes: The data is placed in the queue FIFO (*first-in-first-out*). A null string is placed in the queue if the expression is omitted.

RETURN [expression]

Summary: terminates execution of a subroutine and passes a return value to the caller.

Arguments:

expression: value to be returned to caller.

Notes: RETURN does not terminate a REXX program unless it occurs in the topmost procedure of the program.

SAY [expression]

Summary: writes data to the standard output stream (usually the terminal).

Arguments:

expression: the data to be written.

Notes: A null string is written if the expression is omitted. SAY is generally equivalent to a call to LINEOUT() with the first argument omitted.

SELECT; when-list [OTHERWISE [statement-list]] END

Summary: execute a statement depending on a set of conditional expressions.

Arguments:

when-list: a list of clauses of the form WHEN expression THEN statement.

statement-list: one or more REXX statements, separated by semicolons (if on the same line).

Notes: Each expression following a WHEN is evaluated in sequence. The expression must evaluate to 0 or 1. The statement following THEN is executed for the first expression that has the value 1. THEN is a reserved word which cannot be used in any of the expressions. If none of the expressions has the value 1, the statements following OTHERWISE (if present) are executed.

SIGNAL name
SIGNAL VALUE expression
SIGNAL ON condition [NAME handler]
SIGNAL OFF condition

Summary: either transfers control to a specified label in the program or enables or disables a handler for a specified condition.

Arguments:

name: a label in the program.

expression: a REXX expression whose value is a label in the program.

condition: one of the following condition names: ERROR, FAILURE, HALT, NOTREADY, NOVALUE, or SYNTAX.

handler: the name of a handler for the specified condition.

Notes: The first two forms of SIGNAL are used to transfer control to the specified label. All active DO loops are terminated, but control remains within the currently active procedure. The third form enables a handler for a particular condition. If no handler name is specified, it is the same as the condition name. The fourth form disables any existing handler for the specified condition.

TRACE [VALUE] expression

Summary: controls REXX program tracing.

Arguments:

expression: selects type of tracing as follows:
A—trace all clauses.
C—trace commands to external environments.
E—trace external commands that end with an error.
F—trace external commands that end with a failure.
I—trace all clauses and intermediate results of expressions.
L—trace all labels.
N—same as F (the default).
O—disable tracing.
R—trace all clauses and final results of expressions.

Notes: If the expression is not a symbol or literal but does begin with a symbol or literal, it must be preceded by the keyword VALUE. The value of the expression may be prefixed with ? to indicate that interactive tracing is to be toggled on or off.

REXX Built-in Functions

The same notational conventions apply as in Appendix A.

`ABBREV(string1, string2, [length])`

Summary: indicates whether one string is a beginning segment of another.

Arguments:

> `string1`: the *long form* being checked for abbreviation.
>
> `string2`: the string which is a potential abbreviation.
>
> `length`: the minimum length of `string2` that will qualify as an abbreviation.

Notes: The function returns 1 if `string2` is a substring of `string1`, starting at the first position and if it is at least length characters long, otherwise it returns 0. The default for `length` is the length of `string2`.

`ABS(number)`

Summary: returns the absolute value of its argument.

Arguments:

> `number`: a valid REXX number.

Notes: The result is formatted according to the current setting of NUMERIC DIGITS.

ADDRESS()

Summary: returns the name of the current default environment.

Notes: The default environment name is set with the ADDRESS instruction.

ARG([argument-number], [option])

Summary: returns either the number of arguments, the value of a specific argument, or whether a specific argument has been included or omitted.

Arguments:

argument-number: the number of the argument in question.

option: one of the following:
'E'—test whether argument exists.
'O'—test whether argument was omitted.

Notes: If no argument is specified, ARG() returns the number of arguments passed to the current internal or external procedure. If only the argument number is specified, ARG() returns the value of the designated argument. If option is also specified, ARG() returns 0 or 1 to indicate whether the argument was present.

BITAND(string1, [string2], [pad])

Summary: returns the logical AND of its arguments.

Arguments:

string1: first operand of AND.

string2: second operand of AND. Default is null string.

pad: character appended before the operation to the shorter of the two operands to make them equal in length if the operands are of different lengths.

Notes: BITAND() produces the logical bitwise AND of its operands. If no pad character is specified, the default is 'ff'x.

BITOR(string1, [string2], [pad])

Summary: returns the logical OR of its arguments.

Arguments:

string1: first operand of OR.

string2: second operand of OR. Default is null string.

pad: character appended before the operation to the shorter of the two operands to make them equal in length if the operands are of different lengths.

Notes: BITOR( ) produces the logical bitwise OR of its operands. If no pad character is specified, the default is '00'x.

BITXOR(string1, [string2], [pad])

Summary: returns the logical XOR of its arguments.

Arguments:

string1: first operand of XOR.

string2: second operand of XOR. Default is null string.

pad: character appended before the operation to the shorter of the two operands to make them equal in length if the operands are of different lengths.

Notes: BITXOR( ) produces the logical bitwise XOR of its operands. If no pad character is specified, the default is '00'x.

B2X(binary-string)

Summary: returns the hexadecimal representation of the given binary string.

Arguments:

binary-string: character string consisting of 0s and 1s to be converted.

Notes: Both the argument and the result of B2X( ) are character strings. B2X( ) coverts the input data from base 2 representation to base 16.

CENTER(string, length, [pad])

Summary: centers a string in a field of a specified width.

Arguments:

string: the string to be centered.

length: width of the field.

pad: character to be added if the field width exceeds the length of the string.

Notes: If the string is longer than the width of the field, CENTER() returns the central length characters of the string. If an odd number of characters is to be either added or removed, one more character is added to or removed from the right end than the left end.

CHARIN([stream], [position], [count])

Summary: returns characters read from the specified input stream.

Arguments:

stream: name of the input stream. Default is the standard input stream.

position: location within the input stream at which to begin reading.

count: number of characters to read.

Notes: The default position is the current read position, which is either the first character of the stream or the character following the last one read by CHARIN() or LINEIN(). The default count is 1. With a count of 0, CHARIN() returns a null string but moves the current read position as specified by the second argument.

CHAROUT([stream], [string], [position])

Summary: writes a string of characters to the specified output stream and returns the number of characters (if any) which could not be written.

Arguments:

stream: name of the output stream. Default is the standard output stream.

string: data to be written.

position: location within the output stream at which to begin writing.

Notes: The default position is the current write position, which is the position following either the last character of the stream or the last one written by CHAROUT() or LINEOUT(). If the string is omitted, the current write position is updated to the value specified by position. If both string and position are omitted, the output stream is closed.

CHARS([stream])

Summary: returns the number of characters remaining to be read in the specified input stream.

Arguments:

stream: name of the input stream. Default is the standard input stream.

Notes: The number of characters remaining to be read is defined to be the number of characters from the current read position to the end of the file.

COMPARE(string1, string2, [pad])

Summary: returns the position of the first mismatch between the two input strings.

Arguments:

string1: first string to be compared.

string2: second string to be compared.

pad: character appended before the operation to the shorter of the two operands to make them equal in length if the operands are of different lengths.

Notes: If the two strings are identical (after padding) COMPARE() returns 0.

CONDITION([option])

Summary: returns information associated with the current trapped condition.

Arguments:

option: select type of information, which can be one of the following:

'C'—name of the trapped condition.

'D'—further descriptive information about the trapped condition.

'I'—the instruction that invoked the condition handler.

'S'—state of handling for the condition.

Notes: CONDITION() returns a null string if no condition has been raised.

COPIES(string, count)

Summary: returns a concatenation of the specified number of copies of the input string.

Arguments:

string: the string to be copied.

count: number of copies.

Notes: Count must be a nonnegative whole number. COPIES() returns a null string if count is 0.

C2D(data, [length])

Summary: returns the value of the input data interpreted as a decimal number.

Arguments:

data: the data to be converted.

length: rightmost number of bytes of input data to be converted.

Notes: The data is assumed to be a binary representation of a number with the most significant byte at the left and the least significant byte at the right of the string. If a length is not specified, the number is assumed to be unsigned. If length is specified, the number is assumed to be signed, and only the rightmost length bytes are converted, padded on the left with 0 if necessary. The result must be a valid whole number according to the current setting of NUMERIC DIGITS.

C2X(data)

Summary: returns the hexadecimal representation of the input data.

Arguments:

data: the data to be converted.

Notes: C2X() returns a string consisting of hexadecimal digits (0–9, A–F) which give the internal representation of the input data.

DATATYPE(string, [type])

Summary: returns the type of the input string, or an indication of the class to which the data belongs.

Arguments:

string: the string whose type is needed.

type: a letter which selects a string type to test for, one of the following:

'A'—alphanumeric (a–z, A–Z, or 0–9).

'B'—binary (0 or 1).

'L'—lowercase (a–z).

'M'—mixed case (a–z or A–Z).

'N'—number (a valid REXX number).

'S'—symbol (only characters valid in REXX symbols).

'U'—uppercase (A–Z).

'W'—whole number (valid whole number with current NUMERIC DIGITS).

'X'—hexadecimal (a–f, A–F, 0–9).

Notes: If type is not specified, DATATYPE() returns NUM or CHAR depending on whether or not the string is a valid REXX number. If the type is specified, it returns 1 or 0 depending on whether or not the string belongs to the designated class.

DATE([option])

Summary: returns the current date.

Arguments:

option: a character that indicates the required date format, one of the following:

'B'—base date, number of complete days since January 1, 0001.

'D'—number of the current day of the year, starting with 1.

'E'—date in European format (dd/mm/yy).

'M'—full English name of the current month.

'N'—date in default format (dd Mmm yyyy).

'O'—date in orderable format (yy/mm/dd).

'S'—date in standard format (yyyymmdd).

'U'—date in US format (mm/dd/yy).

'W'—full English name of the current day.

Notes: The default format, which is provided if option is not specified, consists of two digits for the day, the first three characters of the English name of the month, and the year.

DELSTR(string, start, [length])

Summary: returns the input string from which a substring starting at a specified position is deleted.

Arguments:

string: the input string.

start: the starting position of the substring to be deleted.

length: the length of the substring to be deleted.

Notes: If length is not specified, all characters from the start position are deleted. If the start position is beyond the right end of the string, the string is returned unchanged.

DELWORD(string, start, [length])

Summary: returns the input string from which a substring starting at a specified word is deleted.

Arguments:

string: the input string.

start: the number of the word which starts the substring to be deleted.

length: the length in words of the substring to be deleted.

Notes: If length is not specified, the remainder of the string beginning with the specified word is deleted. If the number of the first word to be deleted is greater than the number of words in the string, the string is returned unchanged.

DIGITS()

Summary: retruns the current value of the NUMERIC DIGITS setting.

D2C(number, [length])

Summary: returns the internal representation of a decimal number.

Arguments:

number: whole number to be converted.

length: length of the result.

Notes: D2C() returns the internal representation of a number as a string of characters with the most significant byte at the left. If length is not specified, the number to be converted must be nonnegative. If length is specified and it is less than required for the entire internal representation, the leftmost (most significant) bytes are truncated. If length is longer than required, the result is sign-extended on the left.

D2X(number, [length])

Summary: returns the internal representation of a decimal number in hexadecimal form.

Arguments:

number: whole number to be converted.

length: length of the result in characters.

Notes: D2X() returns the internal representation of number as a string of hexadecimal digits with the most significant digit at the left. If length is not specified, the number to be converted must be nonnegative. If length is specified and it is less than required for the entire internal representation, the leftmost (most significant) digits are truncated. If length is longer than required, the result is sign-extended on the left.

ERRORTEXT(number)

Summary: returns the text of the message associated with the specified error.

Arguments:

number: the number of an error in the range 0–99.

Notes: If no error message is associated with the specified number, a null string is returned.

FORM()

Summary: returns the current value of NUMERIC FORM.

Notes: Possible values of NUMERIC FORM are SCIENTIFIC or ENGINEERING.

FORMAT(number, [m], [n], [exp1], [exp2])

Summary: formats a number with a given number of digits before and after the decimal point, and with a given number of digits in the exponent.

Arguments:

number: the number to be formatted.

m: number of digits before the decimal point in the result.

n: number of digits after the decimal point in the result.

exp1: number of digits in the exponent of the result.

exp2: number of digits required to trigger exponential notation.

Notes: The number is first rounded as in the result of the expression number + 0. The default values of m and n are the number of digits required for the integral and fractional parts, respectively. Exp2 is the trigger for exponential notation, whose default is NUMERIC DIGITS. That is, exponential notation will be used if the number has more than exp2 digits before the decimal point or more than 2*exp2 digits after the decimal point.

FUZZ( )

Summary: returns the current value of NUMERIC FUZZ.

Notes: NUMERIC FUZZ is the number of least significant digits that will be ignored in numeric comparisons of equality or inequality.

INSERT(string1, string2, [pos], [length], [pad])

Summary: inserts one string at a certain position in a second string.

Arguments:

string1: the string to be inserted.

string2: the string inserted into.

pos: the position in the second string at which the first is inserted.

length: length to which inserted string is extended or truncated.

pad: character appended to the first string when its length is to be extended.

Notes: The first string is inserted in the second string after the character identified by pos. The default position is 0, in which case the first string is inserted before the first character of the second. The default value of length is the length of the first string.

LASTPOS(target, string, [start])

Summary: returns the last position of one string in another, searching from right to left.

Arguments:

target: the string being searched for.

string: the string which is searched.

start: the starting position in the second string at which the search begins.

Notes: LASTPOS() returns 0 if the target string is null or if it is not found. The default start position is LENGTH(string).

LEFT(string, length, [pad])

Summary: returns the leftmost part of the input string.

Arguments:

   string: the string to be truncated or extended.

   length: desired length of the result.

   pad: character added to the right of the input string when its length is to be extended.

Notes: The input string is left-justified in a field of specified length or truncated if necessary.

LENGTH(string)

Summary: returns the length in characters of the input string.

Arguments:

   string: the input string.

LINEIN([stream], [position], [count])

Summary: returns a line read from the specified input stream.

Arguments:

   stream: name of the input stream. Default is the standard input stream.

   position: location within the input stream at which to begin reading, specified as a relative line number.

   count: number of whole lines to read (0 or 1 only).

Notes: The default position is the current read position, which is either the first character of the stream or the character following the last one read by CHARIN() or LINEIN(). The default count is 1. With a count of 0, LINEIN() returns a null string but moves the current read position as specified by the second argument.

LINEOUT([stream], [string], [position])

Summary: writes a string of characters to the specified output stream and returns the number of (0 or 1) which could not be written.

Arguments:

stream: name of the output stream. Default is the standard output stream.

string: data to be written.

position: location within the output stream at which to begin writing, specified as a relative line number.

Notes: The default position is the current write position, which is the position following either the last character of the stream or the last one written by CHAROUT( ) or LINEOUT( ). If the string is omitted, the current write position is updated to the value specified by position. If both string and position are omitted, the output stream is closed.

LINES([stream])

Summary: returns the number of lines remaining to be read in the specified input stream.

Arguments:

stream: name of the input stream. Default is the standard input stream.

Notes: The number of lines remaining to be read is defined to be the number of whole or partial lines from the current read position to the end of the file.

MAX(number, [number], . . .)

Summary: returns the largest of a list of numbers.

Arguments:

number: a valid REXX number.

Notes: The result is rounded according to the current setting of NUMERIC DIGITS. That is, like the value of the expression number + 0.

MIN(number, [number], . . .)

Summary: returns the smallest of a list of numbers.

Arguments:

number: a valid REXX number.

Notes: The result is rounded according to the current setting of NUMERIC DIGITS. That is, like the value of the expression number + 0.

OVERLAY(string1, string2, [pos], length], [pad])

Summary: returns the result of replacing the characters of one string by the characters of another, starting at a certain position.

Arguments:

string1: the string of replacement characters.

string2: the string being overlayed.

pos: the position in the second string at which the first overlays it.

length: length to which overlaying string is extended or truncated.

pad: character appended to the first string when its length is to be extended.

Notes: The default position is 1, in which case the first string overlays the second starting at the beginning. The default value of length is the length of the first string.

POS(target, string, [start])

Summary: returns the position of one string in another, searching from left to right.

Arguments:

target: the string being searched for.

string: the string which is searched.

start: the starting position in the second string at which the search begins.

Notes: POS() returns 0 if the target string is null or if it is not found. The default start position is 1.

QUEUED()

Summary: returns the number of lines contained in the external data queue.

RANDOM(max)
RANDOM([min], [max], [seed])

Summary: returns a quasi-random whole number.

Arguments:

max: maximum value that can be returned.

min: minimum (nonnegative) value that can be returned.

seed: a whole number which is used to generate the first of a repeatable sequence of quasi-random numbers.

Notes: If only one argument is specified, it is assumed to be the maximum value, in which case the minimum will be 0. Otherwise the defaults for min and max are 0 and 999.

REVERSE(string)

Summary: returns the input string with the characters reversed end-for-end.

Arguments:

string: the string to be reversed.

RIGHT(string, length, [pad])

Summary: returns the rightmost part of the input string.

Arguments:

string: the string to be truncated or extended.

length: desired length of the result.

pad: character added to the left of the input string when its length is to be extended.

Notes: The input string is right-justified in a field of specified length or truncated if necessary.

SIGN(number)

Summary: returns the arithmetic sign of the input number.

Arguments:

number: a valid **REXX** number.

Notes: SIGN() returns –1 for a negative number, 1 for a positive number, and 0 for 0.

SOURCELINE([number])

Summary: returns number of lines in the program or the specified line of the program's source code.

Arguments:

number: the number of the line to return.

Notes: SOURCELINE( ) returns the number of lines in the program if number is omitted.

SPACE(string, [count], [pad])

Summary: returns the input string reformatted with a specified number of pad characters between each blank-delimited word.

Arguments:

string: the input string.

count: number of pad characters inserted between each blank-delimited word.

pad: the character to be inserted between words of the input string.

Notes: The default count is 1 and the default pad character is a blank. If count is 0, all blanks are removed. SPACE( ) always removes leading and trailing blanks.

STREAM(stream, [option], [command])

Summary: performs an implementation-dependent operation on a specified I/O stream.

Arguments:

stream: name of the I/O stream.

option: determines type of information to be returned or operation to be performed. It may be one of the following:

'C'—perform a command specified by third argument.

'D'—return extended information about the state of the stream.

'S'—return indication about the state of the stream.

command: command to be performed if option is 'C'.

Notes: STREAM( ) returns ERROR, NOTREADY, READY, or UNKNOWN if option is 'S'. All other behavior of STREAM( ) is unstandardized and dependent on the implementation.

STRIP(string, [option], [character])

Summary: returns the input string with specified leading or trailing characters removed.

Arguments:

string: the input string.

option: specifies whether leading or trailing characters are to be removed. It can be one of the following:

'B'—both leading and trailing characters (the default).

'L'—only leading characters.

'T'—only trailing characters.

character: the character to be stripped from the input string. Default is a blank.

SUBSTR(string, start, [length], [pad])

Summary: returns a substring of the input string.

Arguments:

string: the input string.

start: the beginning position in the input string of the desired substring.

length: length of the desired substring.

pad: character added to the left of the substring when its length is to be extended. Default is a blank.

Notes: The substring may extend beyond the right end of the input string, in which case it is extended with pad characters. The start position may be greater than LENGTH(string), in which case the result will consist entirely of pad characters.

SUBWORD(string, start, [length])

Summary: returns a substring of the input string.

Arguments:

string: the input string.

start: the beginning position in the input string of the desired substring, expressed in terms of blank-delimited words.

length: length in words of the desired substring.

Notes: Leading and trailing blanks will be removed from the result. If the length is greater than the number of words remaining in the string, only the remainder is returned. The default for length is the number of words left in the string.

SYMBOL(name)

Summary: returns an indication of whether a given string is a valid symbol, and if so, whether it has an assigned value.

Arguments:

name: a string that represents a possible symbol name.

Notes: SYMBOL() returns BAD if name is not a valid symbol name (for instance, the string contains characters not allowed in a symbol). SYMBOL() returns VAR if the string is the name of a symbol which has been assigned a value. Otherwise it returns LIT.

TIME([option])

Summary: returns the current time.

Arguments:

option: a character that indicates the required time format, one of the following:
'C'—civil format: hh:mm, followed by am or pm.
'E'—elapsed time in seconds since timer was reset ('R' option).
'H'—complete hours since midnight.
'L'—hh:mm:ss.uuuuuu format (fractional seconds).
'M'—complete minutes since midnight.
'N'—normal time format (hh:mm:ss), 24-hour clock (default).
'R'—reset time and return time elapsed since last reset.
'S'—complete seconds since midnight.

Notes: Time values are never affected by NUMERIC DIGITS setting. The 'E' and 'R' options can be used for computing elapsed time without concern for crossing midnight.

TRACE([type])

Summary: returns current trace settings and optionally changes them.

Arguments:

type: new trace setting in the same form as used in the TRACE instruction.

Notes: When the TRACE() function is used to change trace settings it works generally like the TRACE instruction, except that counts cannot be specified, and the settings will be changed even during interactive tracing.

TRANSLATE(string, [output], [input], [pad])

Summary: replaces specified characters in an input string.

Arguments:

string: the string to be modified.

output: the table of output characters.

input: the table of input characters.

pad: pad character used to extend the output table when it is shorter than the input table.

Notes: Every occurrence in the input string of a character from the input table is replaced by the corresponding character from the output table. The pad character, which defaults to a blank, is used as a replacement when there is no corresponding character in the output table because it is shorter than the input table. Characters not present in the input table are not changed. The default input table is XRANGE('00'x, 'ff'x). If neither input nor output table is specified, TRANSLATE() converts all lowercase characters to upper case.

TRUNC(number, [digits])

Summary: formats a number with a given number of digits after the decimal point.

Arguments:

number: the number to be formatted.

digits: number of digits after the decimal point in the result.

Notes: The number is first rounded as in the result of the expression number + 0. The default for digits is 0, in which case the result will be an integer without a decimal point.

VALUE(name, [value], [type])

Summary: returns the value of a specified variable and optionally changes it.

Arguments:

name: a string that is the name of a variable.

value: new value for the specified variable.

type: system-dependent type or class of variable to be accessed.

Notes: The VALUE() function can be used instead of an INTERPRET statement to fetch or set a variable whose name isn't known until run-time. If a new value is not spcified, the variable is not changed. By default (when type is not specified) VALUE() references REXX variables of the current generation. In this case, the specified name is uppercased and subject to substitution if it is a compound name. The types of other variables which may be accessed with VALUE() are dependent on the specific implementation.

VERIFY(string, search, [option], [start])

Summary: indicates whether or not characters from a given set occur in a specified string.

Arguments:

string: the string to be searched.

search: a string composed of the characters to be searched for.

option: either 'N' (nomatch) to find the location of the first character of string that is not in the search string, or 'M' (match) to find the first character of the string that is in the search string. Default is 'N'.

start: the starting position in the string for the search. Default is 1.

Notes: VERIFY() returns 0 if string is entirely composed of characters in search (option 'N'), if string is entirely composed of characters not in search (option 'M'), if the string to be searched is null, or if the start position is beyond the end of the string.

WORD(string, number)

Summary: returns a specific blank-delimited word from a string.

Arguments:

string: the input string.

number: number of the word to select from the string.

Notes: WORD() returns a null string if there are fewer than number words in the string.

WORDINDEX(string, number)

Summary: returns the character position of a specific blank-delimited word in a string.

Arguments:

> string: the input string.
>
> number: number of the word whose index is required.

Notes: WORDINDEX() returns 0 if there are fewer than number words in the string.

WORDLENGTH(string, number)

Summary: returns the length of a specific blank-delimited word in a string.

Arguments:

> string: the input string.
>
> number: number of the word whose length is required.

Notes: WORDLENGTH() returns 0 if there are fewer than number words in the string.

WORDPOS(phrase, string, [start])

Summary: returns the word position of one string of words in another, searching from left to right.

Arguments:

> phrase: the string of words being searched for.
>
> string: the string which is searched.
>
> start: the starting word position in the string at which the search begins. Default is 1.

Notes: WORDPOS() returns 0 if the phrase being searched for is a null string or is not found. Excess blanks between words in the target and search strings are ignored.

WORDS(string)

Summary: returns the number of blank-delimited words in a string.

Arguments:

> string: the string whose length is required.

XRANGE([first], [last])

Summary: returns a string of all characters whose encodings lie in a given range.

Arguments:

first: the first character in the range. Default is '00'x.

last: the last character in the range. Default is 'ff'x.

Notes: The result consists of characters in ascending order if first is less than last. If first is greater than last, the result consists of characters in ascending order, but wrapping at 'ff'x. The result depends on the specific character collating sequence used by the implementation.

X2B(hex-string)

Summary: returns the binary-string representation of a given hexadecimal string.

Arguments:

hex-string: the hex string whose binary-string representation is required.

Notes: Both the argument and the result of X2B() are character strings. X2B() converts the input data from base 16 representation to base 2.

X2C(hex-string)

Summary: returns the binary (internal) representation of a given hexadecimal string.

Arguments:

hex-string: the hex string whose binary representation is required.

Notes: The result of X2C() is the internal representation of the given hex string. It will normally contain nonprintable characters.

X2D(hex-string, [length])

Summary: returns the decimal representation of a given hexadecimal string.

Arguments:

hex-string: the hex string whose decimal representation is required.

length: rightmost number of hex digits to be converted.

Notes: The input string must consist of valid hex digits. The digits may be separated by spaces as long as each blank-delimited group except the first contains an even number of hex digits. The spaces are ignored in selecting the rightmost digits when length is specified. If length is specified, the result is a signed number. Otherwise the result will be unsigned. If `length` exceeds `LENGTH(hex-string)`, the string is first padded on the left with 0.

Further Reading

Cowlishaw, Michael F., *The REXX Language: A Practical Approach to Programming* , 2d ed. (1988). This is the standard definition of REXX, by its inventor.

Daney, Charles, "REXX in Charge," *Byte*, Vol. 15, No. 8 (August 1990). Introduction to REXX as a general purpose macro language for personal computer applications.

Goldberg, Gabriel; Smith, Philip H. III, *The REXX Handbook* (1992). Contains 45 separate chapter with general information, usage notes, descriptions of different implementations, details of REXX-related products, and an extensive bibliography.

O'Hara, Robert P.; Gomberg, David R., *Modern Programming Using REXX*, 2d ed. (1988). A very good introduction to programming concepts and techniques which uses REXX.

Quercus Systems, *Personal REXX User's Guide, Version 3.0* (1991). Quercus Systems, P.O. Box 2157, Saratoga CA 95070. Contains a long tutorial chapter with many examples of REXX programs.

Operators and Special Characters

+
addition operator, 63
in positional parsing patterns, 153, 158
unary plus, 63

−
in positional parsing patterns, 153, 158
subtraction operator, 63
unary minus, 63

*
multiplication operator, 63

/
division operator, 63

//
remainder of integer division, 63

**
exponentiation operator, 63

\
negation operator, 64

%
integer division operator, 63

|
logical or operator, 64

| |
concatentation operator, 61

&
logical and operator, 64

&&
logical exclusive or operator, 64

=
assignment, 45, 59
comparison, equality, 62
in positional parsing patterns, 153, 158

==
comparison, strict equality, 62–63

>
comparison, first operand greater than, 62

>>
comparison, first operand strictly greater than, 63

<
comparison, first operand less than, 62

<<
comparison, first operand strictly less than, 63

>=
comparison, first operand greater than or equal to, 62

>>=
comparison, first operand strictly greater than or equal to, 63

<=
comparison, first operand less than or equal to, 62

<<=
comparison, first operand strictly less than or equal to, 63

Index

ABOUT THE AUTHOR

Charles Daney is President of Quercus Systems, a software development company in Saratoga, California that specializes in REXX-related products and applications involving communications, electronic mail and conferencing, textual databases, and augmentation of knowledge work. He is a developer of Personal REXX for MS-DOS and OS/2, and of the REXXTERM communication package for MS-DOS and OS/2. He worked for a number of years as developer and administrator of the VMSHARE computer conferencing facility, but now spends most of his on-line time on CompuServe and the WELL. He has a B.S. degree in mathematics from M.I.T. and an M.A. in political science from Yale.